APOSIMZ

07

**TSUTOMU
NIHEI**

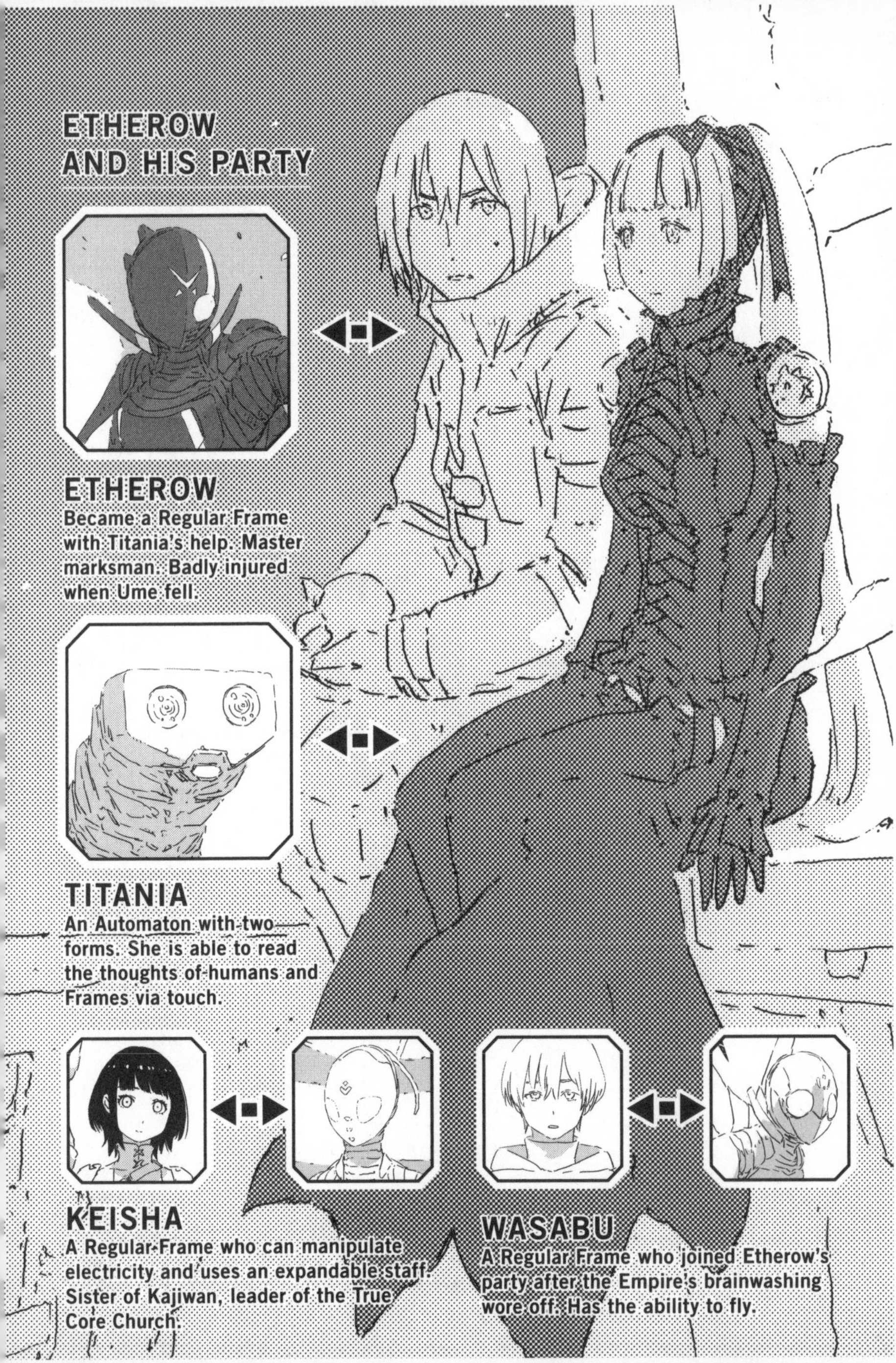

ETHEROW AND HIS PARTY

ETHEROW
Became a Regular Frame with Titania's help. Master marksman. Badly injured when Ume fell.

TITANIA
An Automaton with two forms. She is able to read the thoughts of humans and Frames via touch.

KEISHA
A Regular Frame who can manipulate electricity and uses an expandable staff. Sister of Kajiwan, leader of the True Core Church.

WASABU
A Regular Frame who joined Etherow's party after the Empire's brainwashing wore off. Has the ability to fly.

PLOT AND CHARACTER INTRO

REBEDOAN EMPIRE

A militant state with powerful, heavily-armed forces that continues to invade various regions. Has many Regular Frames in its ranks.

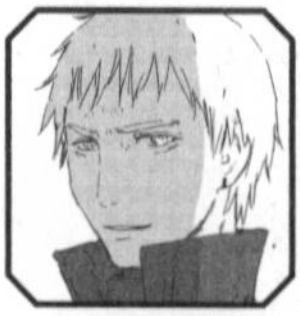

NICHIKO SUOU

The Emperor of Rebedoa. Has the ability to predict the future.

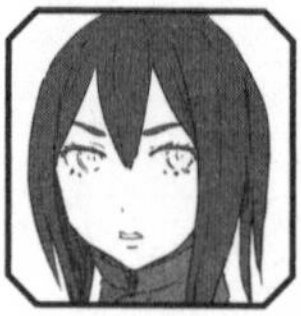

JATE

A high-level Reincarnated of the Rebedoan Empire. Has the ability to manipulate automatons.

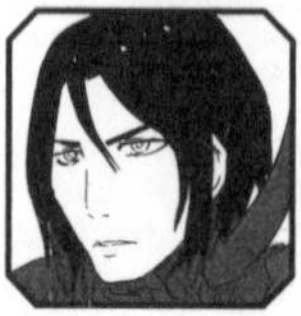

TOSU

A high-level Reincarnated of the Rebedoan Empire. Has the ability to manipulate metal.

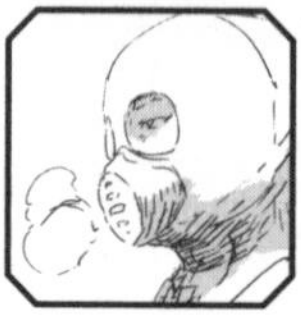

TASHITSUMA

Member of the Imperial Science Division. Successfully created a Regular Frame clone of Jate named Ajate.

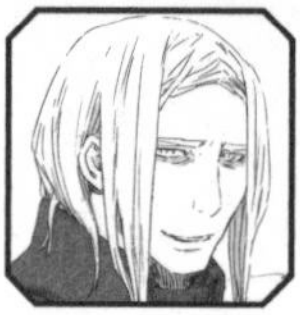

RINAI

Reincarnated.
An old friend of Jate.

TRUE CORE CHURCH

Organization created by Kajiwan to gather those afflicted with Frame disease. Bestows certain sufferers with knowledge and power, turning them into "Regenerateds." Views both the Empire and humans as enemies.

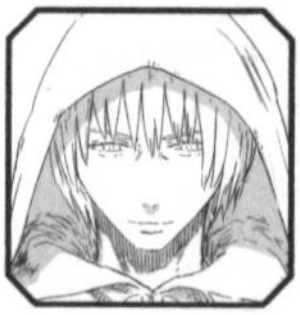

KAJIWAN

The last King of Irf Nikk. Using the powers of the mysterious Frame created from Titania's stolen arm, he became a Regular Frame himself. Has the ability to produce fireballs.

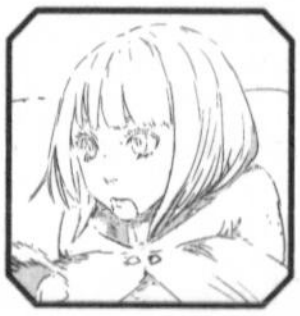

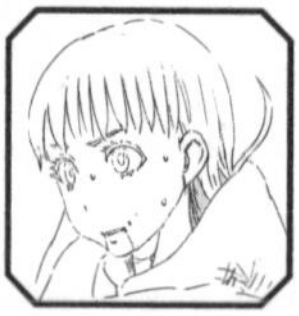

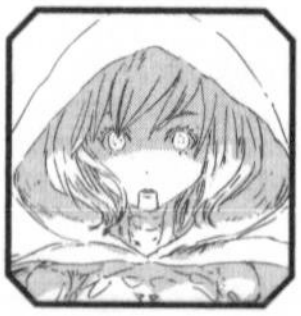

JINATA, TASURI, FIISA

Regular Frames of the Church. Their abilities only allow them to fight against other Regular Frames.

Previously

After much devoted care by Keisha, Etherow has recovered, only to be surrounded by the Empire's forces. After destroying several High-Level Reincarnateds, Etherow and his party were able to drive the Imperial forces into a corner. However, just as victory was within their grasp, a mistake allows Nichiko Suou to escape. Meanwhile, Kajiwan of the True Core Church has suffered total defeat, and heads underground with a small party of followers...

APOSIMZ

CHAPTER 37

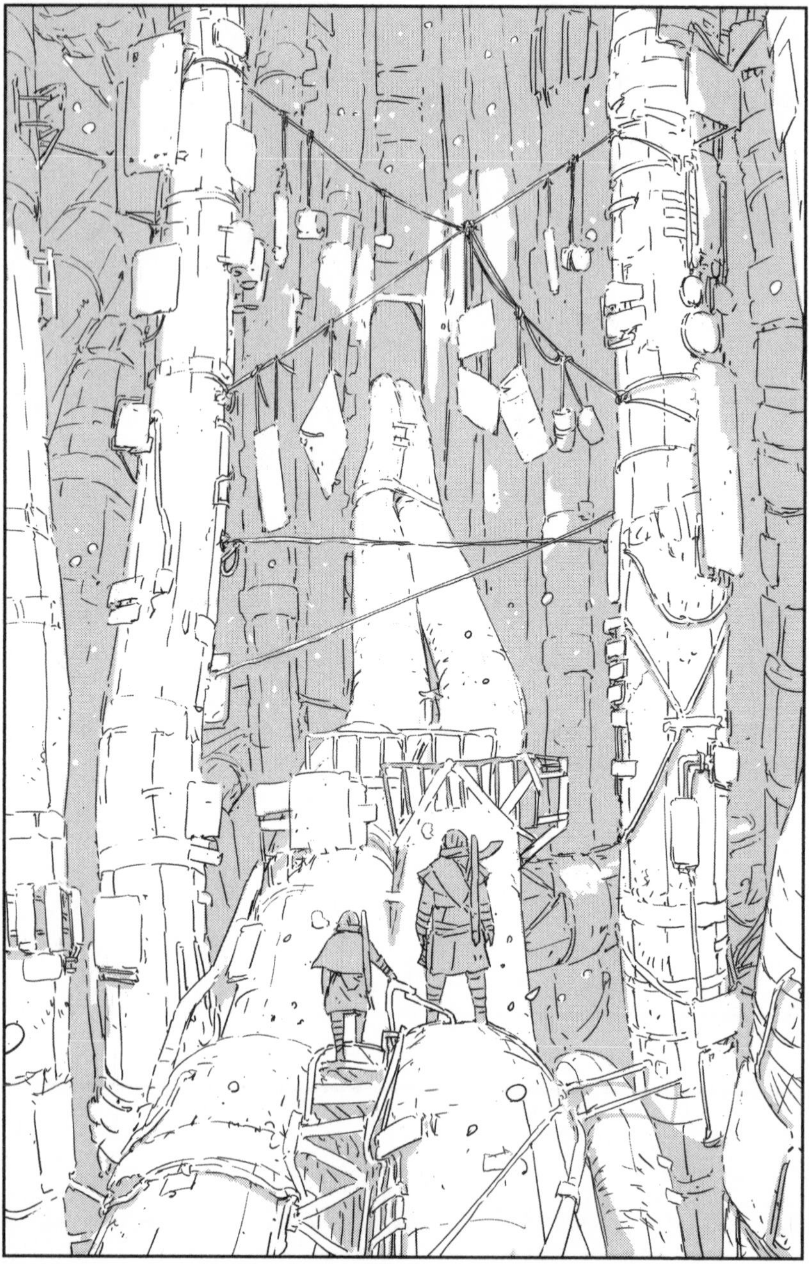

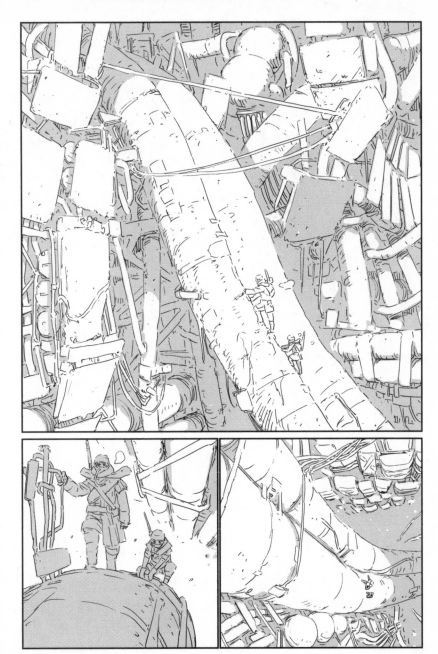

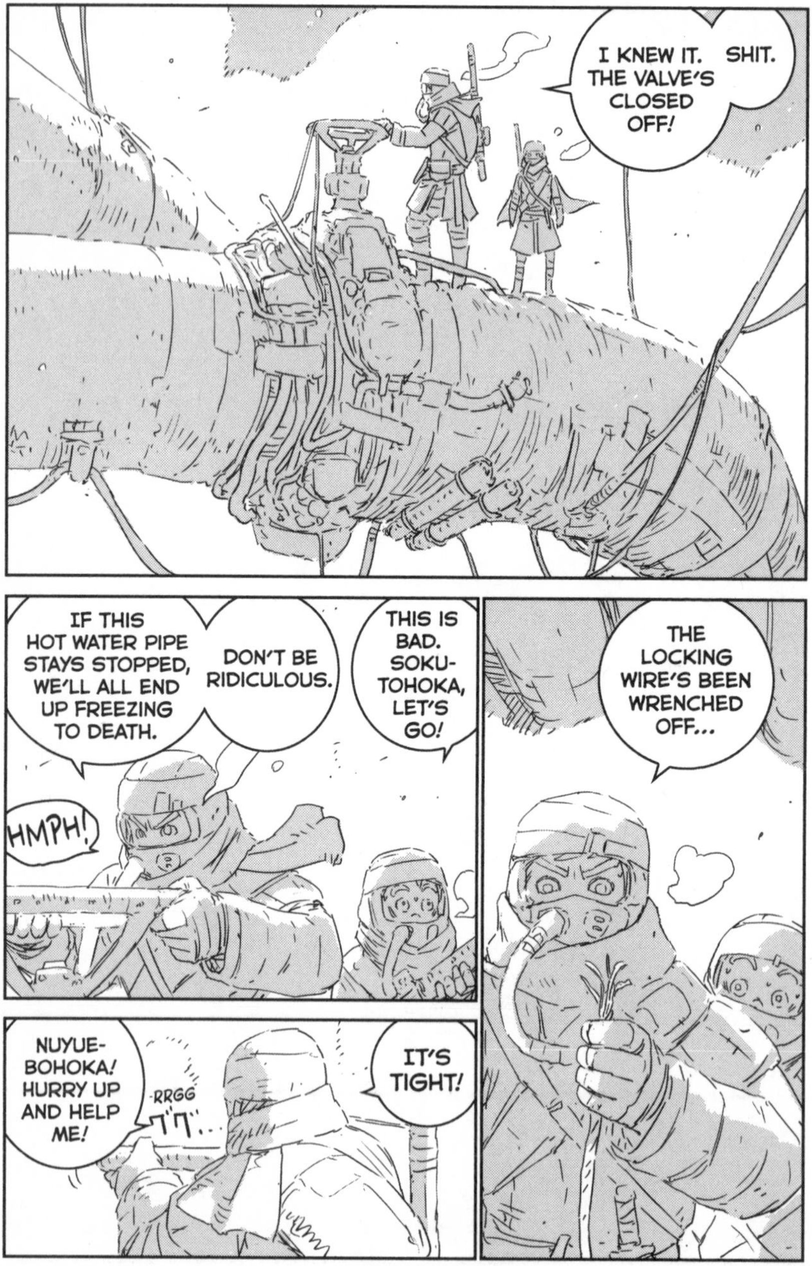
SHIT.
I KNEW IT. THE VALVE'S CLOSED OFF!
THE LOCKING WIRE'S BEEN WRENCHED OFF...
THIS IS BAD. SOKU-TOHOKA, LET'S GO!
DON'T BE RIDICULOUS.
IF THIS HOT WATER PIPE STAYS STOPPED, WE'LL ALL END UP FREEZING TO DEATH.
HMPH!
IT'S TIGHT!
-RRGG
NUYUE-BOHOKA! HURRY UP AND HELP ME!

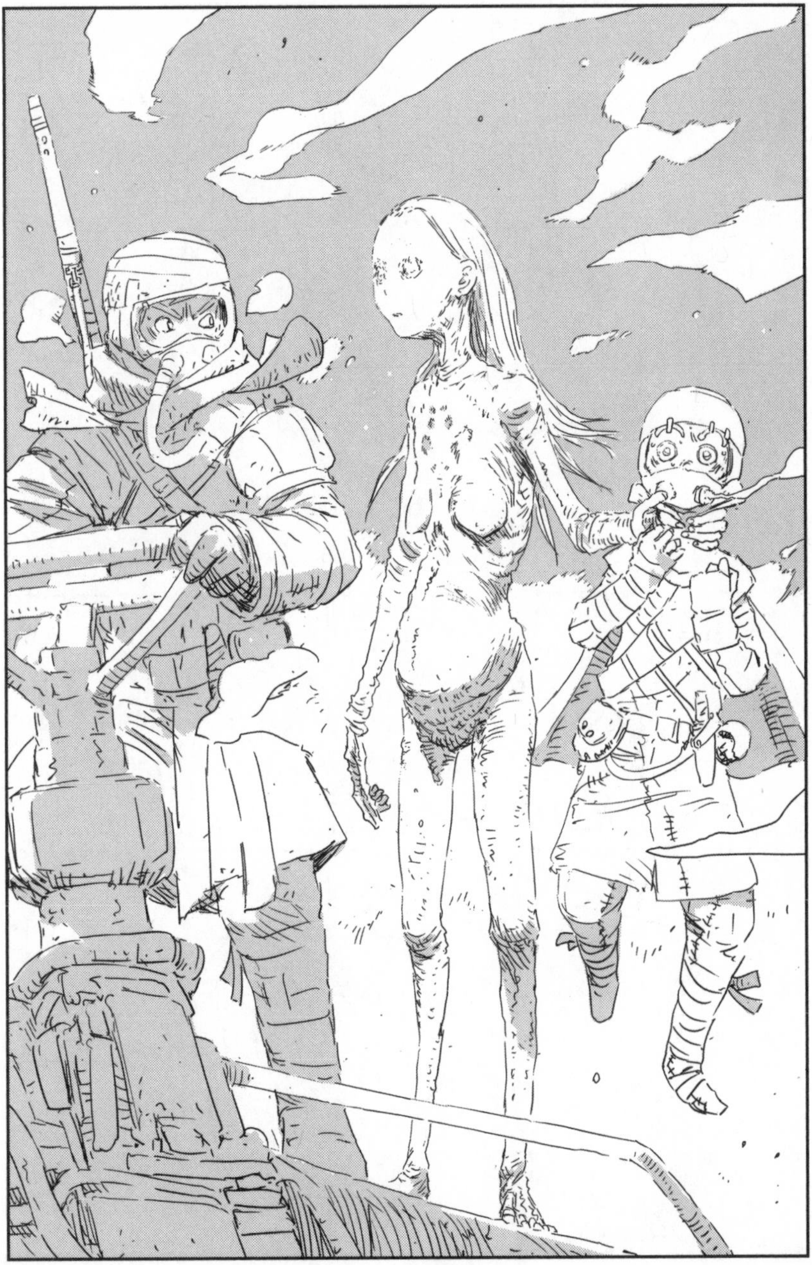

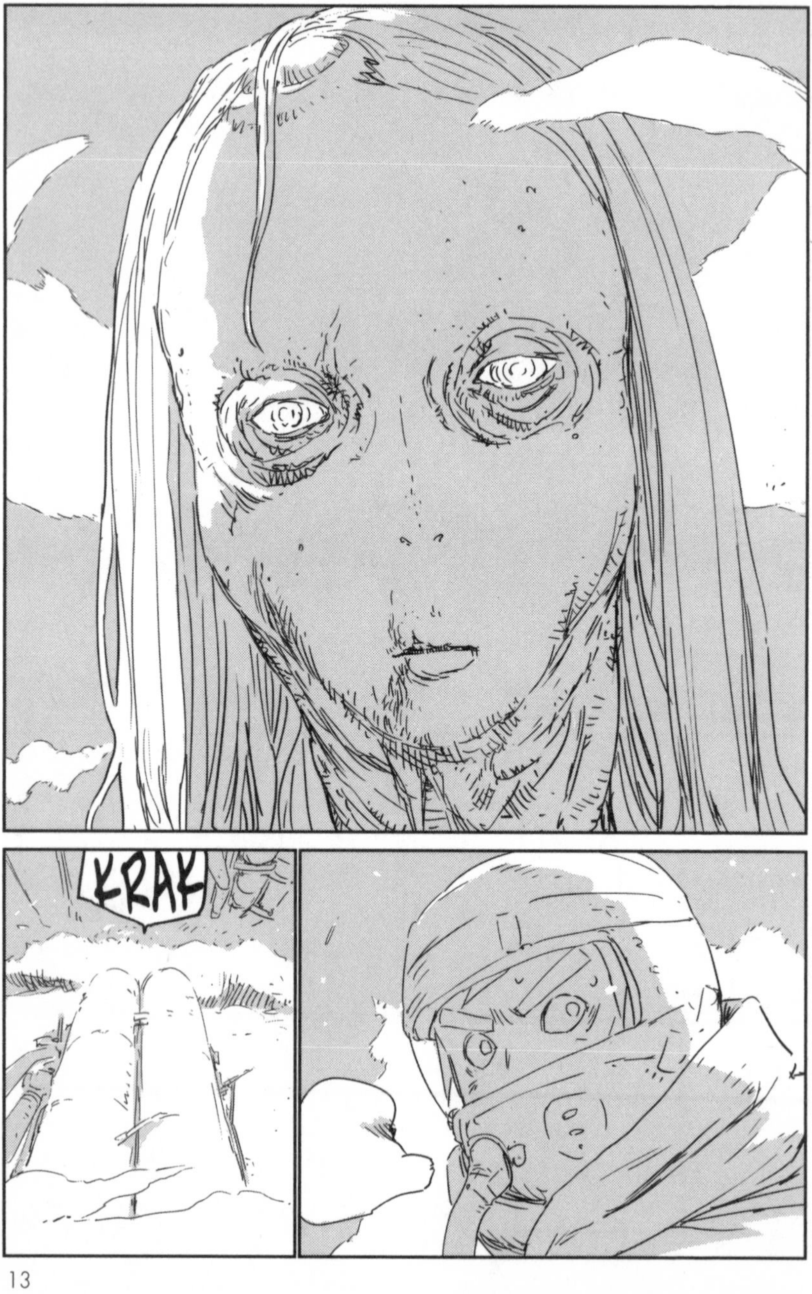
KRAK

GAAAH!
WHAT IS IT? WHAT'S WRONG ?!

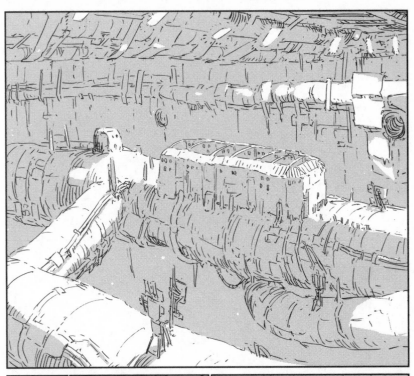

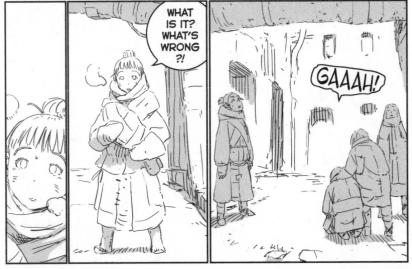

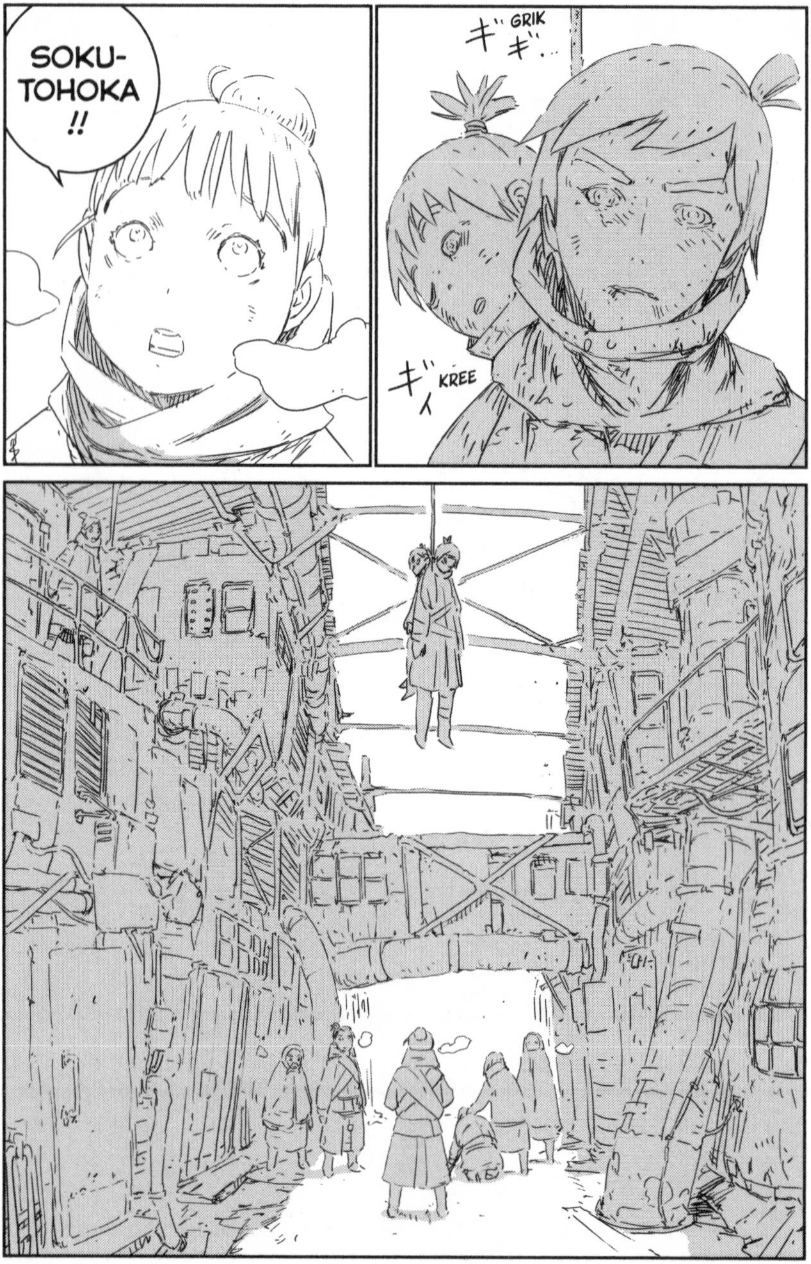
ギギ…
GRIK
ギイ
KREE
SOKU-TOHOKA!!

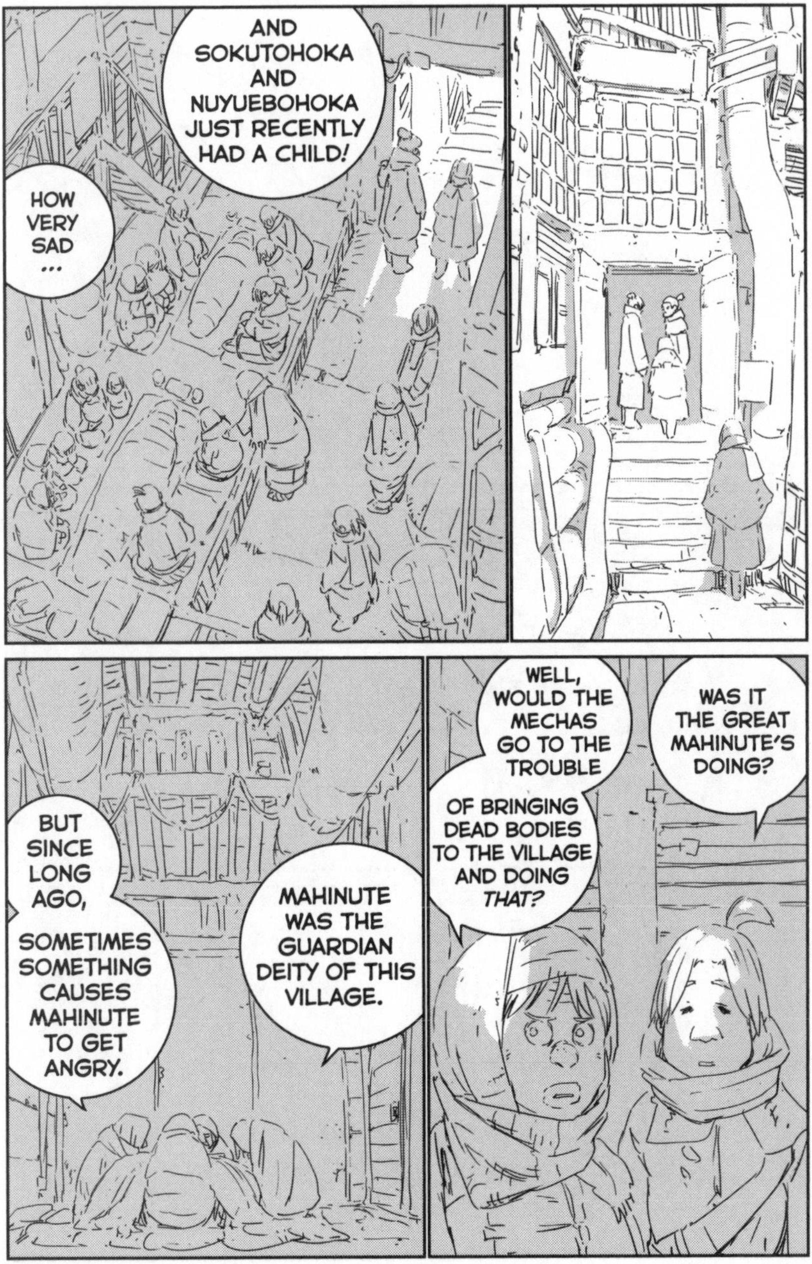
AND SOKUTOHOKA AND NUYUEBOHOKA JUST RECENTLY HAD A CHILD!
HOW VERY SAD ...
WAS IT THE GREAT MAHINUTE'S DOING?
WELL, WOULD THE MECHAS GO TO THE TROUBLE
OF BRINGING DEAD BODIES TO THE VILLAGE AND DOING *THAT?*
MAHINUTE WAS THE GUARDIAN DEITY OF THIS VILLAGE.
BUT SINCE LONG AGO,
SOMETIMES SOMETHING CAUSES MAHINUTE TO GET ANGRY.

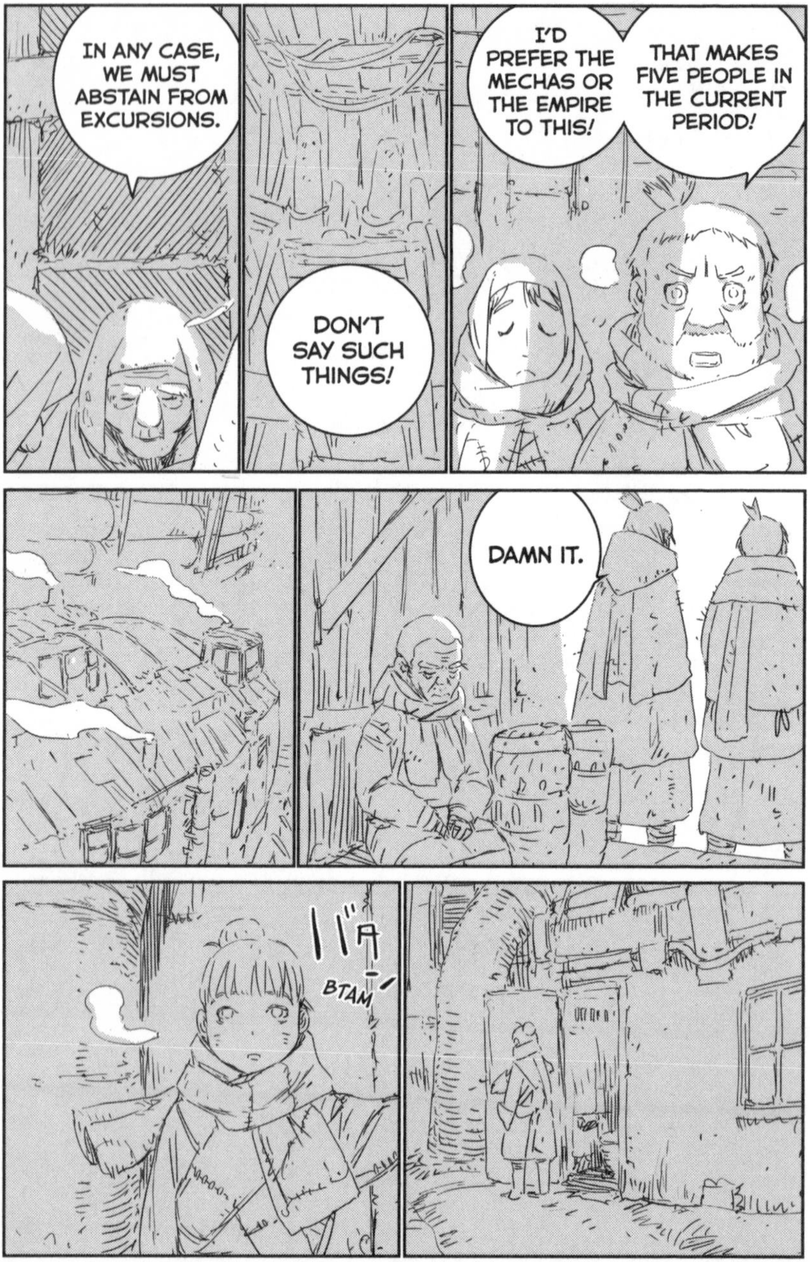
THAT MAKES FIVE PEOPLE IN THE CURRENT PERIOD!
I'D PREFER THE MECHAS OR THE EMPIRE TO THIS!
DON'T SAY SUCH THINGS!
IN ANY CASE, WE MUST ABSTAIN FROM EXCURSIONS.
DAMN IT.
BTAM

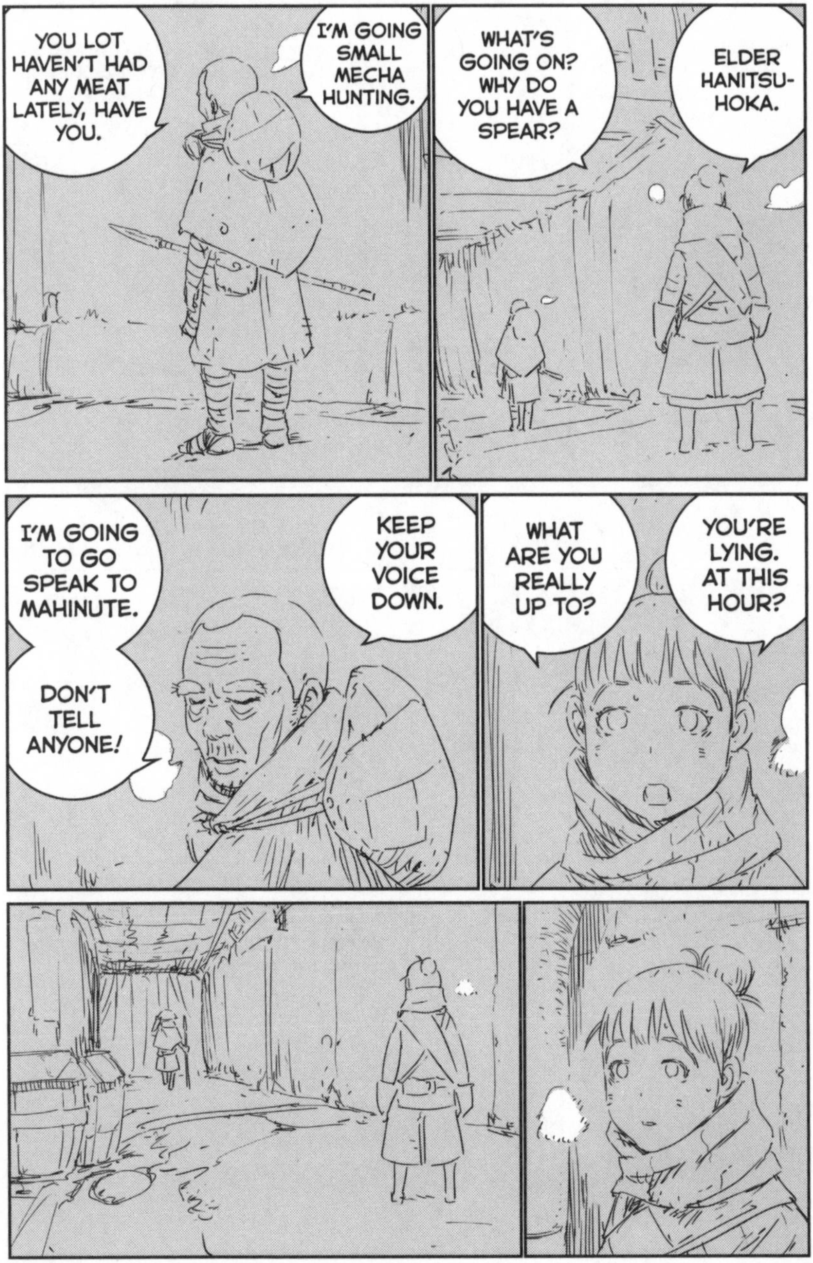
ELDER HANITSU-HOKA.
WHAT'S GOING ON? WHY DO YOU HAVE A SPEAR?
I'M GOING SMALL MECHA HUNTING.
YOU LOT HAVEN'T HAD ANY MEAT LATELY, HAVE YOU.
YOU'RE LYING. AT THIS HOUR?
WHAT ARE YOU REALLY UP TO?
KEEP YOUR VOICE DOWN.
I'M GOING TO GO SPEAK TO MAHINUTE.
DON'T TELL ANYONE!

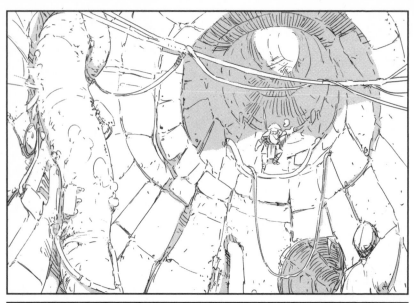

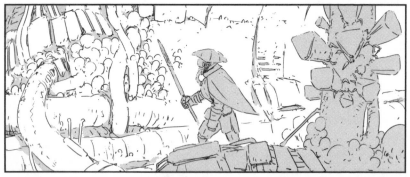

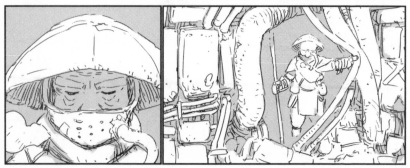

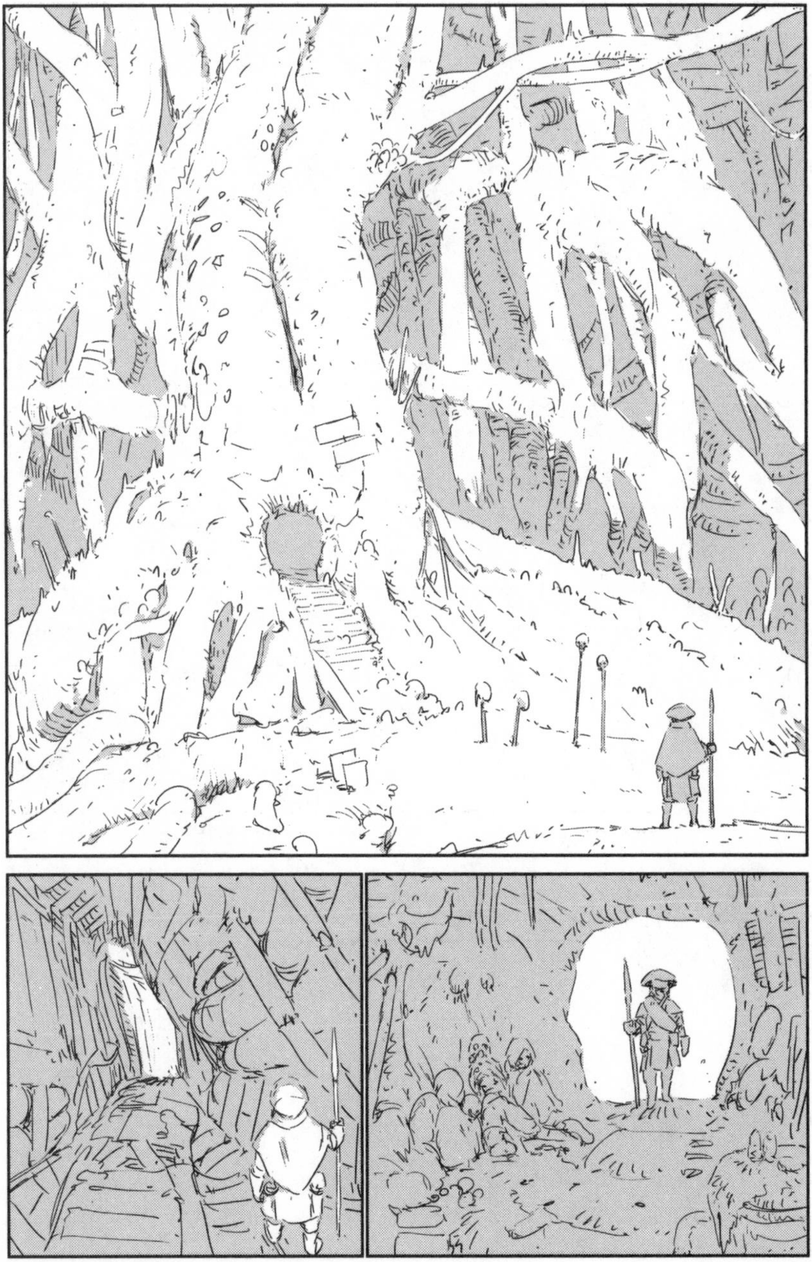

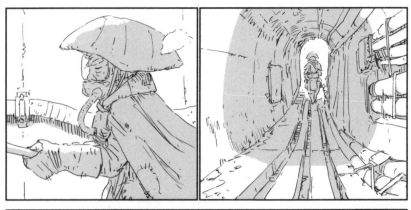

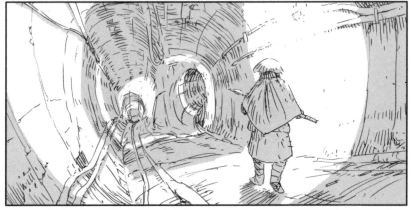

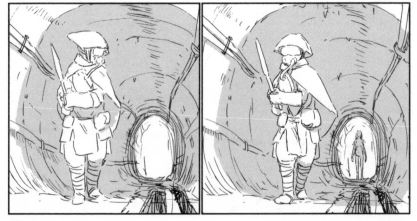

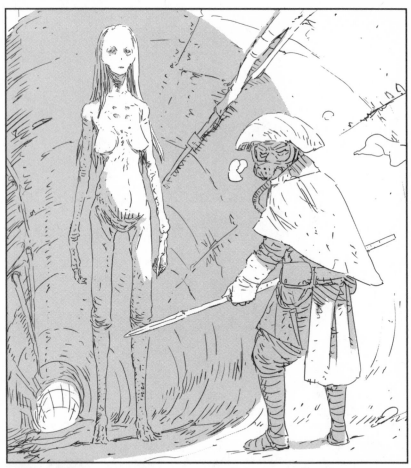

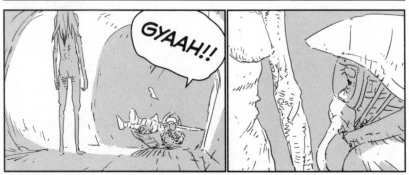

GYAAH!!

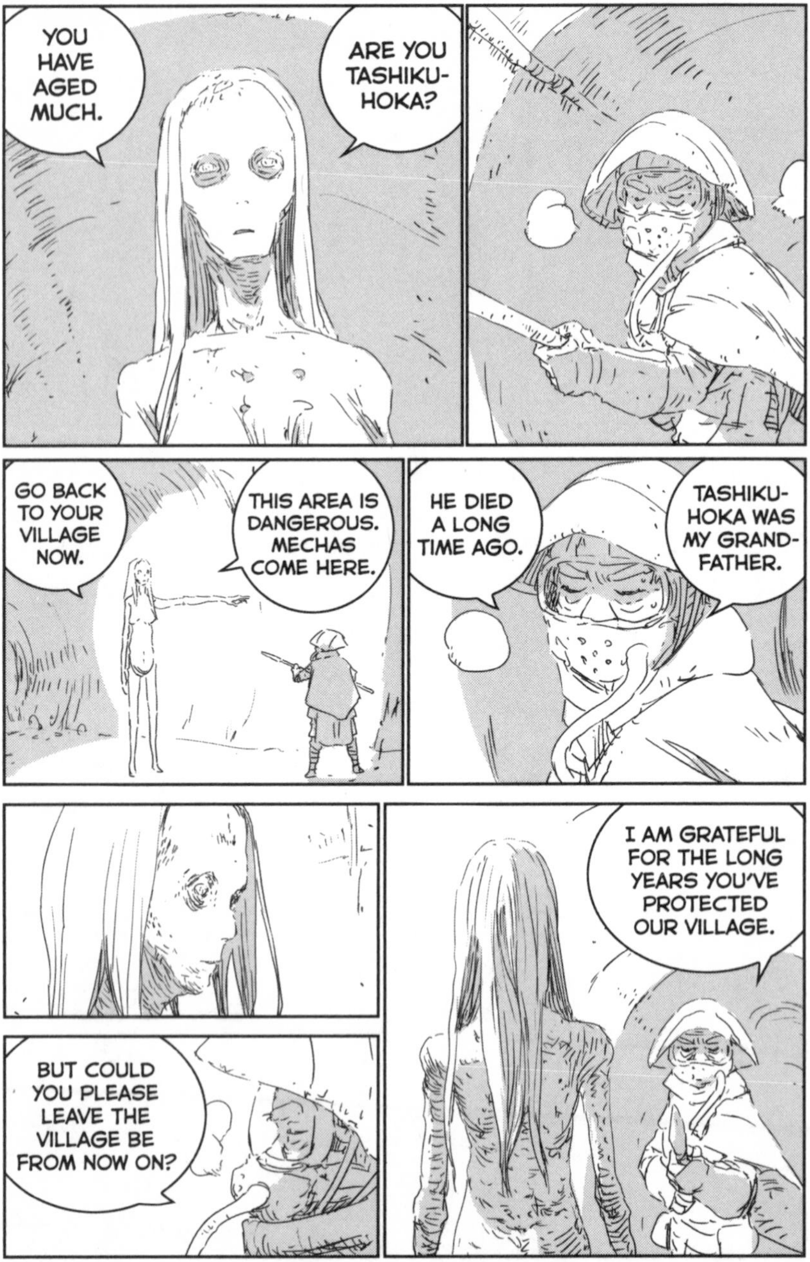
ARE YOU TASHIKU-HOKA?
YOU HAVE AGED MUCH.
TASHIKU-HOKA WAS MY GRAND-FATHER.
HE DIED A LONG TIME AGO.
THIS AREA IS DANGEROUS. MECHAS COME HERE.
GO BACK TO YOUR VILLAGE NOW.
I AM GRATEFUL FOR THE LONG YEARS YOU'VE PROTECTED OUR VILLAGE.
BUT COULD YOU PLEASE LEAVE THE VILLAGE BE FROM NOW ON?

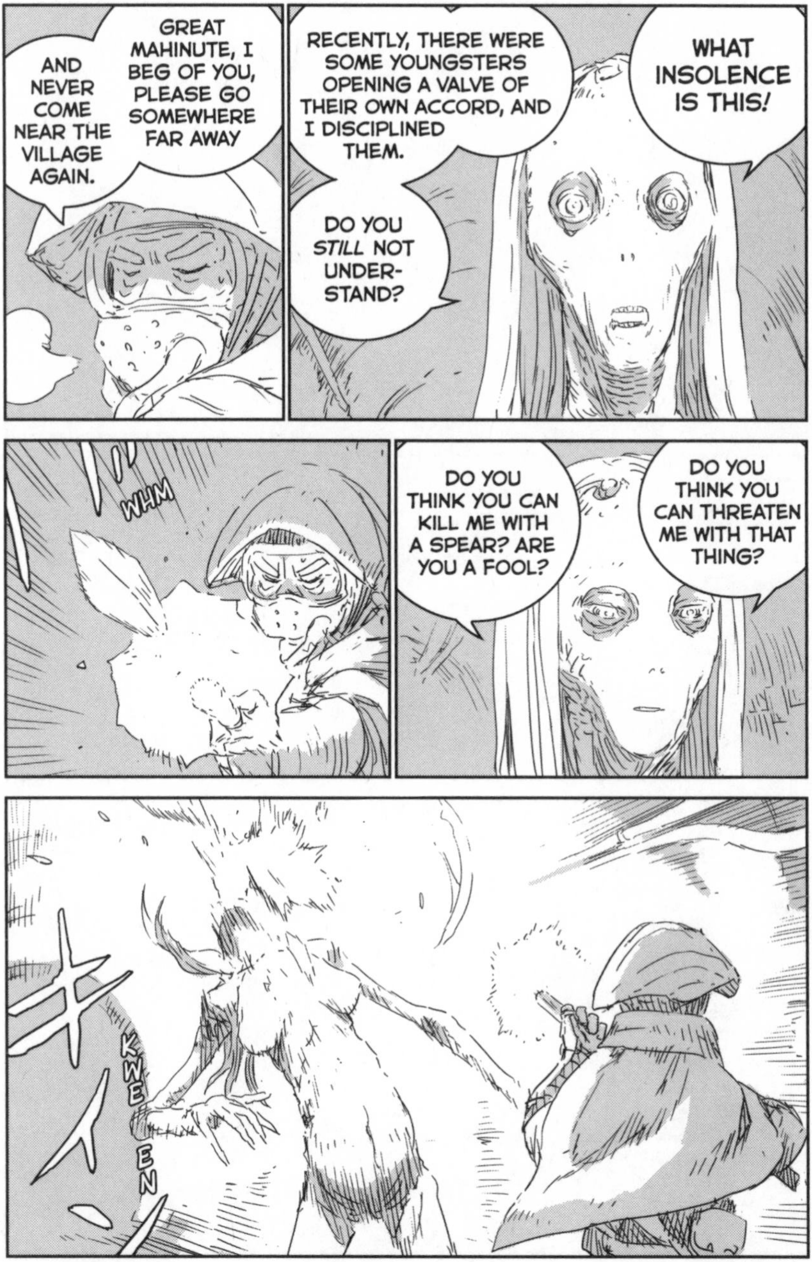
WHAT INSOLENCE IS THIS!
RECENTLY, THERE WERE SOME YOUNGSTERS OPENING A VALVE OF THEIR OWN ACCORD, AND I DISCIPLINED THEM.
DO YOU STILL NOT UNDER-STAND?
GREAT MAHINUTE, I BEG OF YOU, PLEASE GO SOMEWHERE FAR AWAY
AND NEVER COME NEAR THE VILLAGE AGAIN.
DO YOU THINK YOU CAN THREATEN ME WITH THAT THING?
DO YOU THINK YOU CAN KILL ME WITH A SPEAR? ARE YOU A FOOL?
WHM
KWEEN

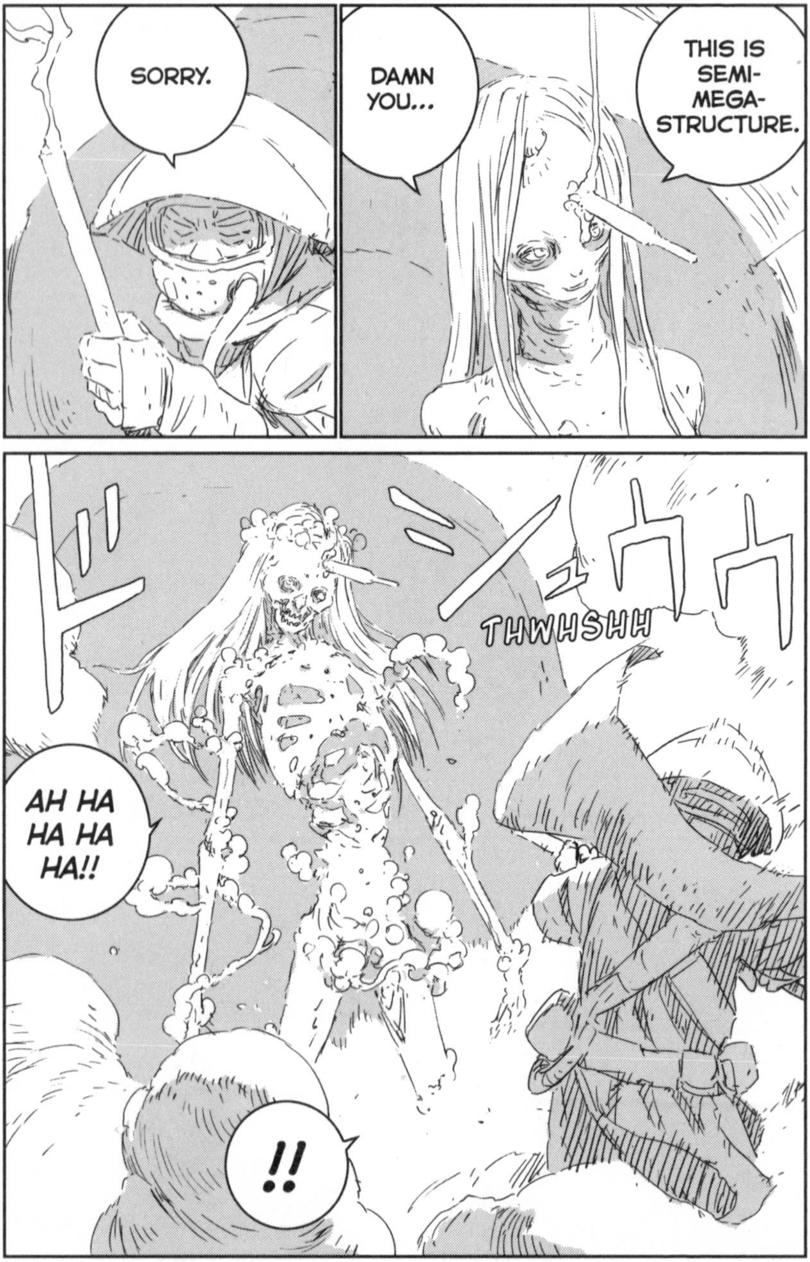
THIS IS SEMI-MEGA-STRUCTURE.
DAMN YOU...
SORRY.
THWHSHH
AH HA HA HA HA!!
!!

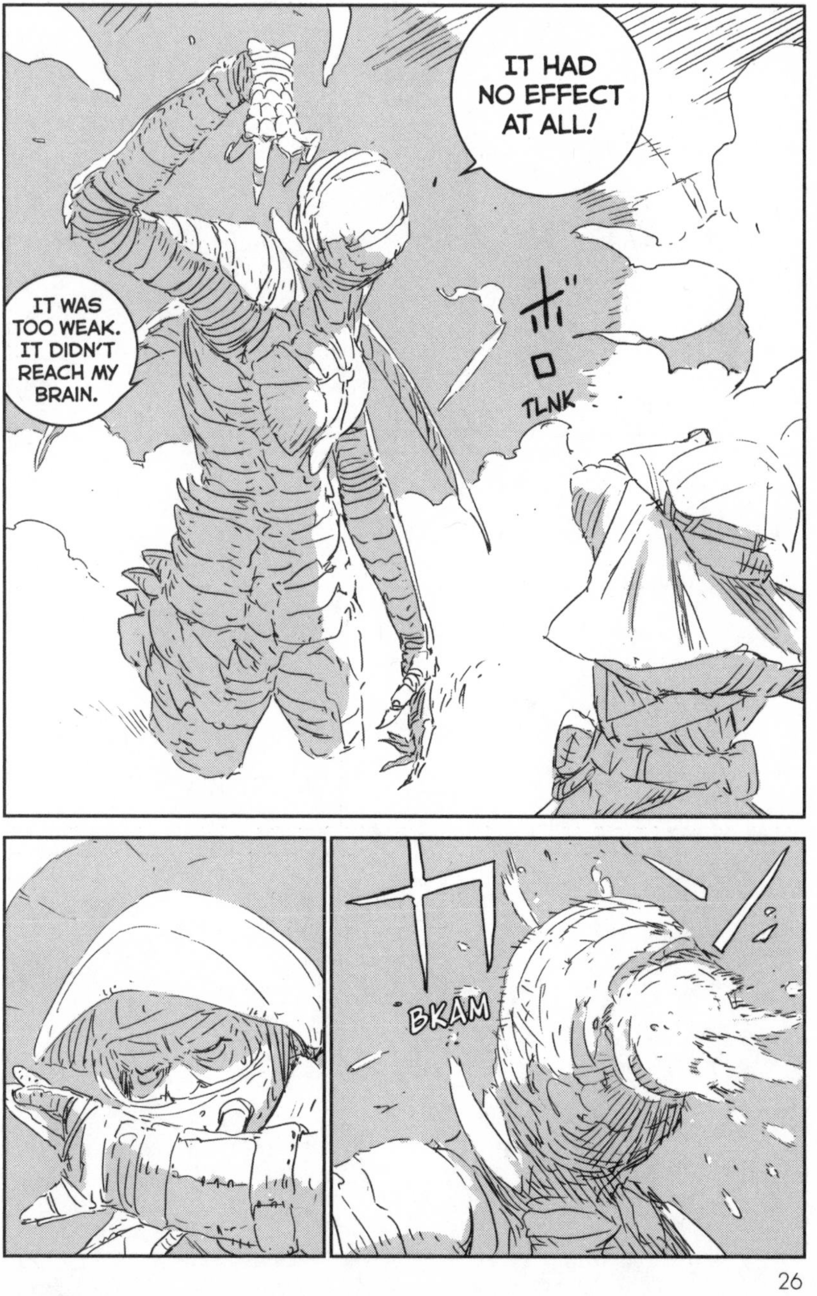
IT HAD NO EFFECT AT ALL!
IT WAS TOO WEAK. IT DIDN'T REACH MY BRAIN.
TLNK
BKAM

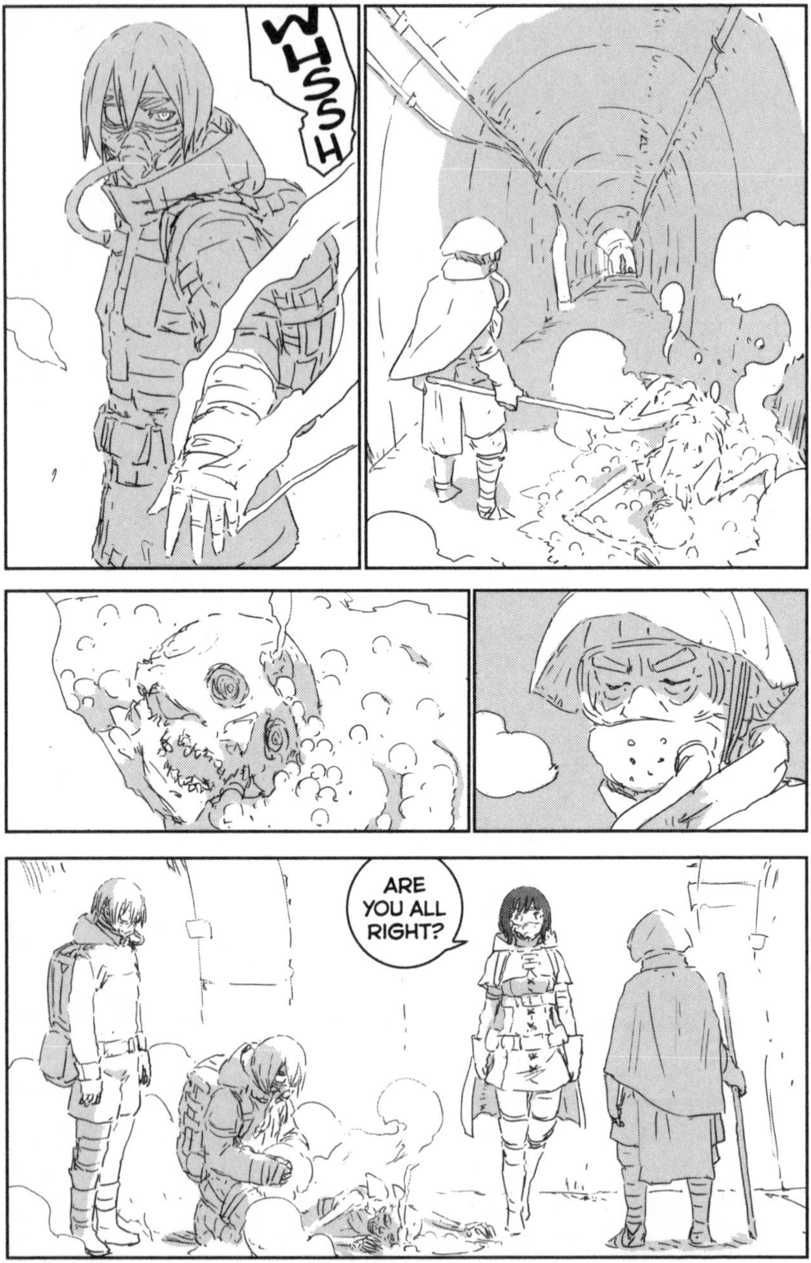
WHSSH
ARE YOU ALL RIGHT?

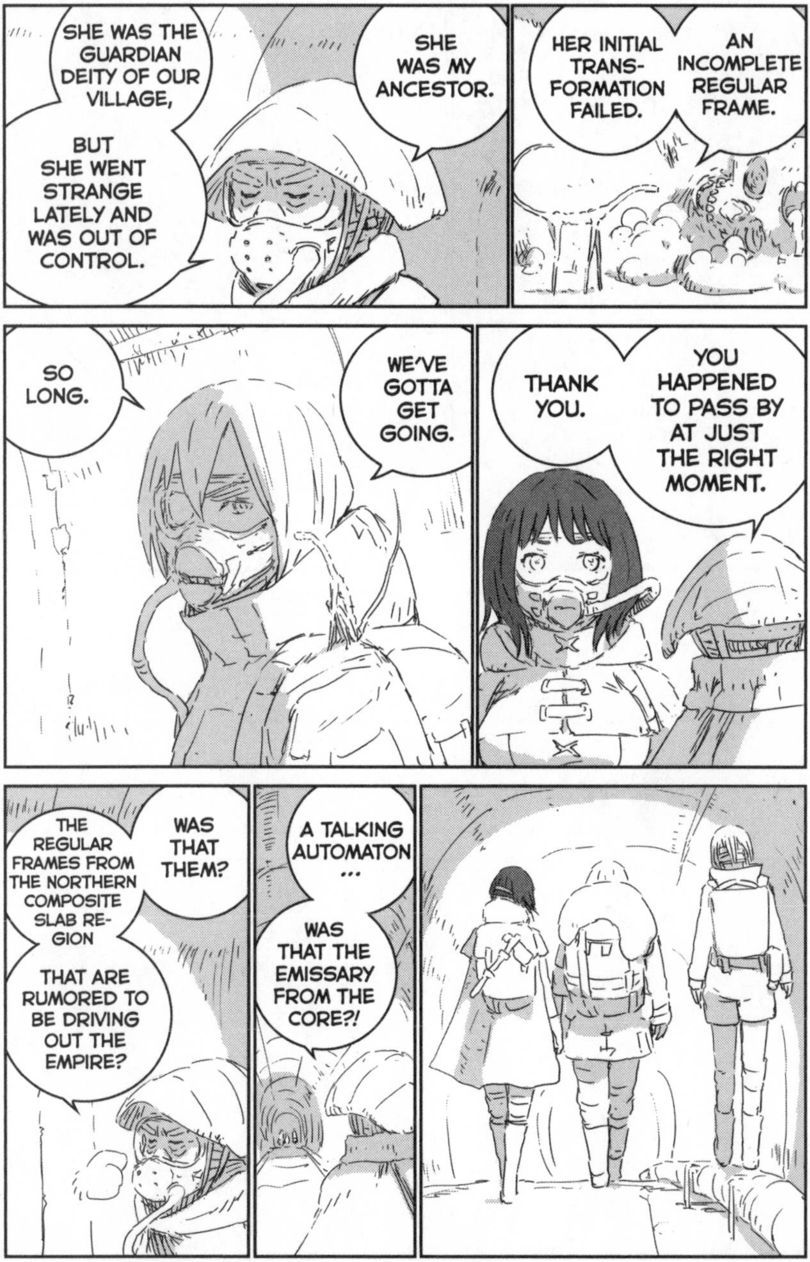
AN INCOMPLETE REGULAR FRAME.
HER INITIAL TRANS- FORMATION FAILED.
SHE WAS MY ANCESTOR.
SHE WAS THE GUARDIAN DEITY OF OUR VILLAGE,
BUT SHE WENT STRANGE LATELY AND WAS OUT OF CONTROL.
YOU HAPPENED TO PASS BY AT JUST THE RIGHT MOMENT.
THANK YOU.
WE'VE GOTTA GET GOING.
SO LONG.
A TALKING AUTOMATON ...
WAS THAT THE EMISSARY FROM THE CORE?!
WAS THAT THEM?
THE REGULAR FRAMES FROM THE NORTHERN COMPOSITE SLAB RE- GION
THAT ARE RUMORED TO BE DRIVING OUT THE EMPIRE?

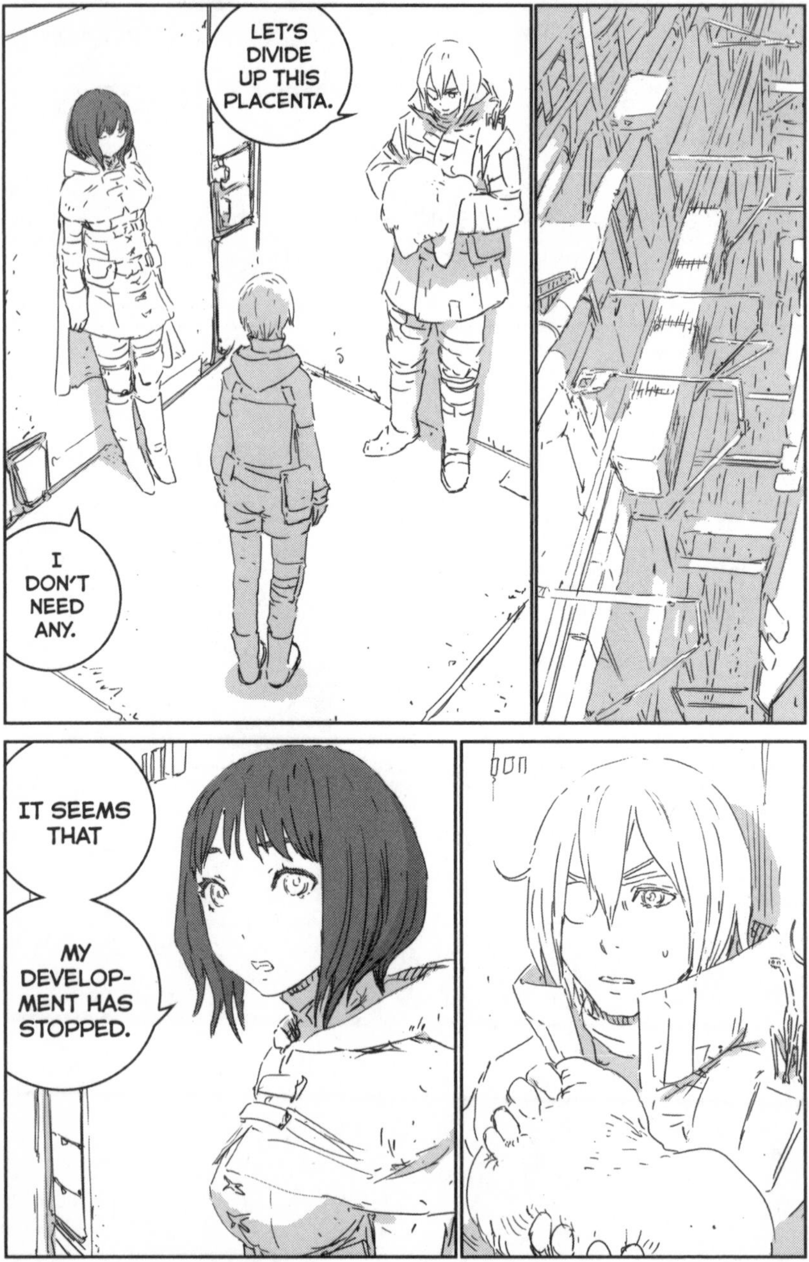
LET'S DIVIDE UP THIS PLACENTA.
I DON'T NEED ANY.
IT SEEMS THAT
MY DEVELOPMENT HAS STOPPED.

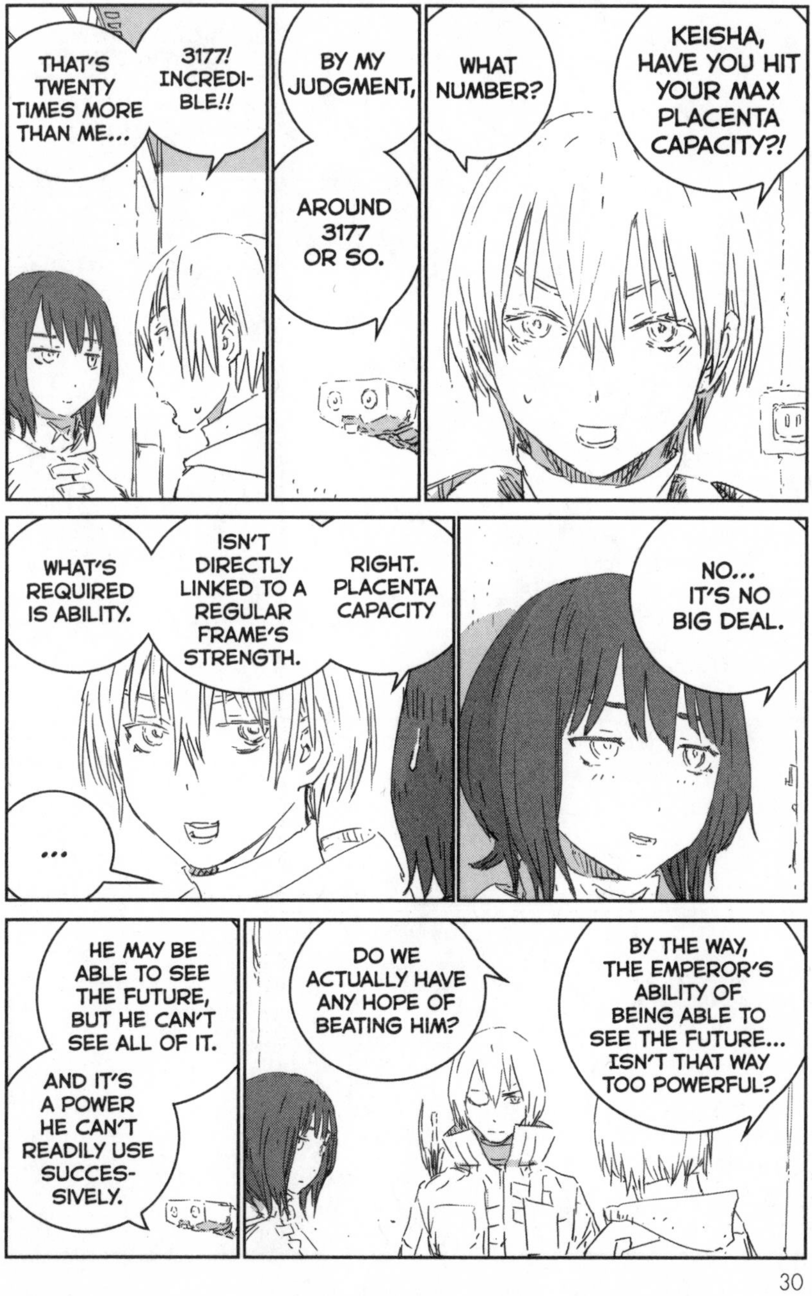
KEISHA, HAVE YOU HIT YOUR MAX PLACENTA CAPACITY?!
WHAT NUMBER?
BY MY JUDGMENT,
AROUND 3177 OR SO.
3177! INCREDI-BLE!!
THAT'S TWENTY TIMES MORE THAN ME...
NO... IT'S NO BIG DEAL.
RIGHT. PLACENTA CAPACITY
ISN'T DIRECTLY LINKED TO A REGULAR FRAME'S STRENGTH.
WHAT'S REQUIRED IS ABILITY.
...
BY THE WAY, THE EMPEROR'S ABILITY OF BEING ABLE TO SEE THE FUTURE... ISN'T THAT WAY TOO POWERFUL?
DO WE ACTUALLY HAVE ANY HOPE OF BEATING HIM?
HE MAY BE ABLE TO SEE THE FUTURE, BUT HE CAN'T SEE ALL OF IT.
AND IT'S A POWER HE CAN'T READILY USE SUCCES-SIVELY.

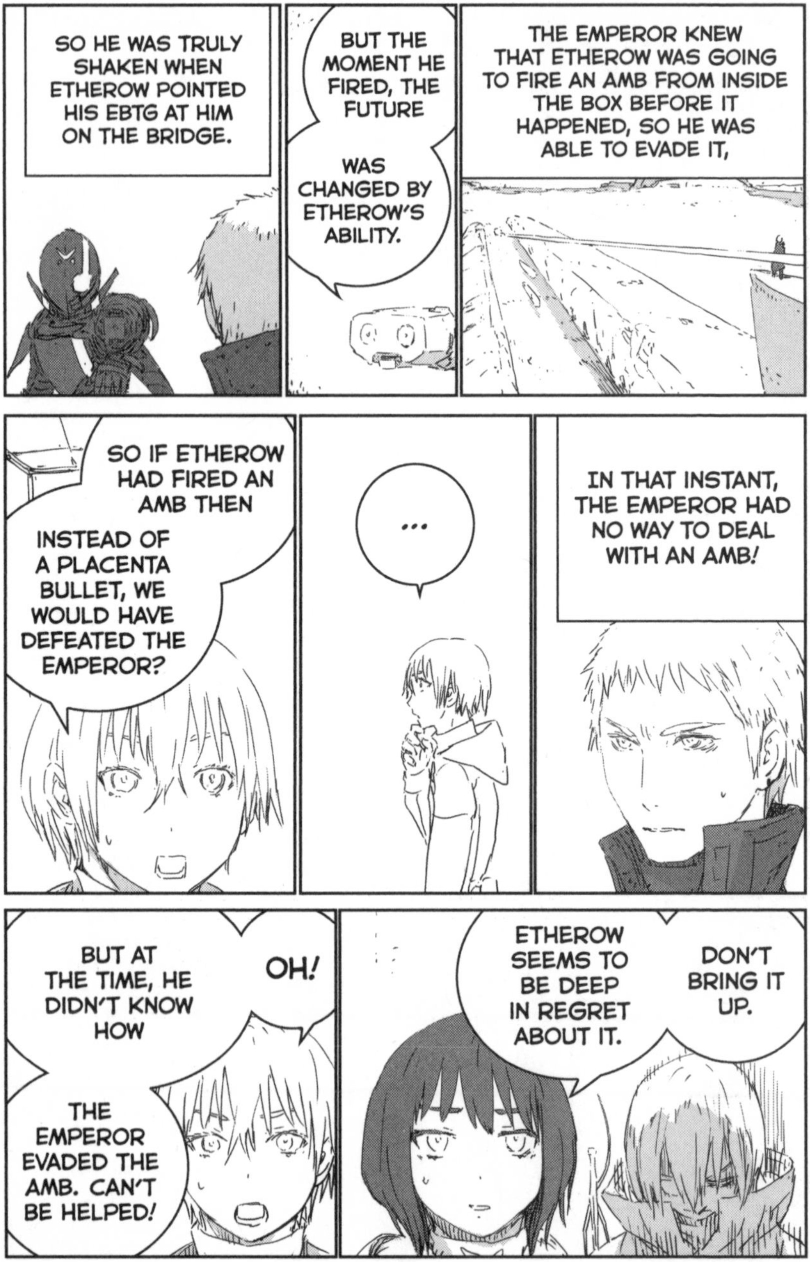
THE EMPEROR KNEW THAT ETHEROW WAS GOING TO FIRE AN AMB FROM INSIDE THE BOX BEFORE IT HAPPENED, SO HE WAS ABLE TO EVADE IT,
BUT THE MOMENT HE FIRED, THE FUTURE
WAS CHANGED BY ETHEROW'S ABILITY.
SO HE WAS TRULY SHAKEN WHEN ETHEROW POINTED HIS EBTG AT HIM ON THE BRIDGE.
IN THAT INSTANT, THE EMPEROR HAD NO WAY TO DEAL WITH AN AMB!
...
SO IF ETHEROW HAD FIRED AN AMB THEN
INSTEAD OF A PLACENTA BULLET, WE WOULD HAVE DEFEATED THE EMPEROR?
DON'T BRING IT UP.
ETHEROW SEEMS TO BE DEEP IN REGRET ABOUT IT.
OH!
BUT AT THE TIME, HE DIDN'T KNOW HOW
THE EMPEROR EVADED THE AMB. CAN'T BE HELPED!

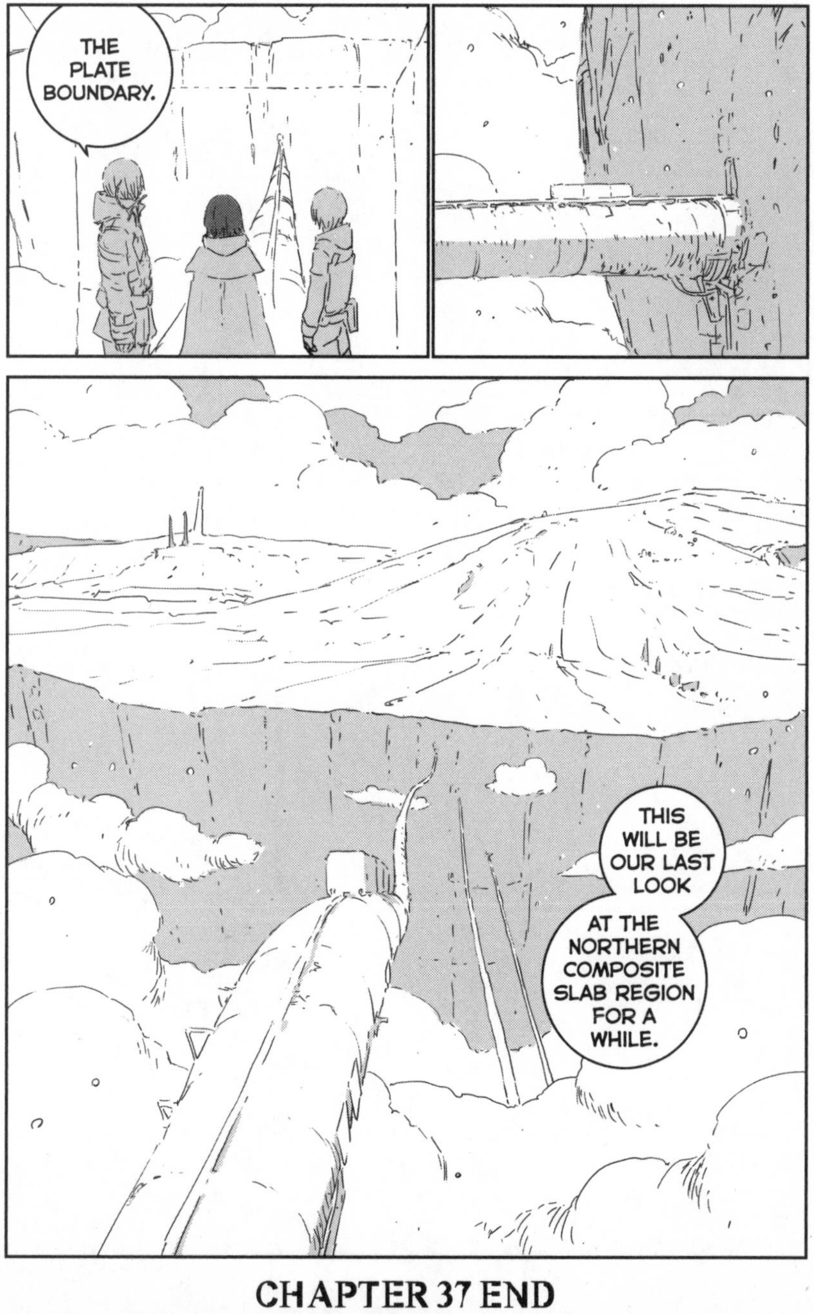
THE PLATE BOUNDARY.
THIS WILL BE OUR LAST LOOK AT THE NORTHERN COMPOSITE SLAB REGION FOR A WHILE.

CHAPTER 37 END

APOSIMZ

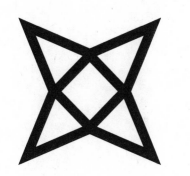

CHAPTER 38

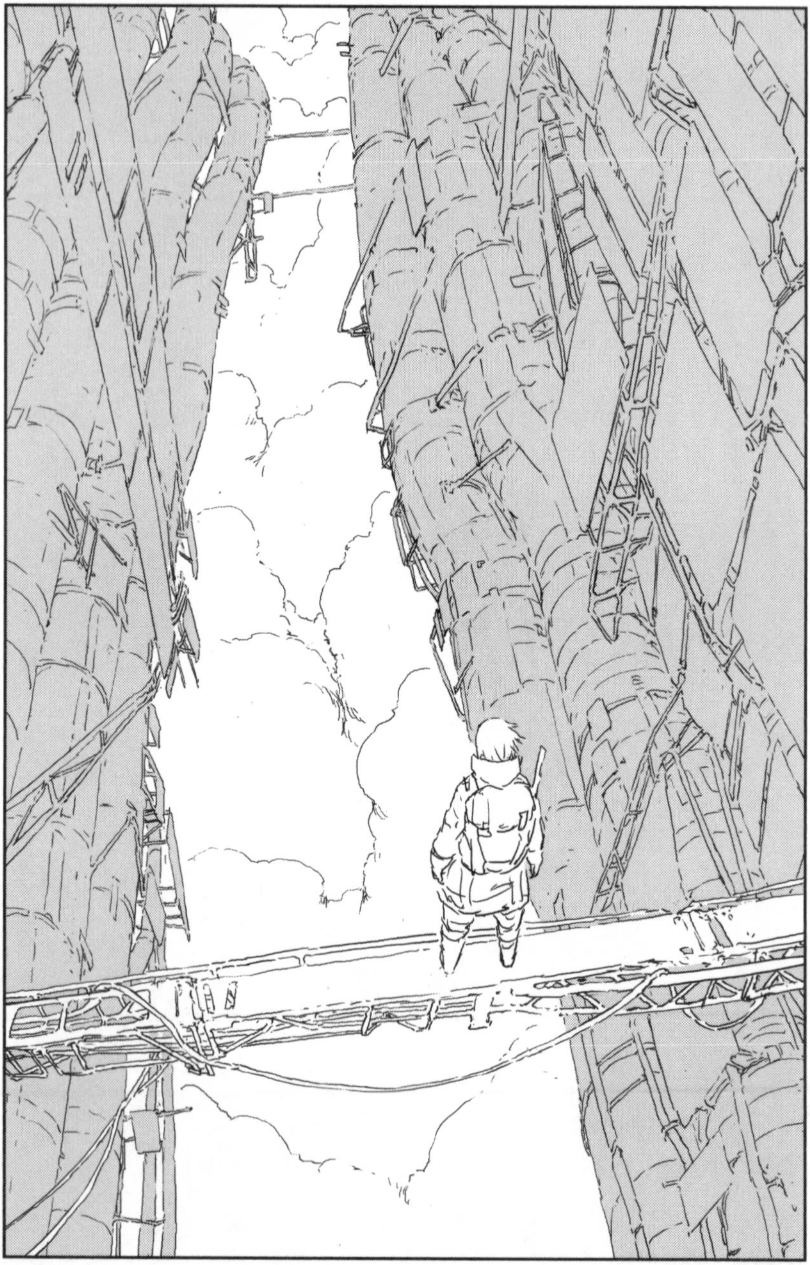

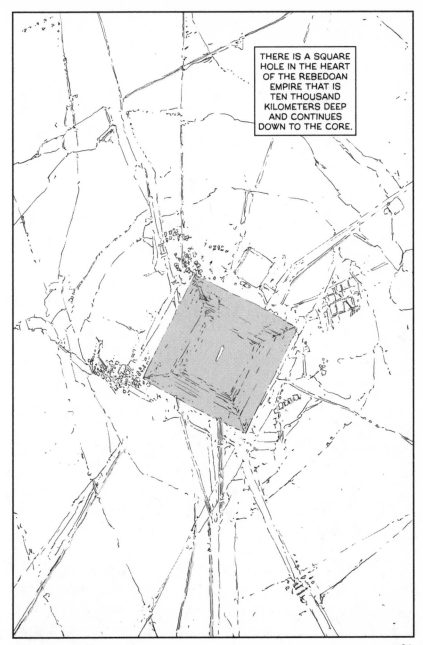

THERE IS A SQUARE
HOLE IN THE HEART
OF THE REBEDOAN
EMPIRE THAT IS
TEN THOUSAND
KILOMETERS DEEP
AND CONTINUES
DOWN TO THE CORE.

36

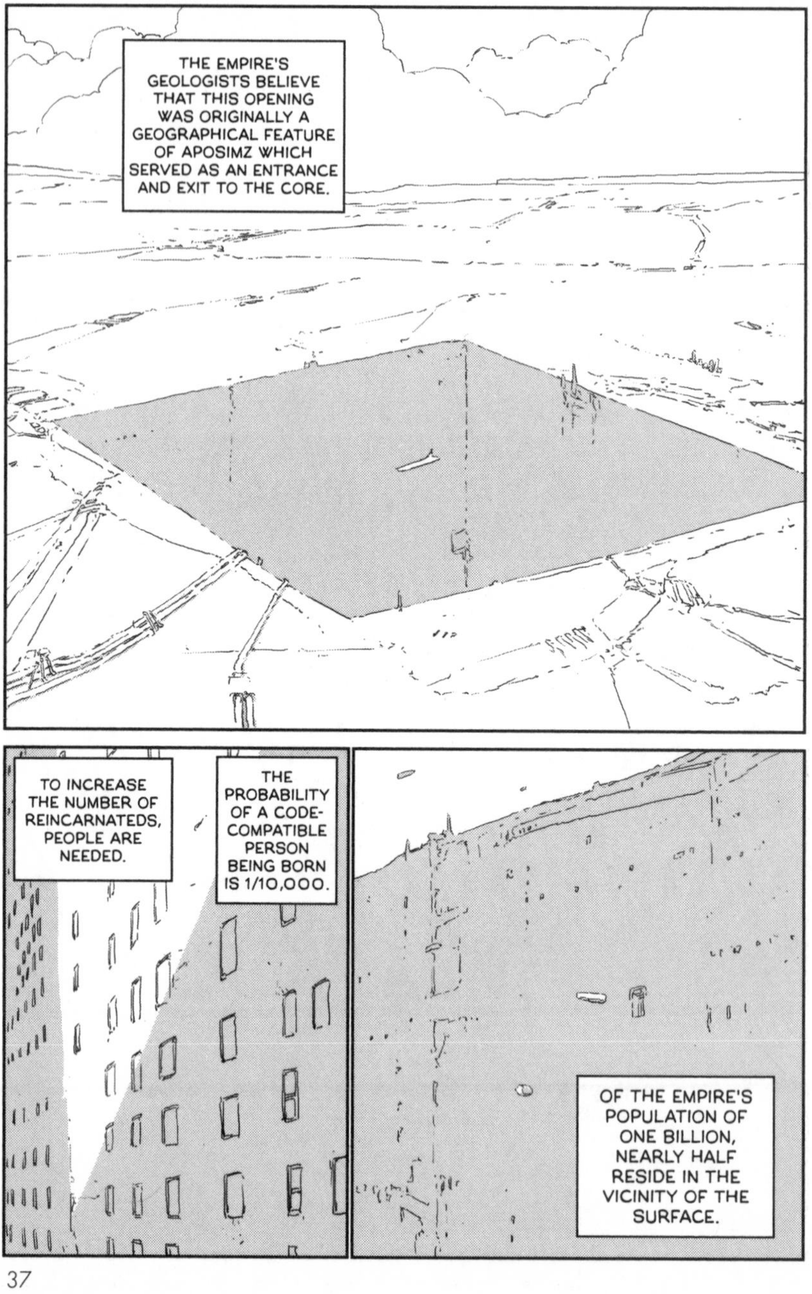
THE EMPIRE'S GEOLOGISTS BELIEVE THAT THIS OPENING WAS ORIGINALLY A GEOGRAPHICAL FEATURE OF APOSIMZ WHICH SERVED AS AN ENTRANCE AND EXIT TO THE CORE.
OF THE EMPIRE'S POPULATION OF ONE BILLION, NEARLY HALF RESIDE IN THE VICINITY OF THE SURFACE.
THE PROBABILITY OF A CODE-COMPATIBLE PERSON BEING BORN IS 1/10,000.
TO INCREASE THE NUMBER OF REINCARNATEDS, PEOPLE ARE NEEDED.

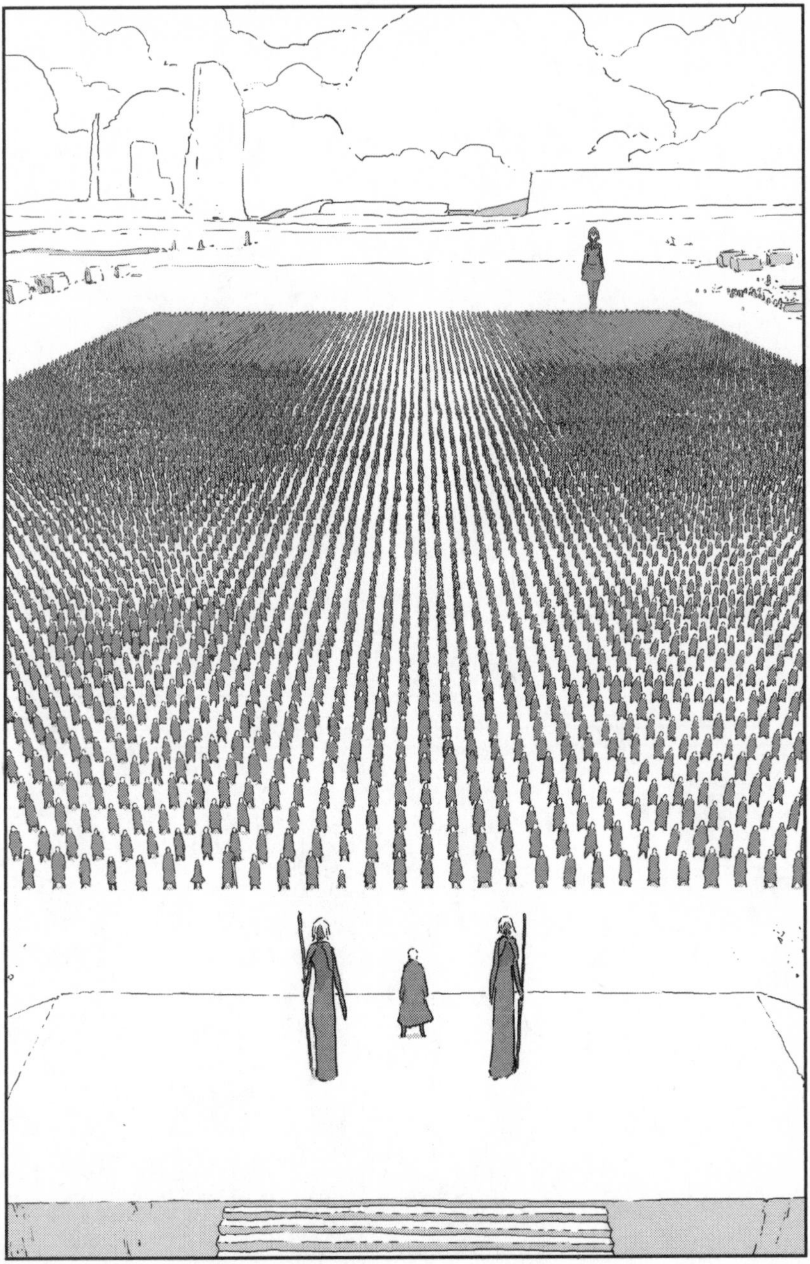

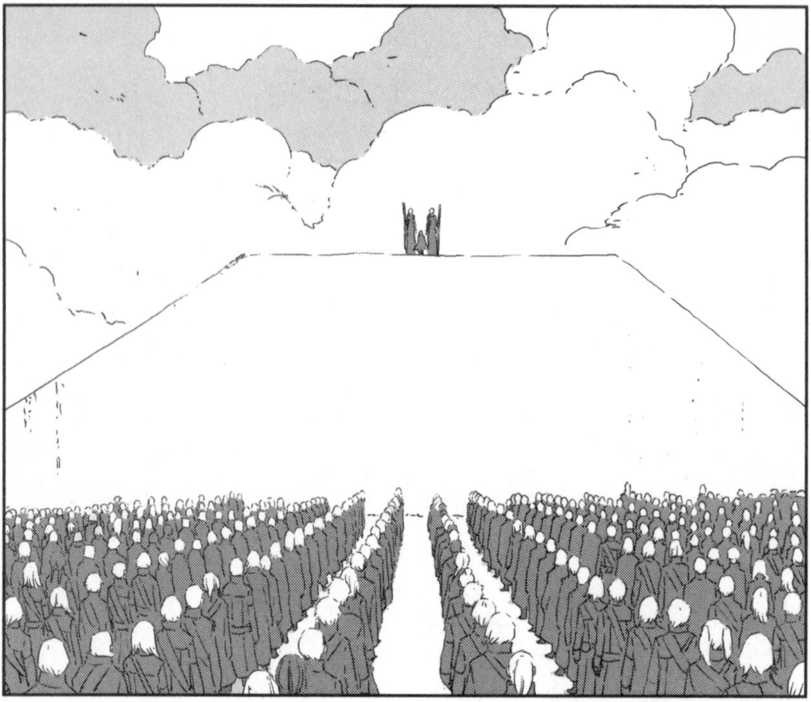

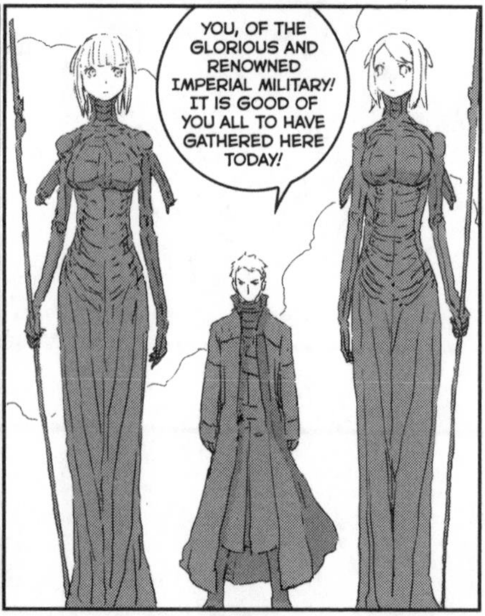
YOU, OF THE GLORIOUS AND RENOWNED IMPERIAL MILITARY! IT IS GOOD OF YOU ALL TO HAVE GATHERED HERE TODAY!

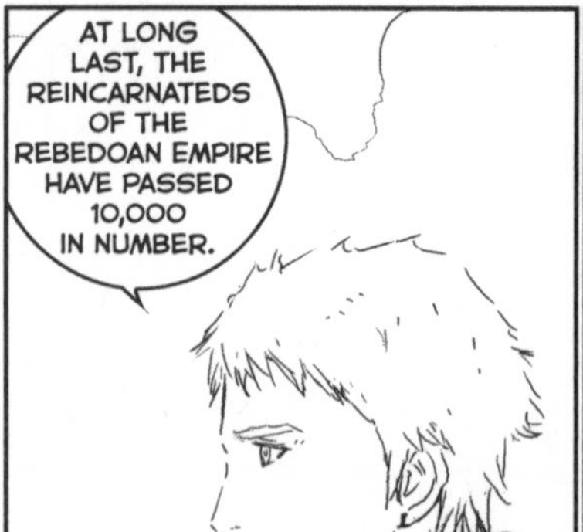
AT LONG LAST, THE REINCARNATEDS OF THE REBEDOAN EMPIRE HAVE PASSED 10,000 IN NUMBER.

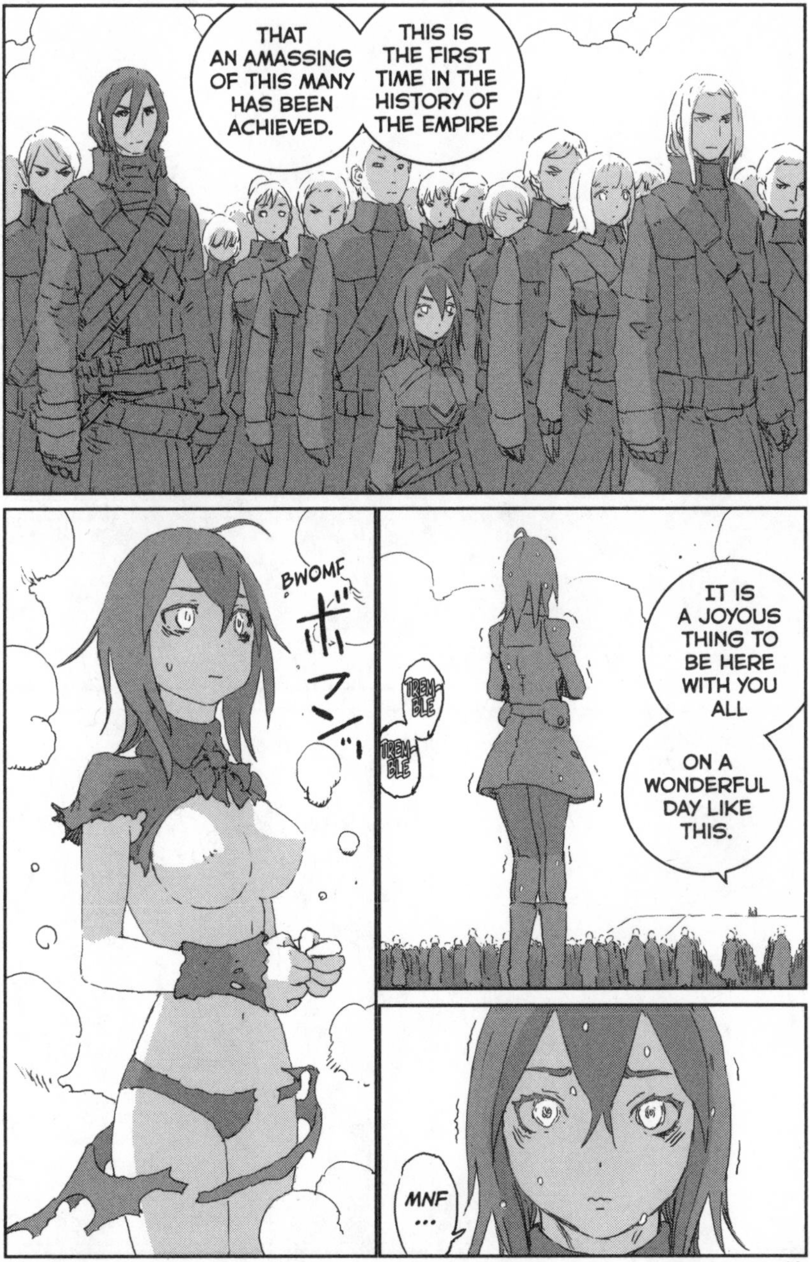
THIS IS THE FIRST TIME IN THE HISTORY OF THE EMPIRE
THAT AN AMASSING OF THIS MANY HAS BEEN ACHIEVED.
IT IS A JOYOUS THING TO BE HERE WITH YOU ALL
ON A WONDERFUL DAY LIKE THIS.
TREMBLE
TREMBLE
MNF ...
BWOMF
ボフンッ

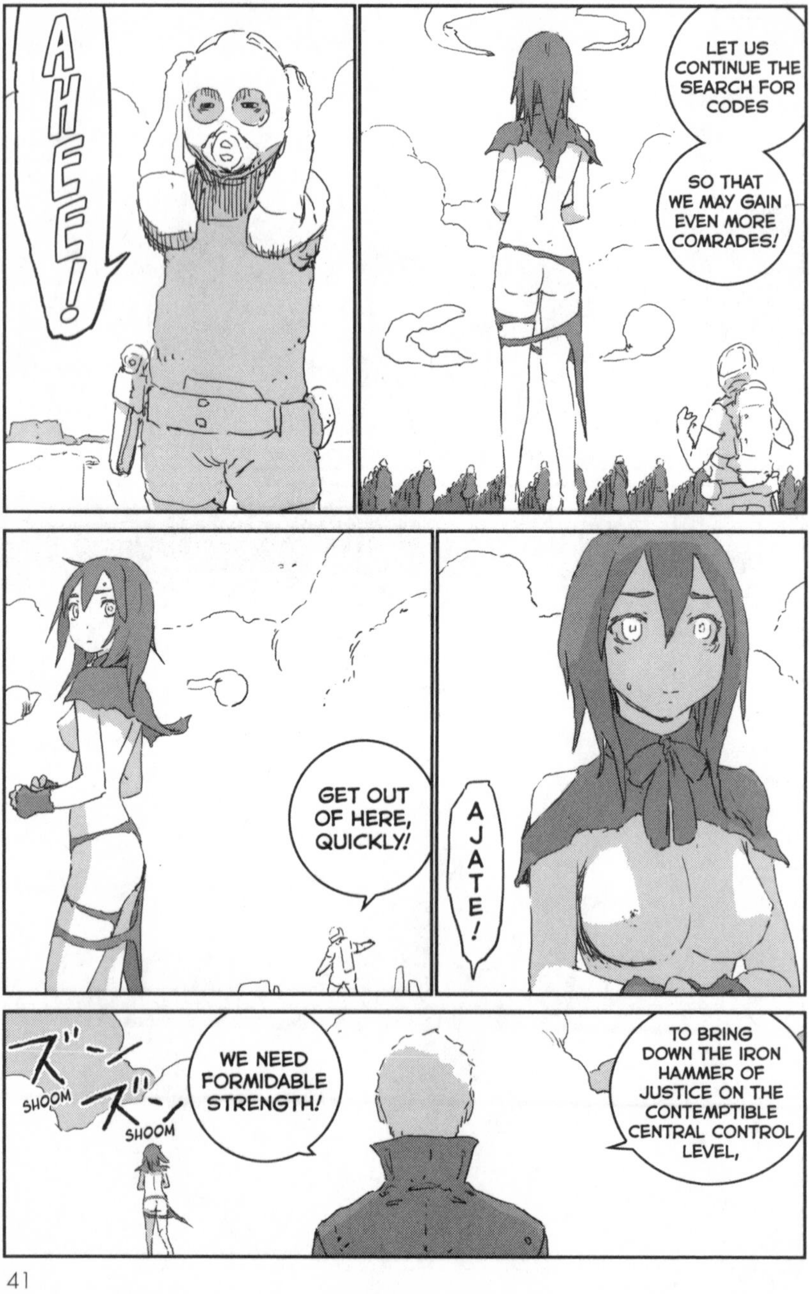
LET US CONTINUE THE SEARCH FOR CODES
SO THAT WE MAY GAIN EVEN MORE COMRADES!
AHEE!
AJATE!
GET OUT OF HERE, QUICKLY!
TO BRING DOWN THE IRON HAMMER OF JUSTICE ON THE CONTEMPTIBLE CENTRAL CONTROL LEVEL,
WE NEED FORMIDABLE STRENGTH!
ズーン SHOOM
ズーン SHOOM

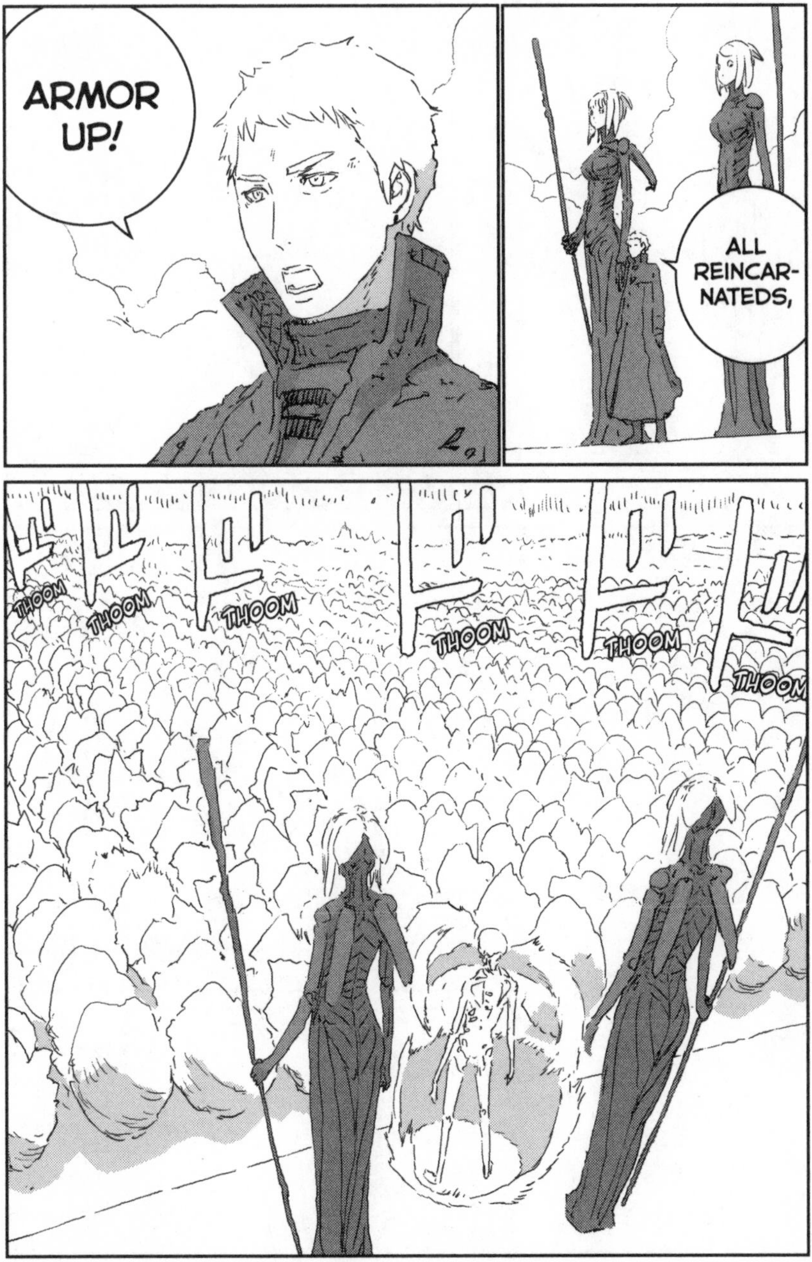
ALL REINCARNATEDS,
ARMOR UP!
THOOM
THOOM
THOOM
THOOM
THOOM
THOOM

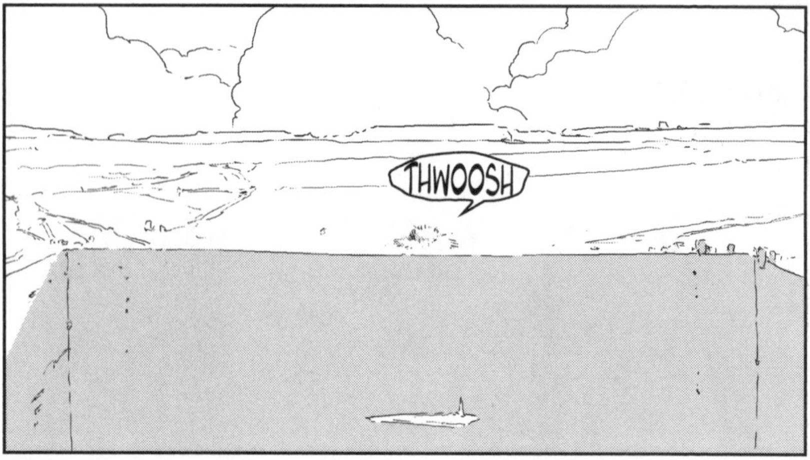
THWOOSH
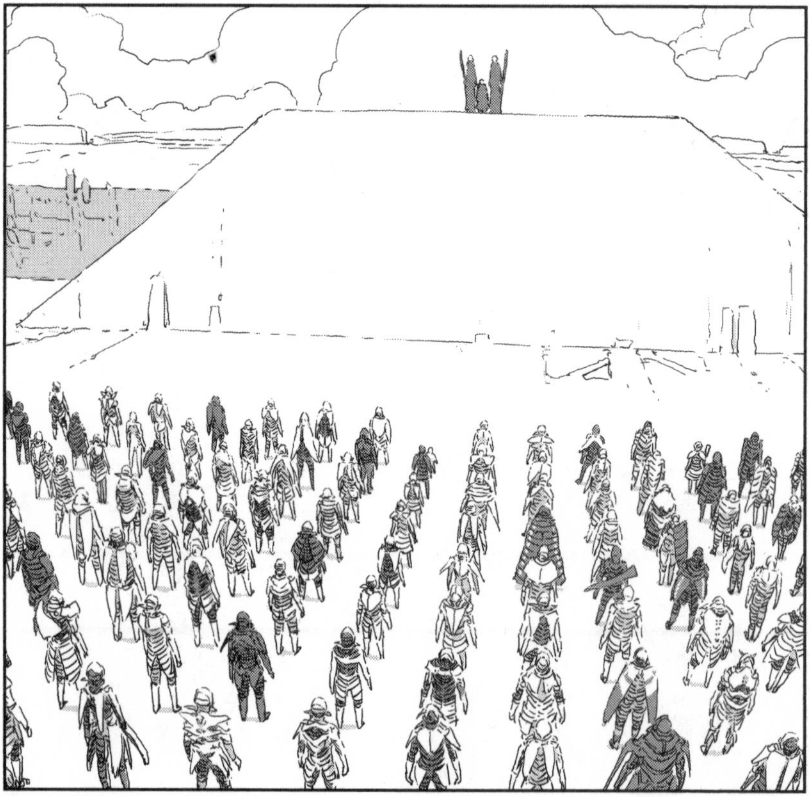

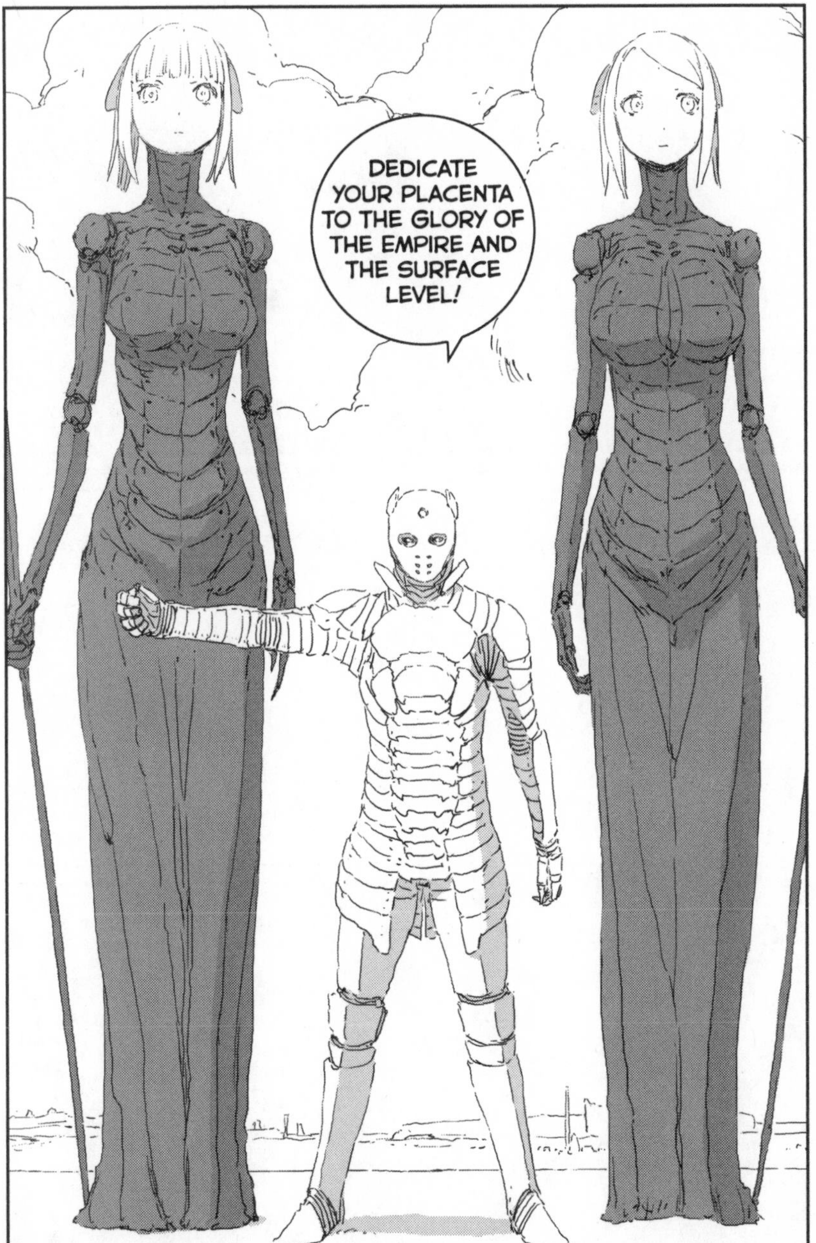
DEDICATE YOUR PLACENTA TO THE GLORY OF THE EMPIRE AND THE SURFACE LEVEL!

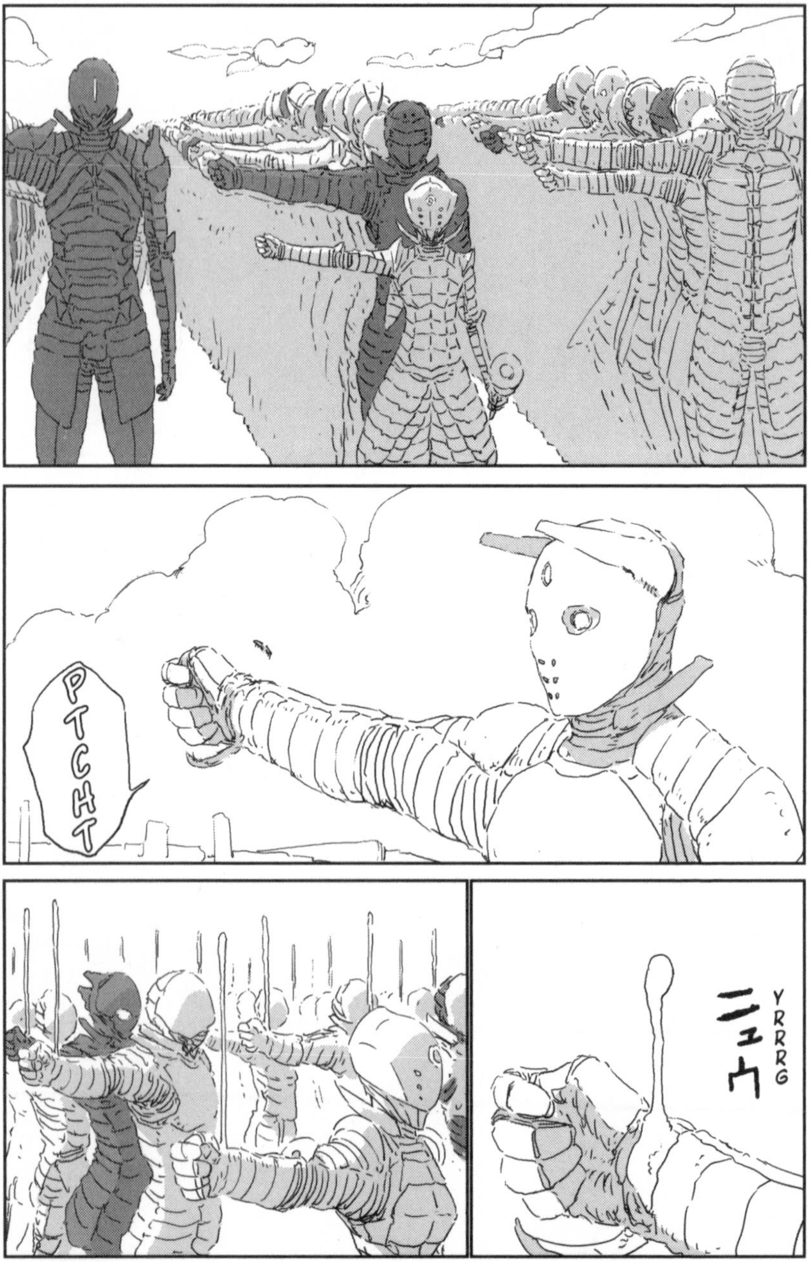
PTCHT
ニュウ
YRRRG

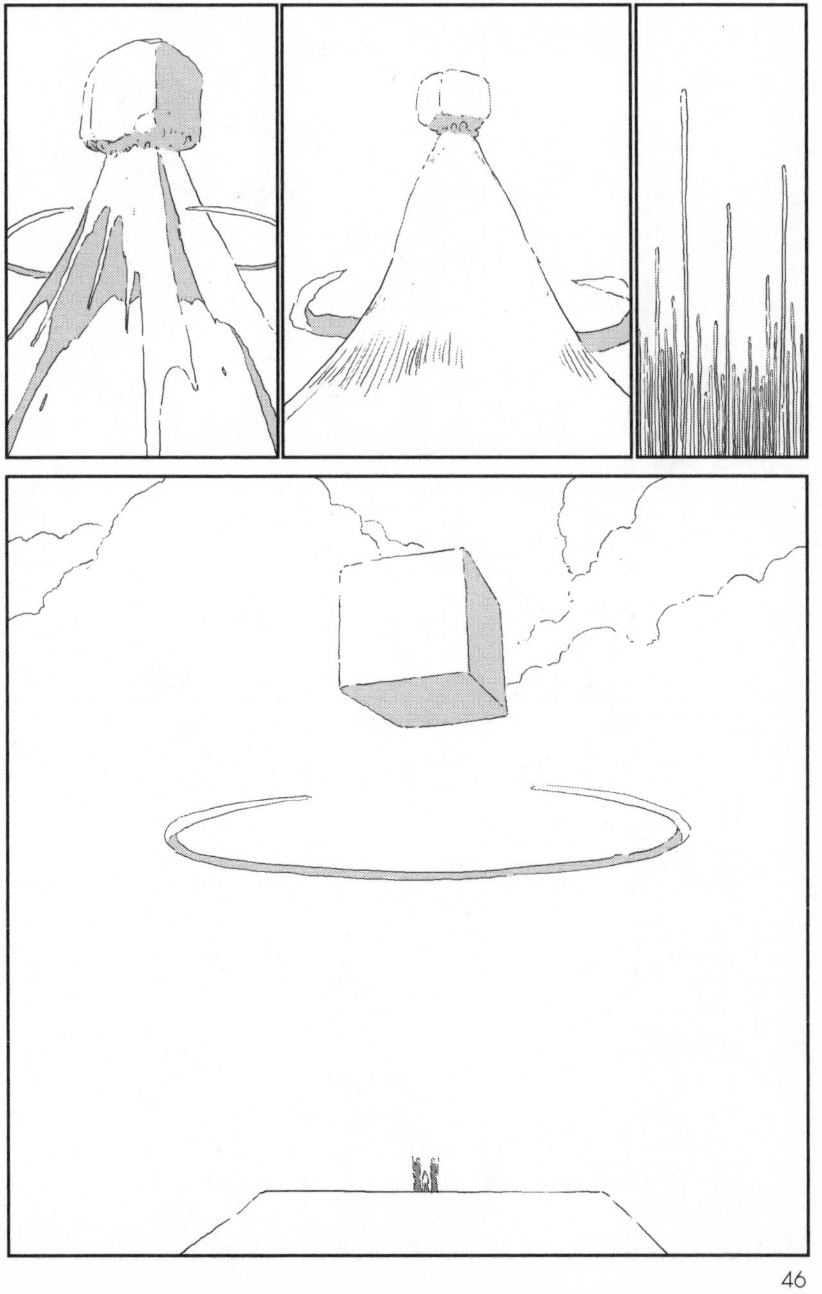

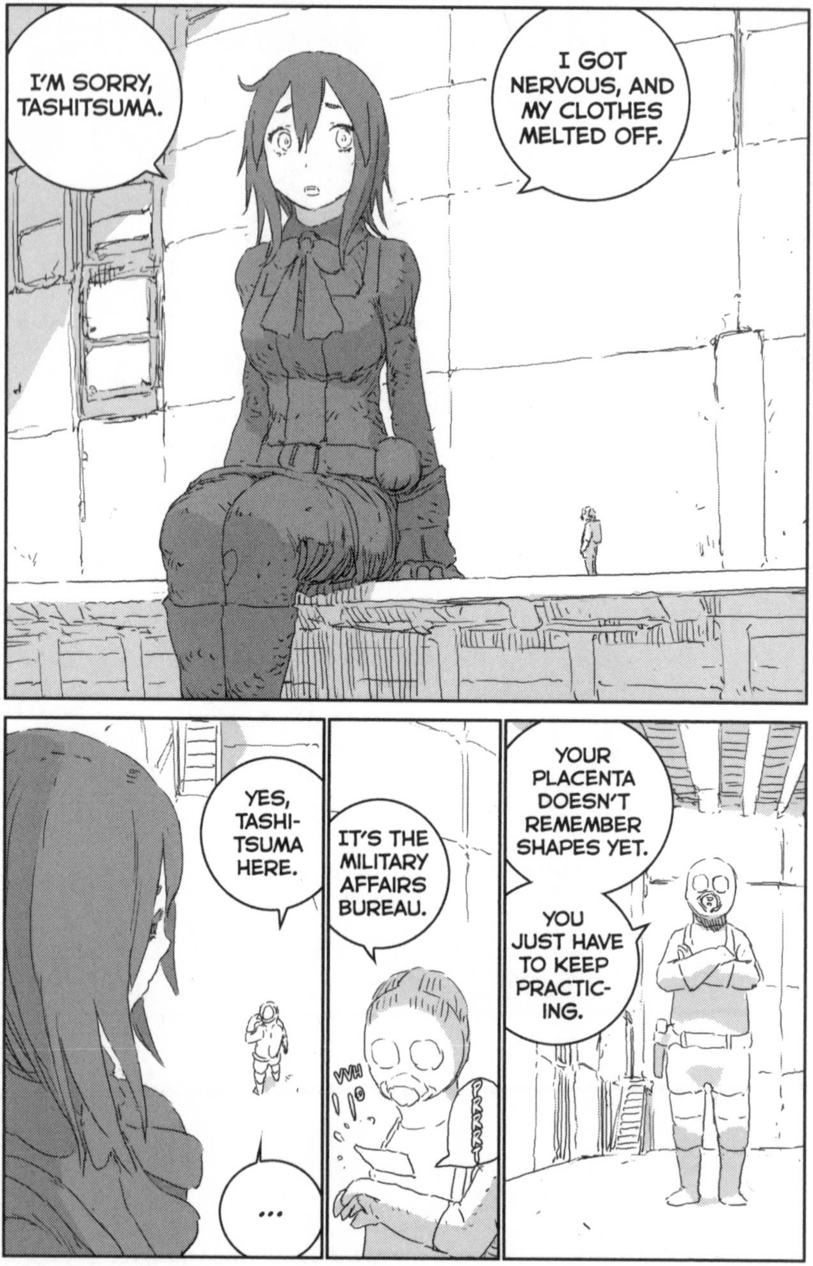
I GOT NERVOUS, AND MY CLOTHES MELTED OFF.
I'M SORRY, TASHITSUMA.
YOUR PLACENTA DOESN'T REMEMBER SHAPES YET.
YOU JUST HAVE TO KEEP PRACTIC-ING.
IT'S THE MILITARY AFFAIRS BUREAU.
VVH
PRRRT
YES, TASHI-TSUMA HERE.
...

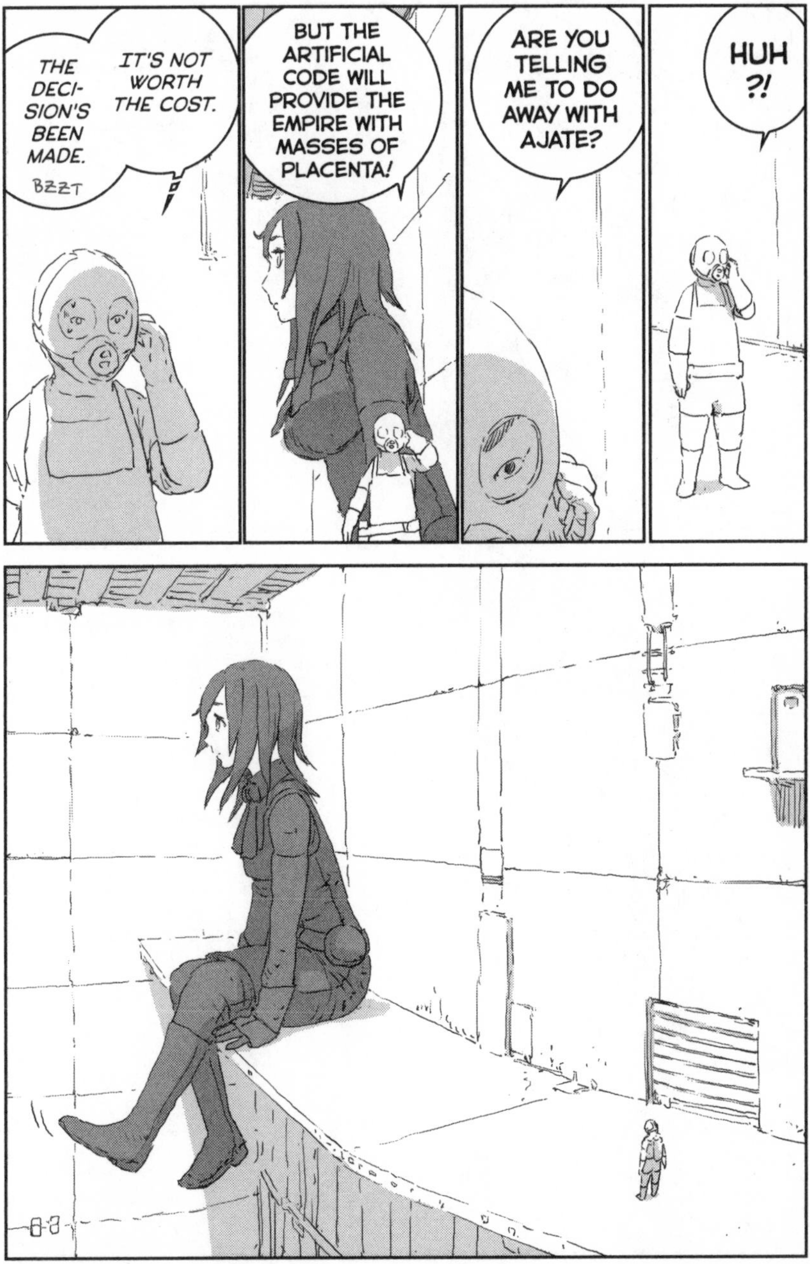
HUH ?!
ARE YOU TELLING ME TO DO AWAY WITH AJATE?
BUT THE ARTIFICIAL CODE WILL PROVIDE THE EMPIRE WITH MASSES OF PLACENTA!
IT'S NOT WORTH THE COST.
THE DECISION'S BEEN MADE.
BZZT

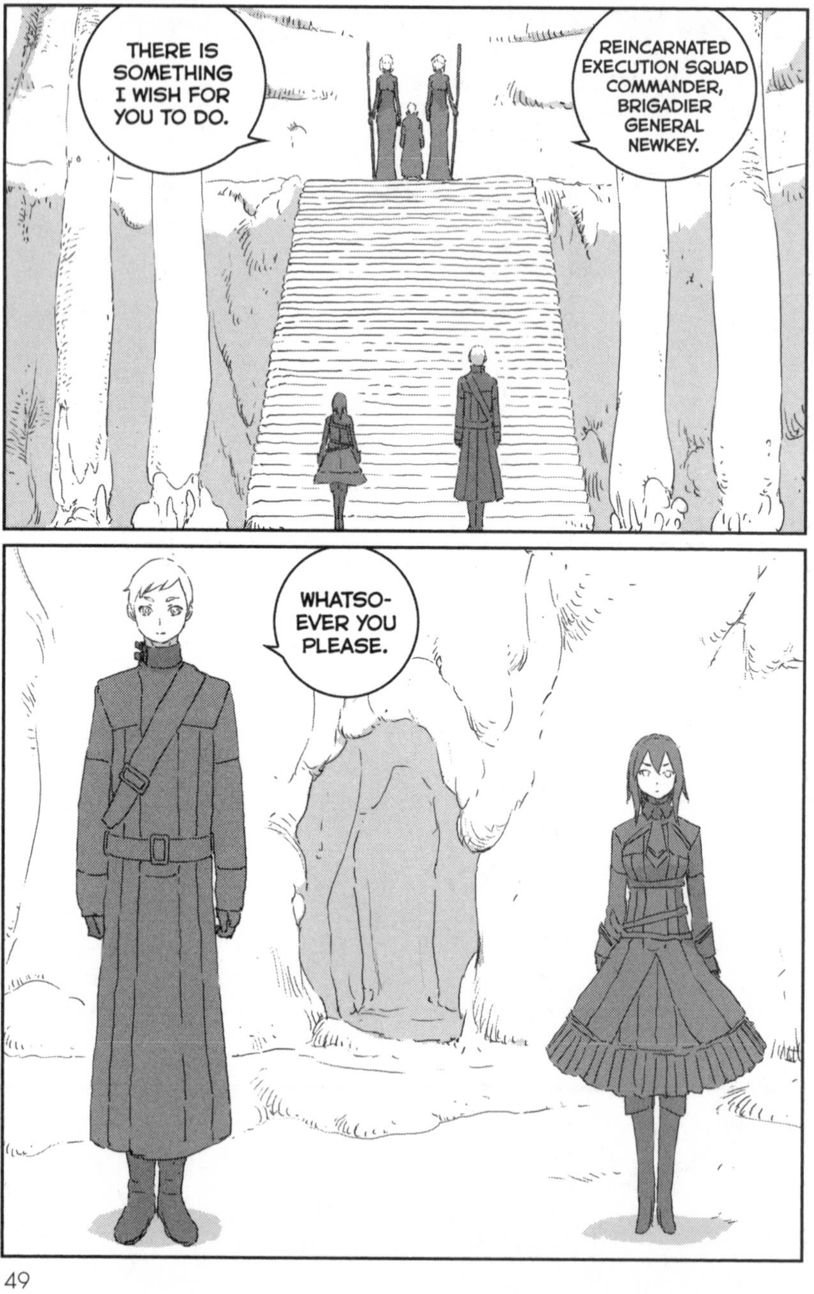
REINCARNATED EXECUTION SQUAD COMMANDER, BRIGADIER GENERAL NEWKEY.
THERE IS SOMETHING I WISH FOR YOU TO DO.
WHATSO-EVER YOU PLEASE.

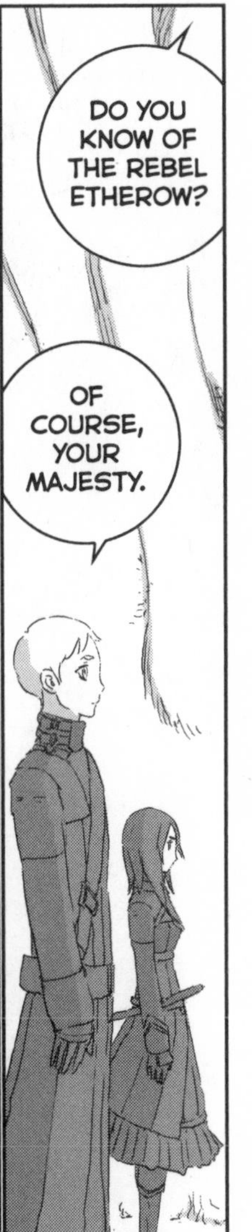
DO YOU KNOW OF THE REBEL ETHEROW?
OF COURSE, YOUR MAJESTY.

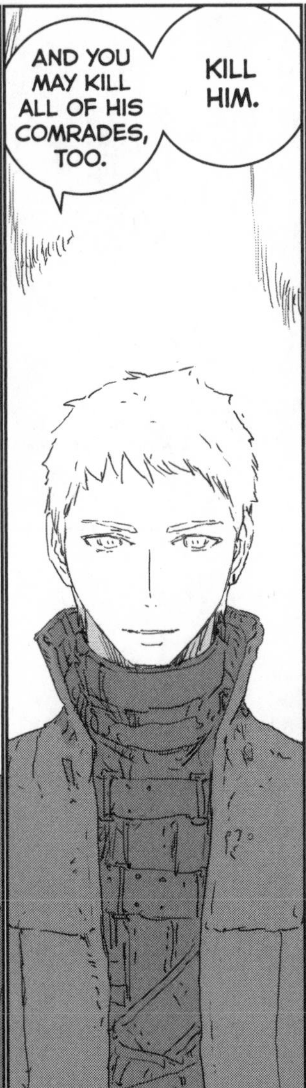
KILL HIM.
AND YOU MAY KILL ALL OF HIS COMRADES, TOO.

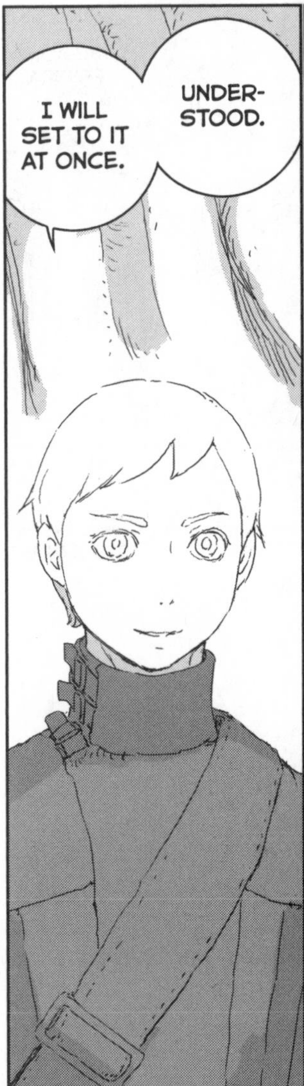
UNDER-STOOD.
I WILL SET TO IT AT ONCE.

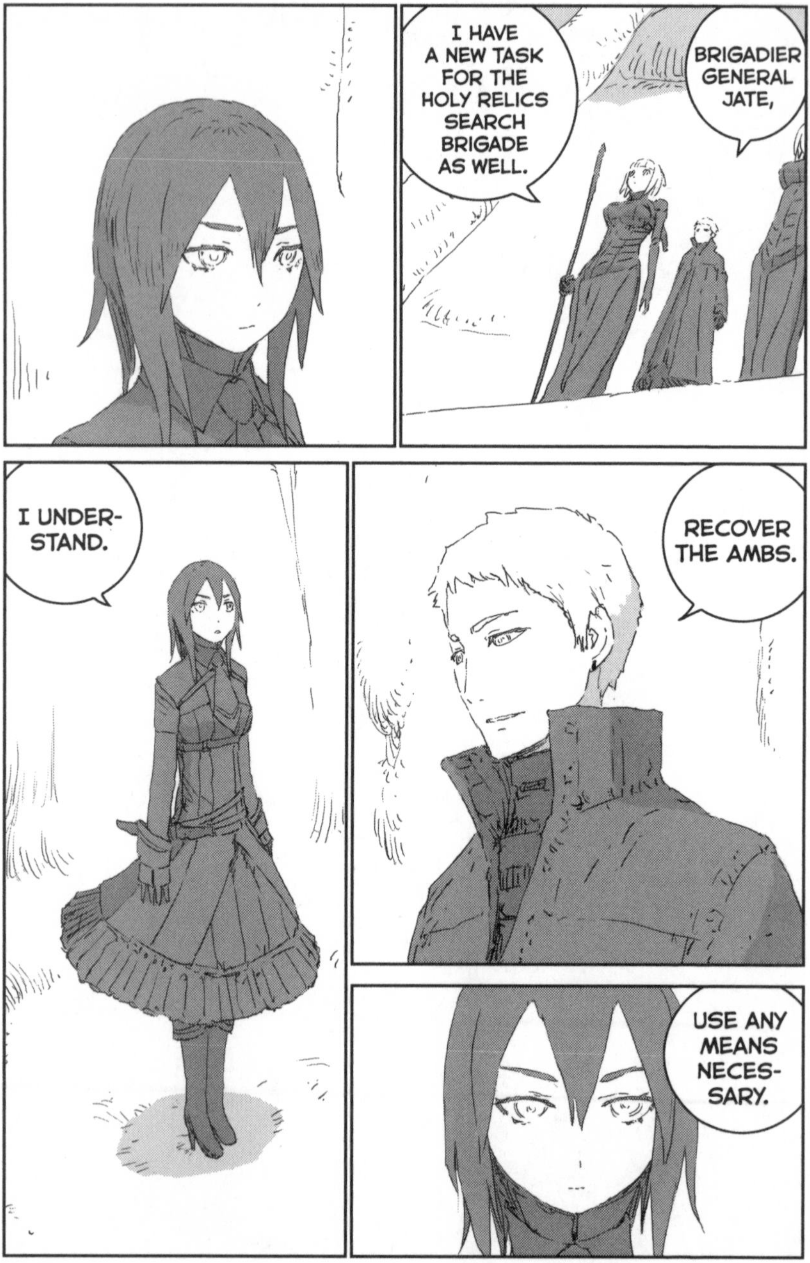
BRIGADIER GENERAL JATE,
I HAVE A NEW TASK FOR THE HOLY RELICS SEARCH BRIGADE AS WELL.
RECOVER THE AMBS.
USE ANY MEANS NECES-SARY.
I UNDER-STAND.

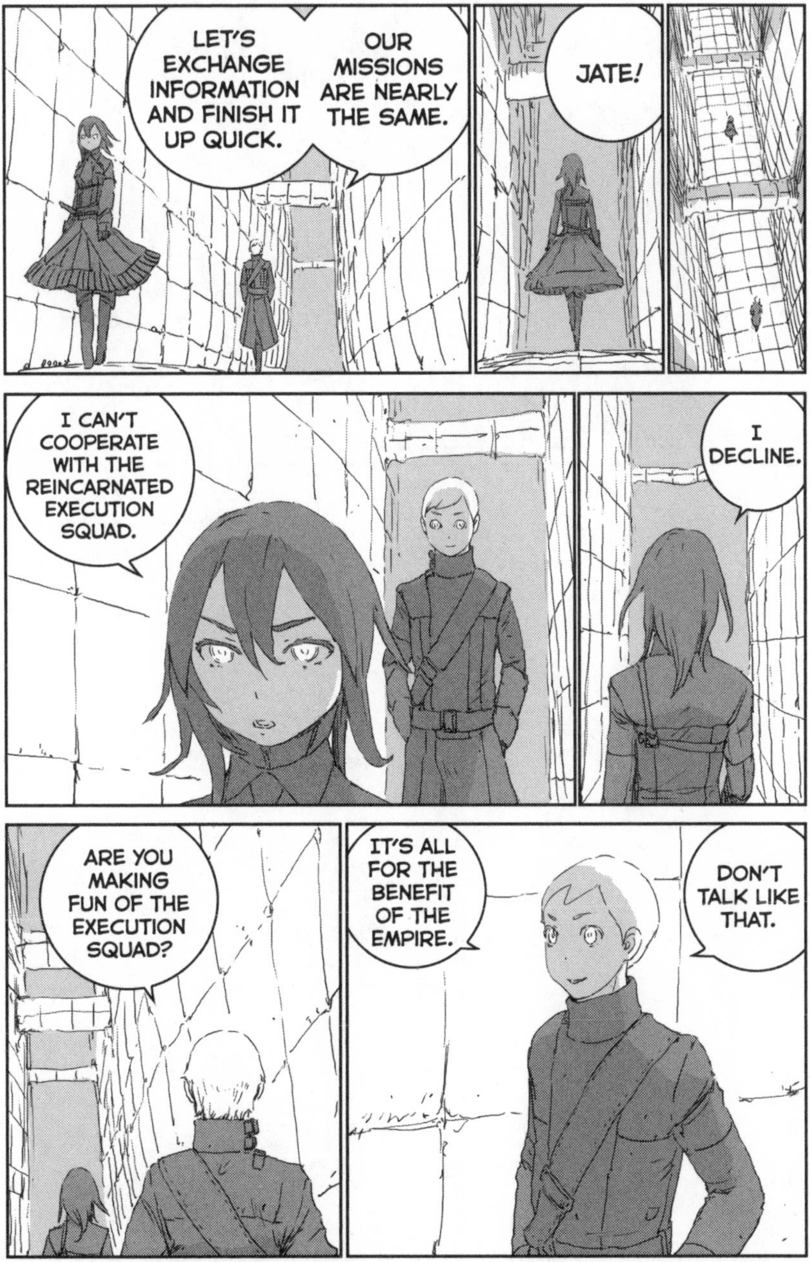
JATE!
OUR MISSIONS ARE NEARLY THE SAME.
LET'S EXCHANGE INFORMATION AND FINISH IT UP QUICK.
I DECLINE.
I CAN'T COOPERATE WITH THE REINCARNATED EXECUTION SQUAD.
DON'T TALK LIKE THAT.
IT'S ALL FOR THE BENEFIT OF THE EMPIRE.
ARE YOU MAKING FUN OF THE EXECUTION SQUAD?

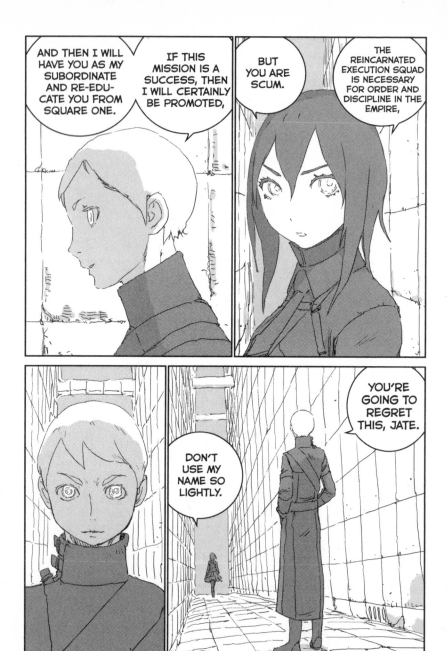

THE REINCARNATED EXECUTION SQUAD IS NECESSARY FOR ORDER AND DISCIPLINE IN THE EMPIRE,
BUT YOU ARE SCUM.
IF THIS MISSION IS A SUCCESS, THEN I WILL CERTAINLY BE PROMOTED,
AND THEN I WILL HAVE YOU AS MY SUBORDINATE AND RE-EDU-CATE YOU FROM SQUARE ONE.
YOU'RE GOING TO REGRET THIS, JATE.
DON'T USE MY NAME SO LIGHTLY.

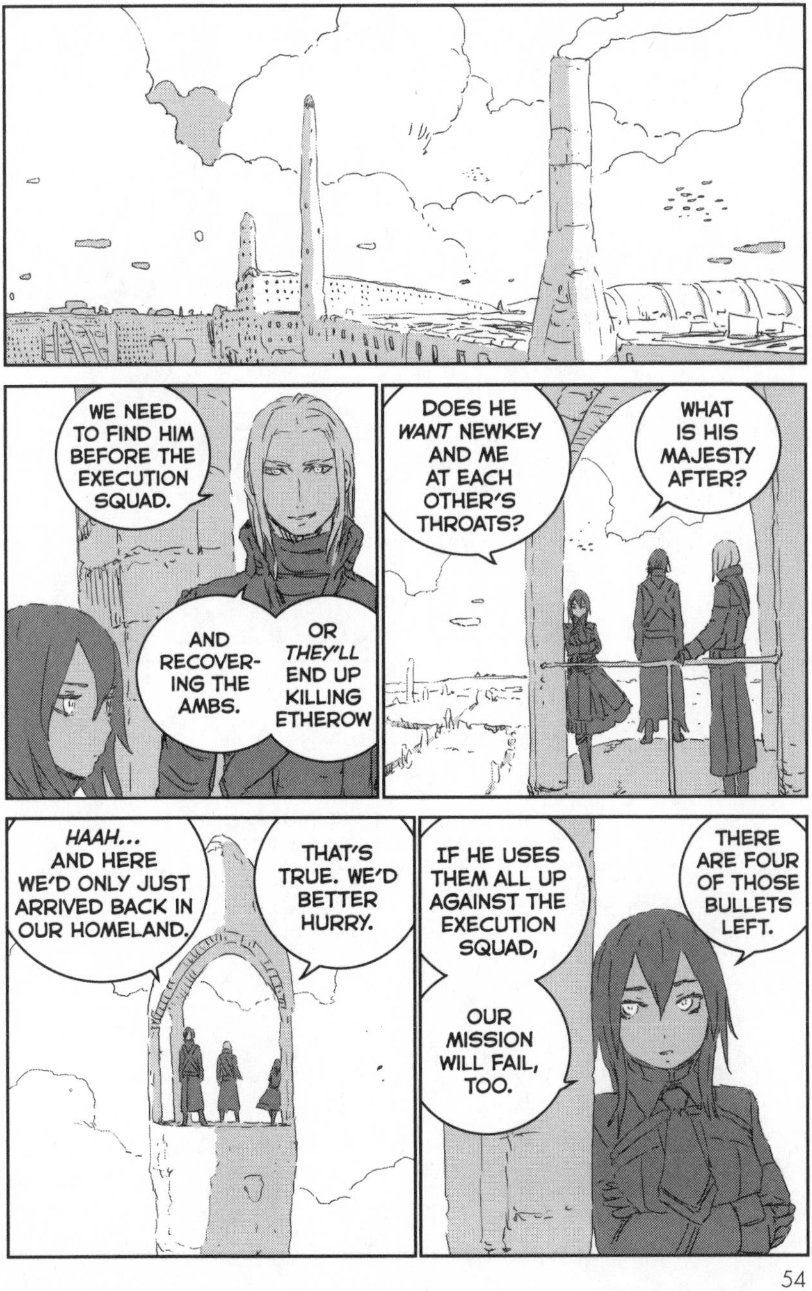
WHAT IS HIS MAJESTY AFTER?
DOES HE *WANT* NEWKEY AND ME AT EACH OTHER'S THROATS?
WE NEED TO FIND HIM BEFORE THE EXECUTION SQUAD.
OR *THEY'LL* END UP KILLING ETHEROW
AND RECOVER-ING THE AMBS.
THERE ARE FOUR OF THOSE BULLETS LEFT.
IF HE USES THEM ALL UP AGAINST THE EXECUTION SQUAD,
OUR MISSION WILL FAIL, TOO.
THAT'S TRUE. WE'D BETTER HURRY.
HAAH... AND HERE WE'D ONLY JUST ARRIVED BACK IN OUR HOMELAND.

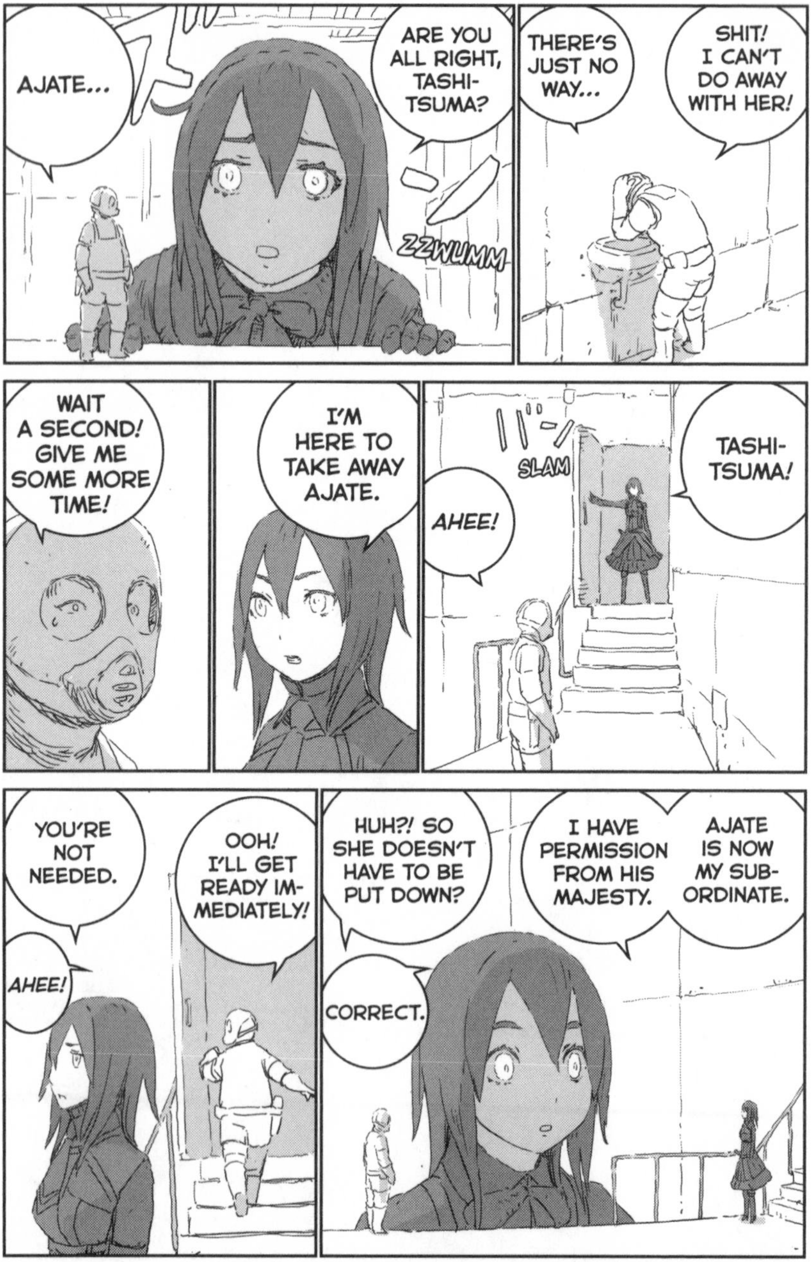
SHIT! I CAN'T DO AWAY WITH HER!
THERE'S JUST NO WAY...
ARE YOU ALL RIGHT, TASHI-TSUMA?
ZZWUMM
AJATE...
TASHI-TSUMA!
SLAM
AHEE!
I'M HERE TO TAKE AWAY AJATE.
WAIT A SECOND! GIVE ME SOME MORE TIME!
AJATE IS NOW MY SUB-ORDINATE.
I HAVE PERMISSION FROM HIS MAJESTY.
HUH?! SO SHE DOESN'T HAVE TO BE PUT DOWN?
CORRECT.
OOH! I'LL GET READY IM-MEDIATELY!
YOU'RE NOT NEEDED.
AHEE!

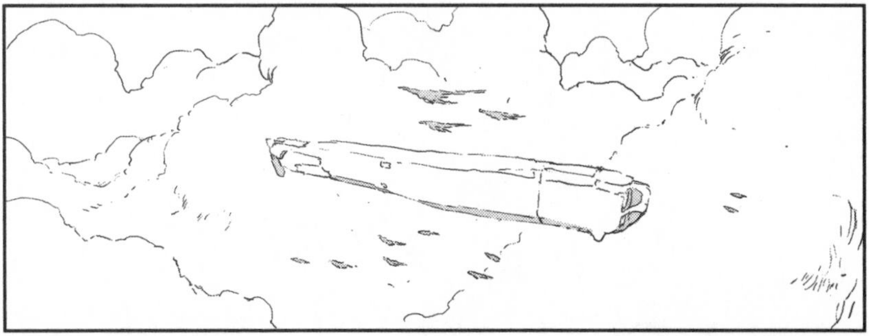

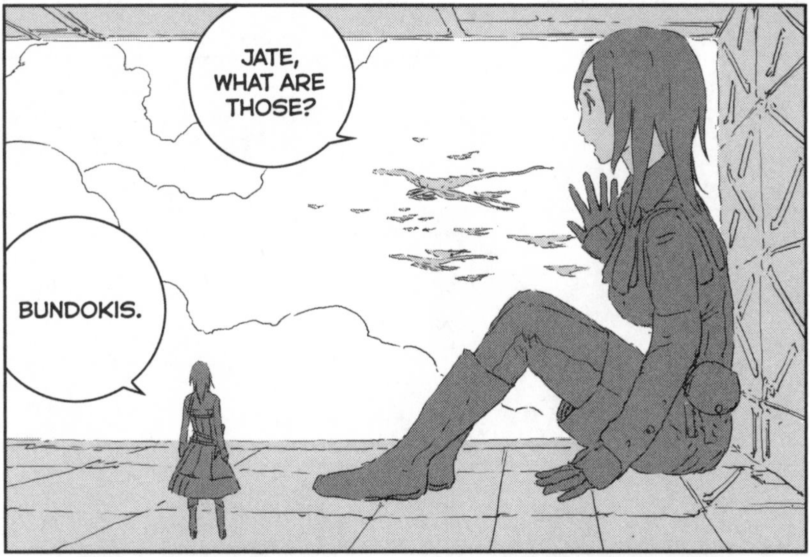
JATE, WHAT ARE THOSE?
BUNDOKIS.

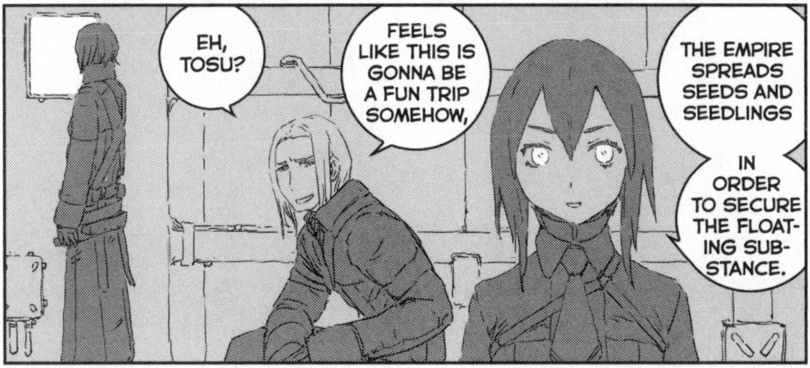
THE EMPIRE SPREADS SEEDS AND SEEDLINGS
IN ORDER TO SECURE THE FLOAT-ING SUB-STANCE.
FEELS LIKE THIS IS GONNA BE A FUN TRIP SOMEHOW,
EH, TOSU?

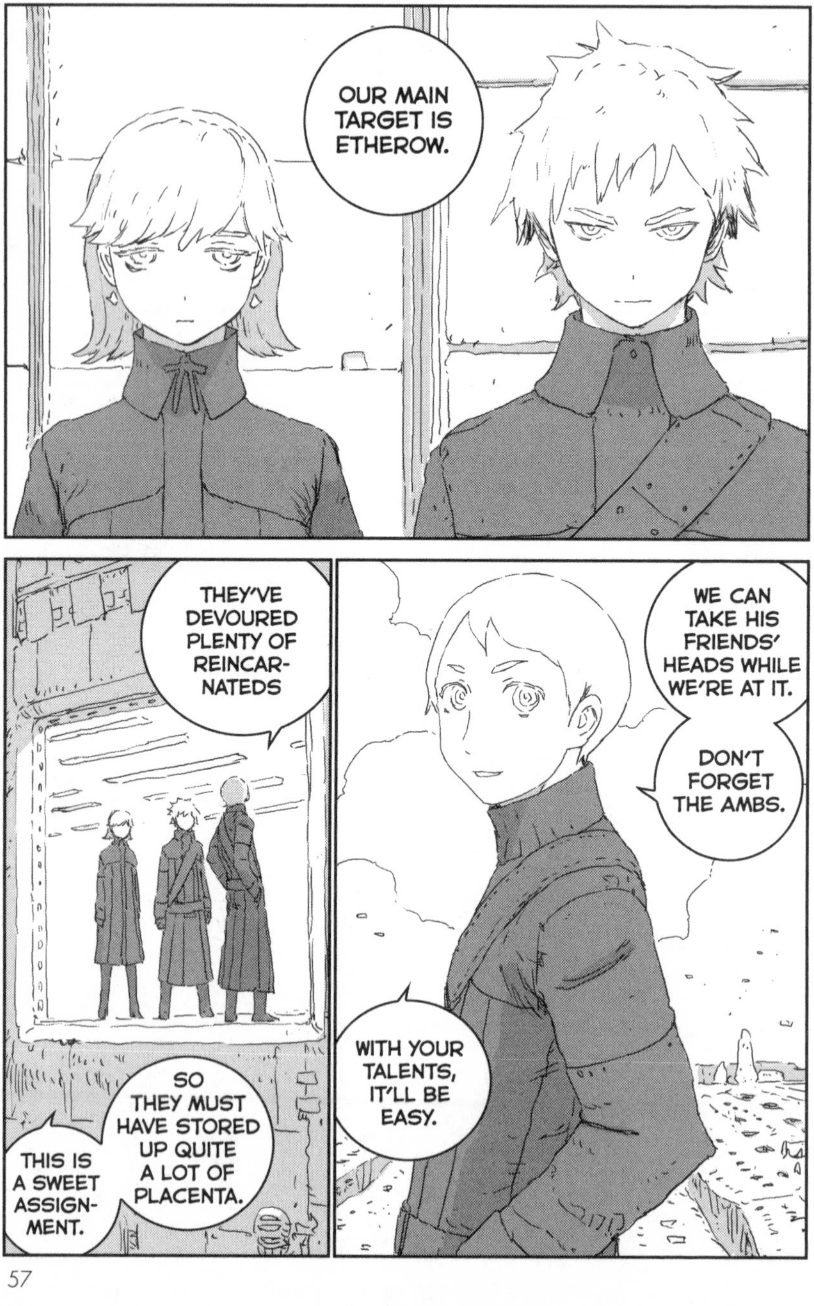
OUR MAIN TARGET IS ETHEROW.
WE CAN TAKE HIS FRIENDS' HEADS WHILE WE'RE AT IT.
DON'T FORGET THE AMBS.
WITH YOUR TALENTS, IT'LL BE EASY.
THEY'VE DEVOURED PLENTY OF REINCAR- NATEDS
SO THEY MUST HAVE STORED UP QUITE A LOT OF PLACENTA.
THIS IS A SWEET ASSIGN- MENT.

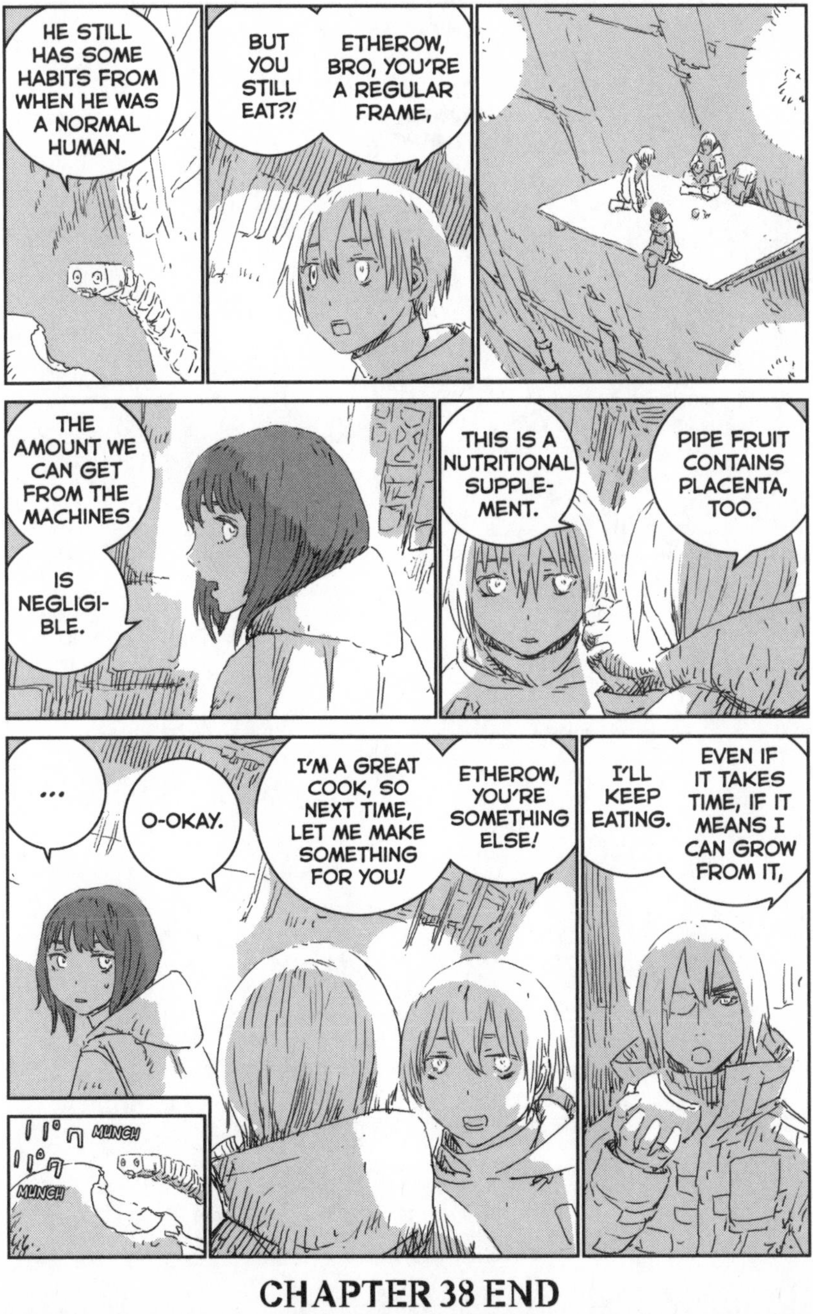
ETHEROW, BRO, YOU'RE A REGULAR FRAME,
BUT YOU STILL EAT?!
HE STILL HAS SOME HABITS FROM WHEN HE WAS A NORMAL HUMAN.
PIPE FRUIT CONTAINS PLACENTA, TOO.
THIS IS A NUTRITIONAL SUPPLEMENT.
THE AMOUNT WE CAN GET FROM THE MACHINES
IS NEGLIGIBLE.
EVEN IF IT TAKES TIME, IF IT MEANS I CAN GROW FROM IT,
I'LL KEEP EATING.
ETHEROW, YOU'RE SOMETHING ELSE!
I'M A GREAT COOK, SO NEXT TIME, LET ME MAKE SOMETHING FOR YOU!
O-OKAY.
...
MUNCH
MUNCH

CHAPTER 38 END

APOSIMZ

X

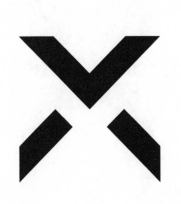

CHAPTER 39

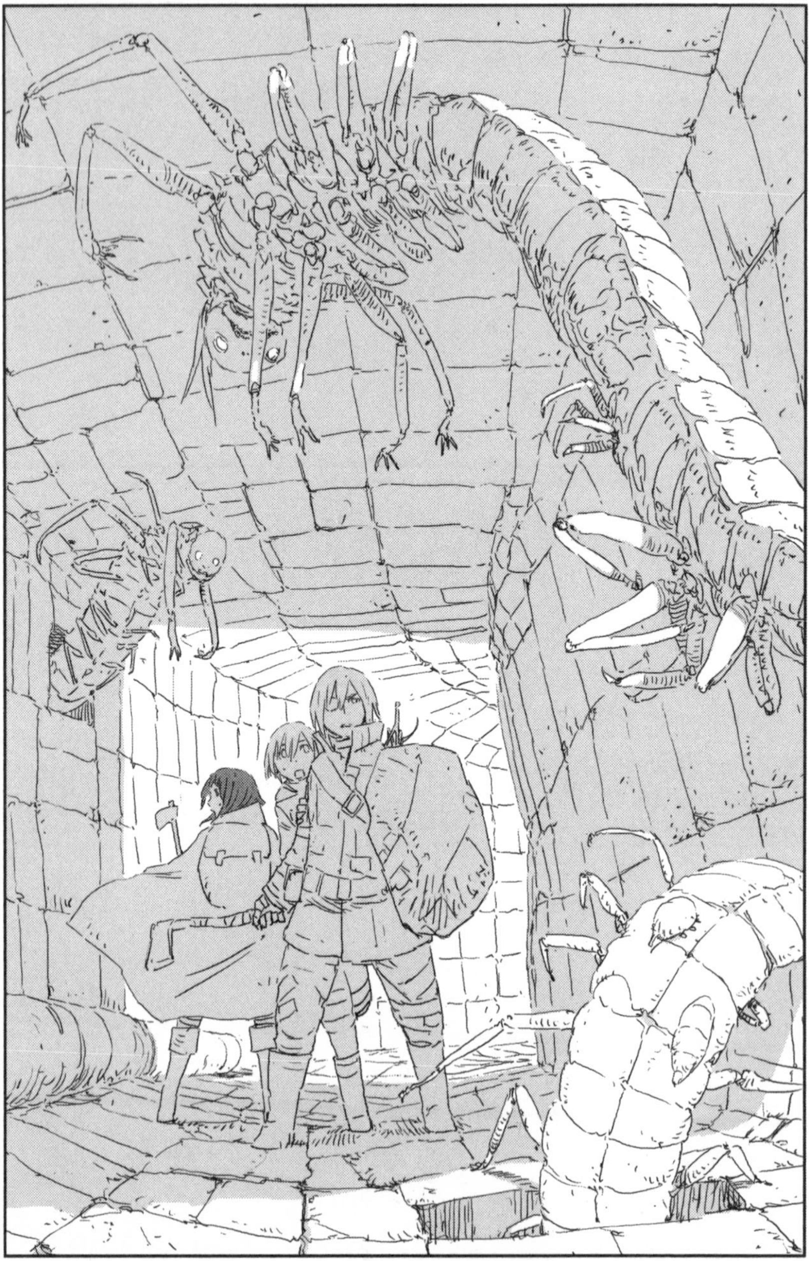

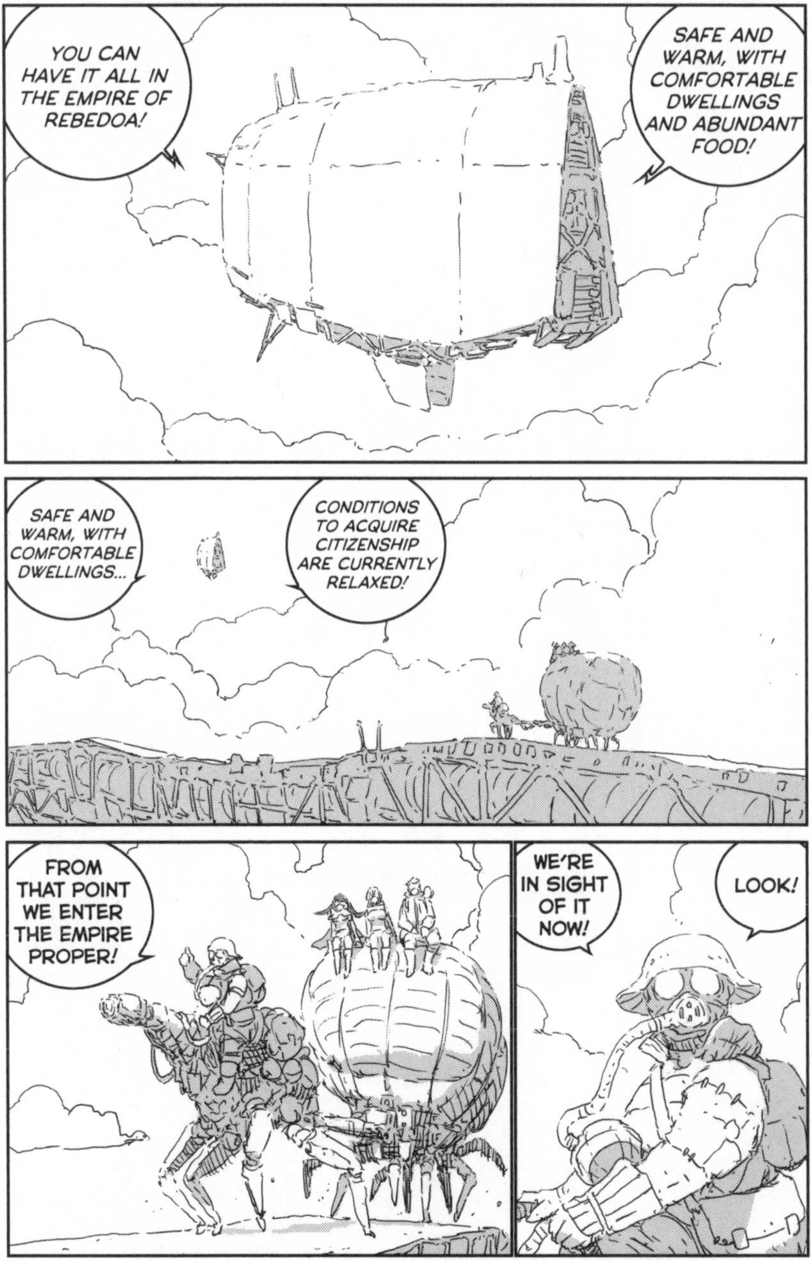
SAFE AND WARM, WITH COMFORTABLE DWELLINGS AND ABUNDANT FOOD!
YOU CAN HAVE IT ALL IN THE EMPIRE OF REBEDOA!
CONDITIONS TO ACQUIRE CITIZENSHIP ARE CURRENTLY RELAXED!
SAFE AND WARM, WITH COMFORTABLE DWELLINGS...
LOOK!
WE'RE IN SIGHT OF IT NOW!
FROM THAT POINT WE ENTER THE EMPIRE PROPER!

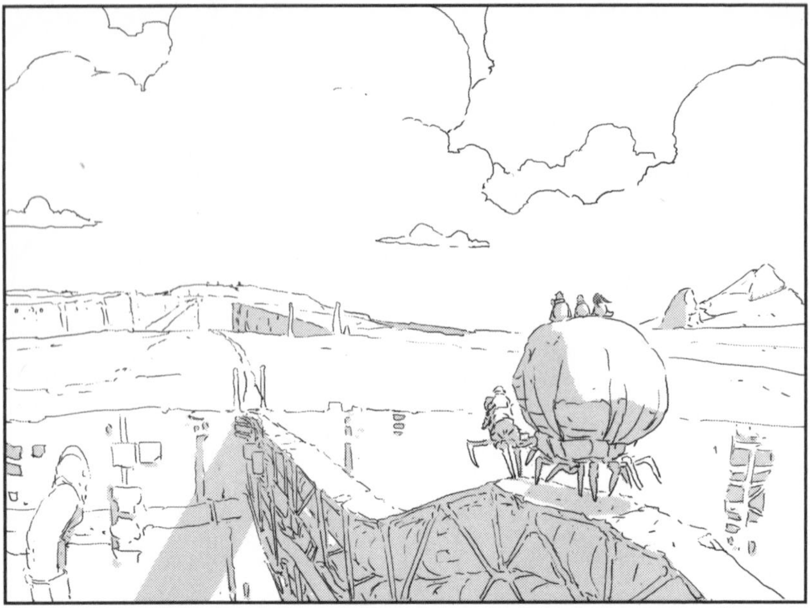
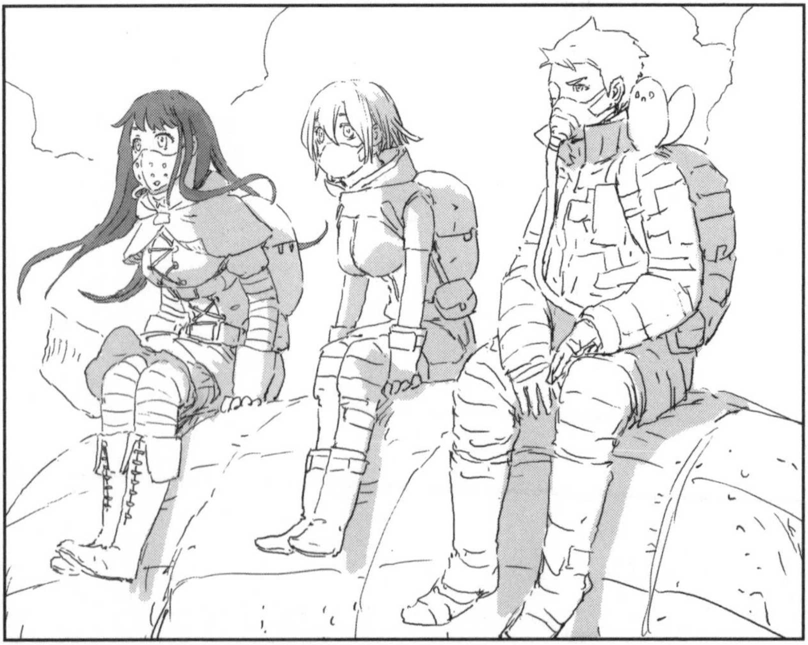

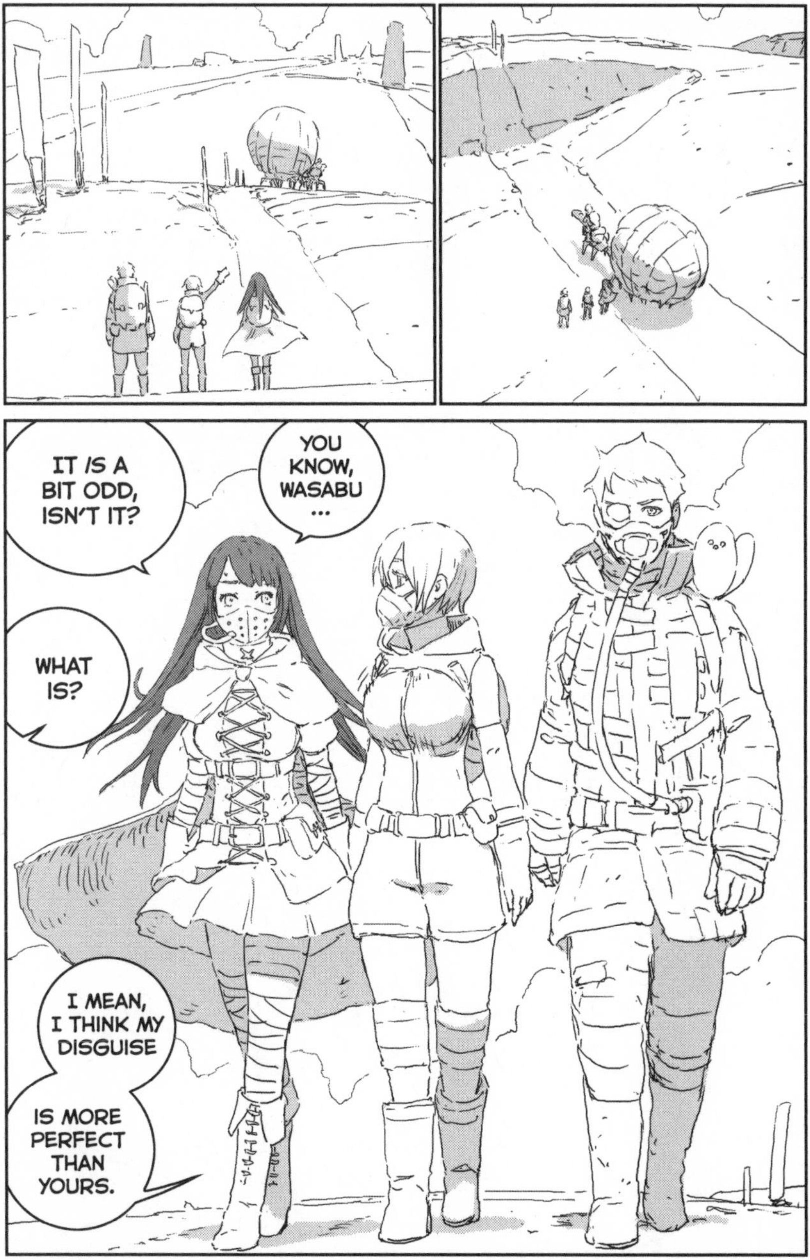
YOU KNOW, WASABU...
IT IS A BIT ODD, ISN'T IT?
WHAT IS?
I MEAN, I THINK MY DISGUISE
IS MORE PERFECT THAN YOURS.

ガシャーン
GASHOOM
WHOA!!
WHAT IS IT?!
A FROST-PLANE. THEY GRAZE ALL OVER THE EMPIRE.

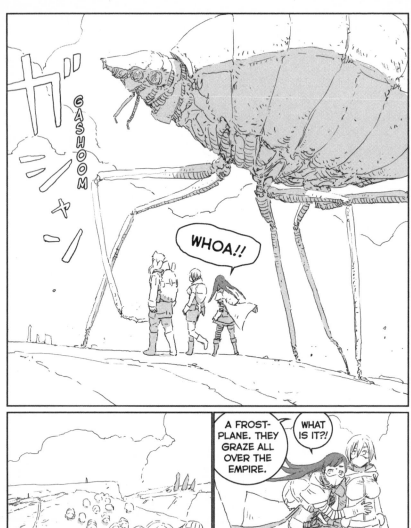

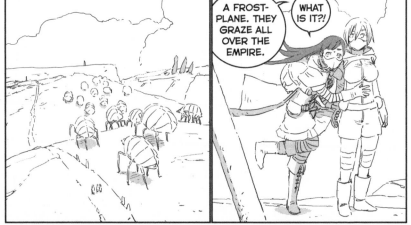

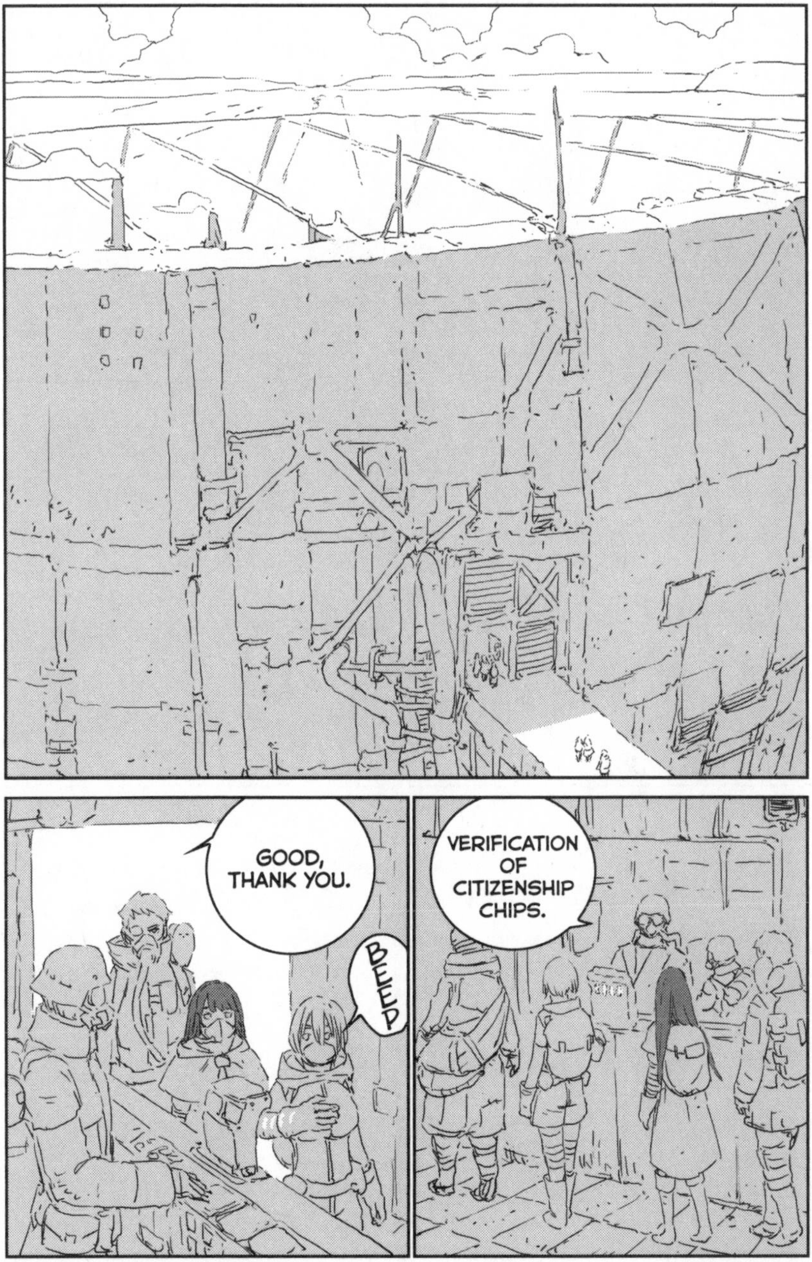
VERIFICATION OF CITIZENSHIP CHIPS.
GOOD, THANK YOU.
BEEP

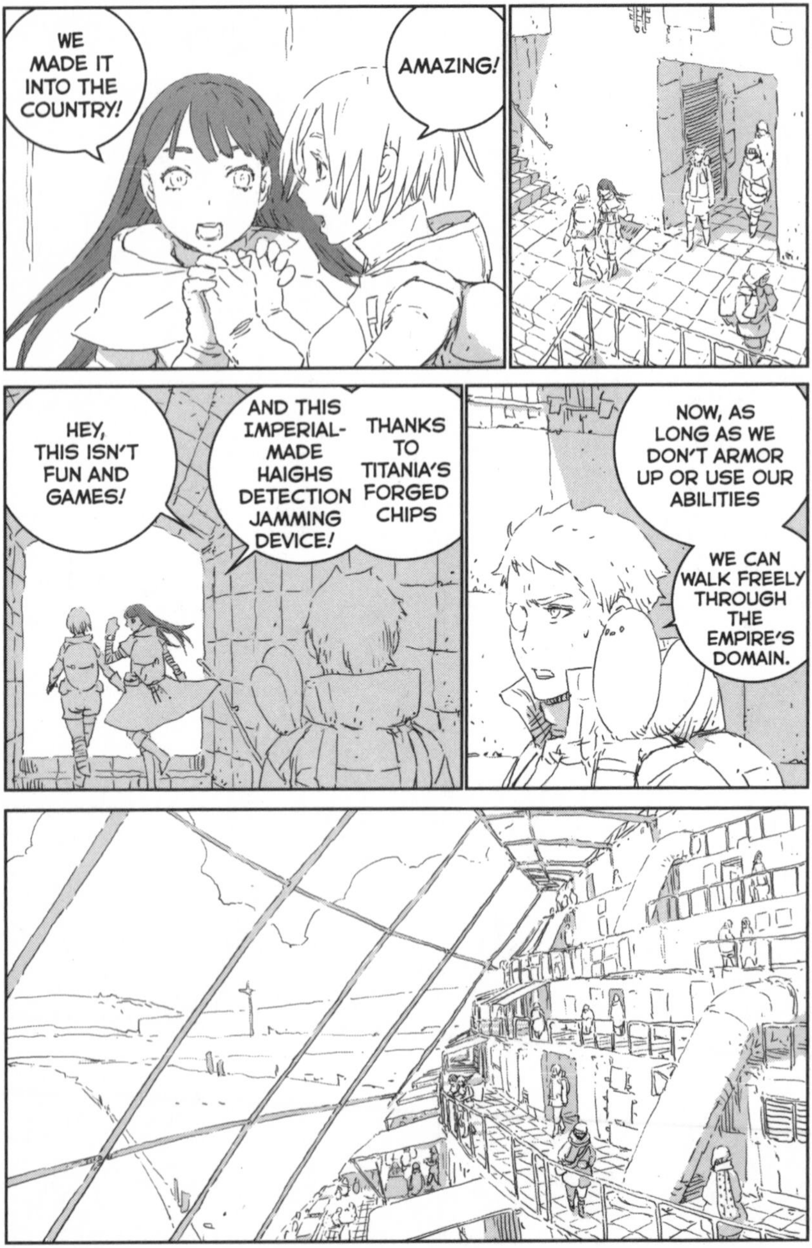
AMAZING!
WE MADE IT INTO THE COUNTRY!
NOW, AS LONG AS WE DON'T ARMOR UP OR USE OUR ABILITIES
WE CAN WALK FREELY THROUGH THE EMPIRE'S DOMAIN.
THANKS TO TITANIA'S FORGED CHIPS
AND THIS IMPERIAL-MADE HAIGHS DETECTION JAMMING DEVICE!
HEY, THIS ISN'T FUN AND GAMES!

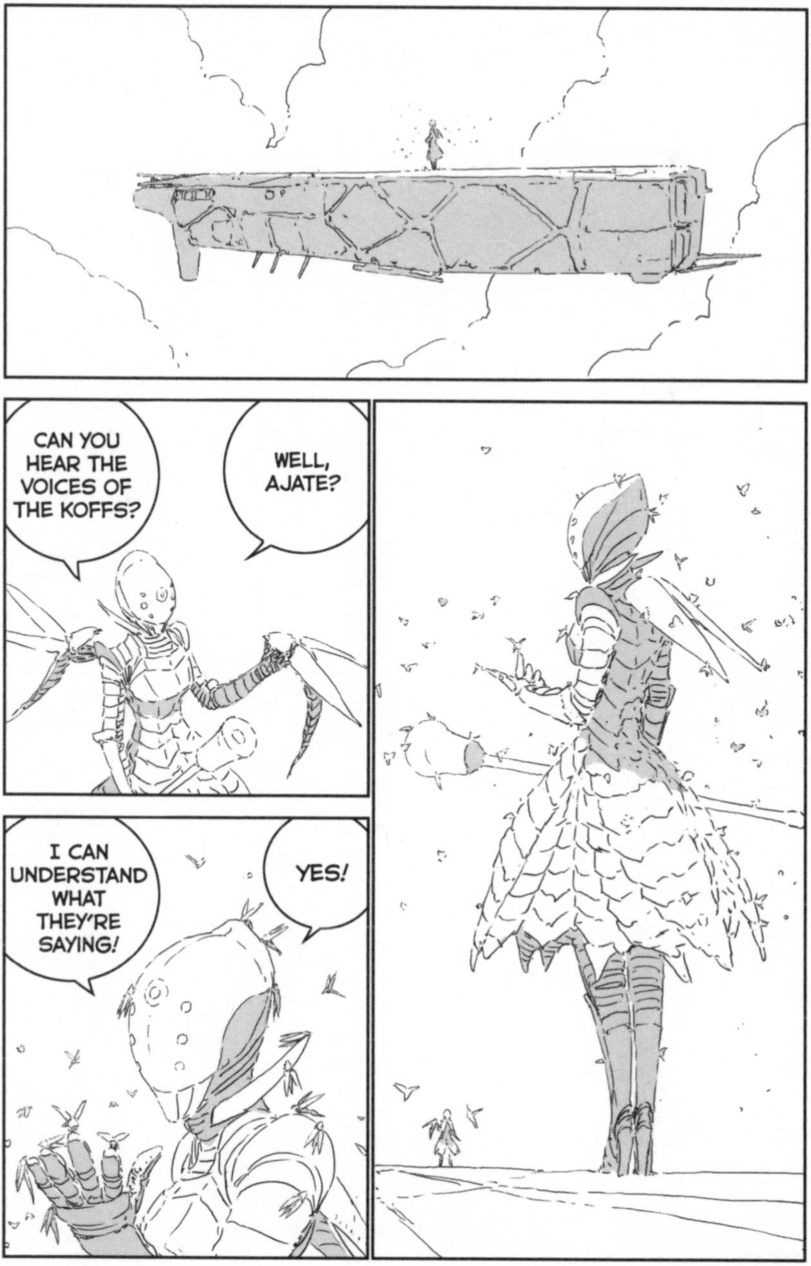
WELL, AJATE?
CAN YOU HEAR THE VOICES OF THE KOFFS?
YES!
I CAN UNDERSTAND WHAT THEY'RE SAYING!

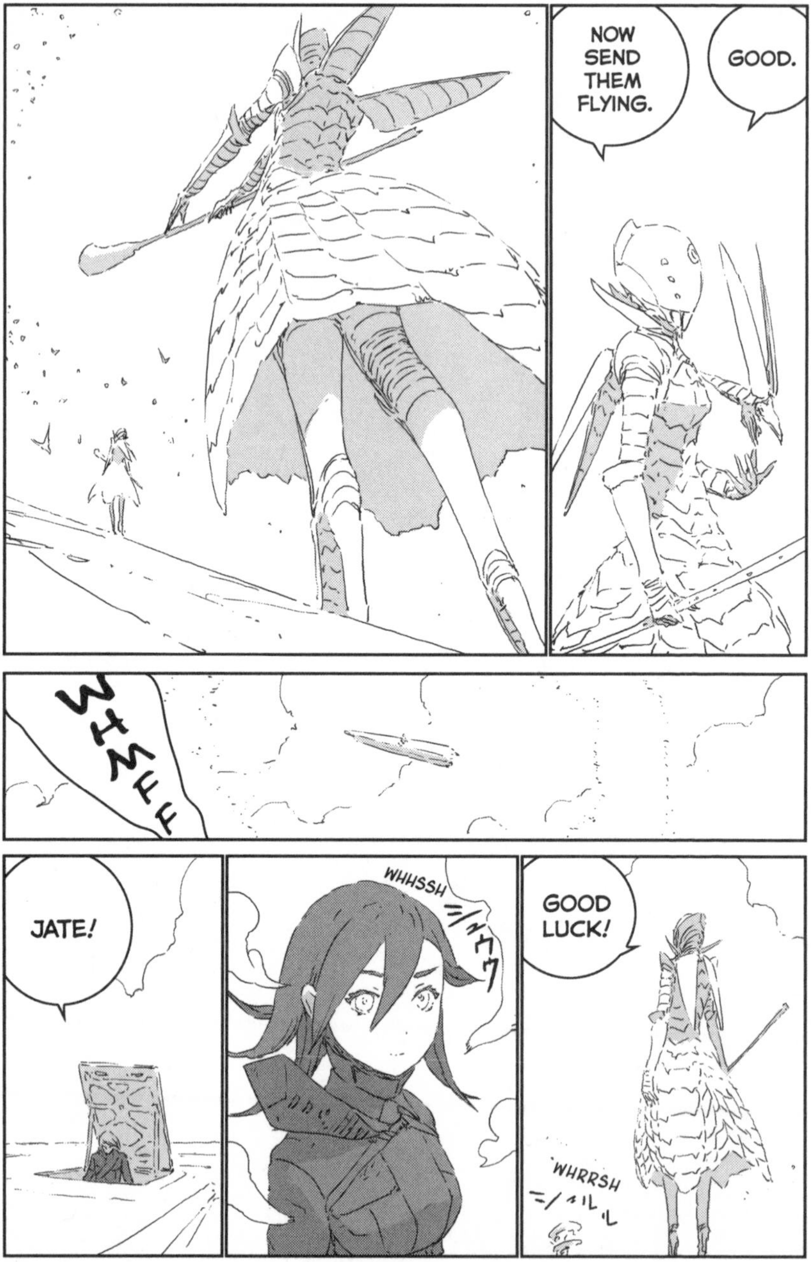
GOOD.
NOW SEND THEM FLYING.
WHMFF
GOOD LUCK!
WHRRSH
WHHSSH
JATE!

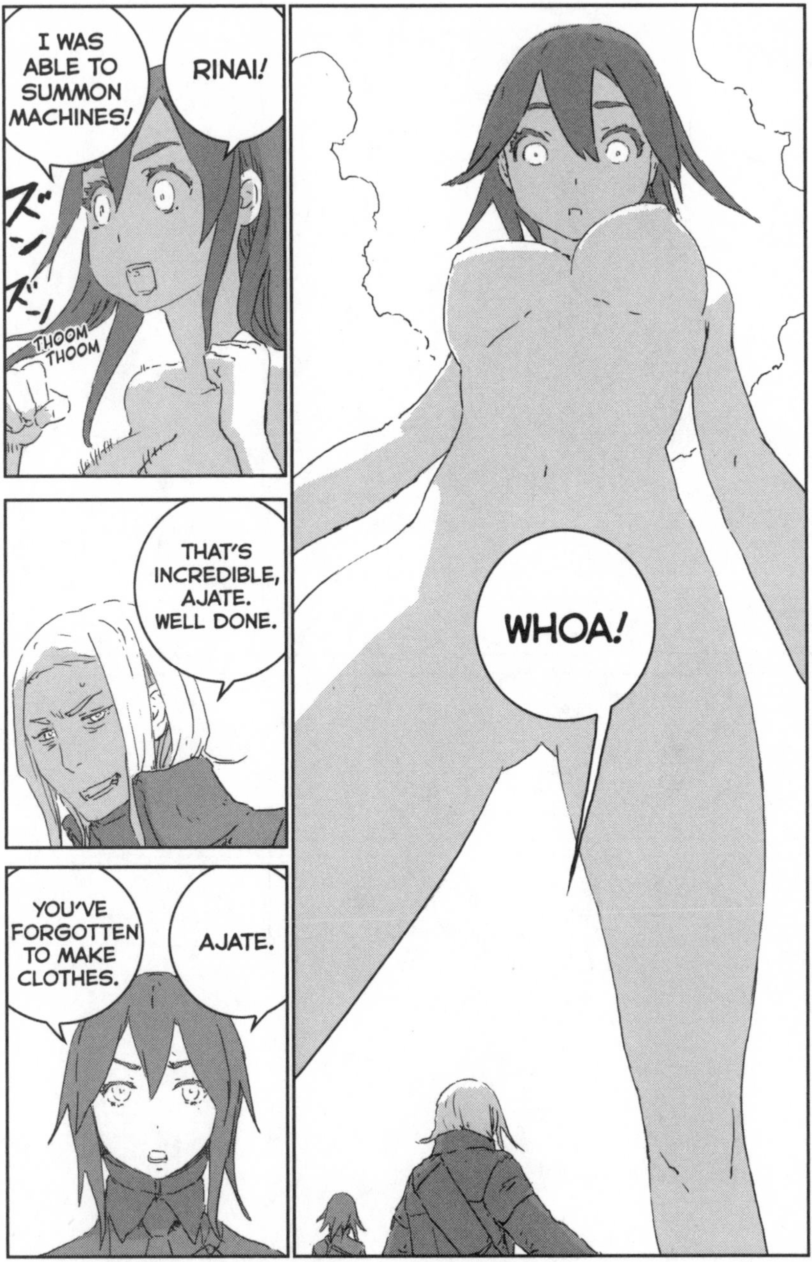
WHOA!
RINAI!
I WAS ABLE TO SUMMON MACHINES!
ズンズン
THOOM THOOM
THAT'S INCREDIBLE, AJATE. WELL DONE.
AJATE.
YOU'VE FORGOTTEN TO MAKE CLOTHES.

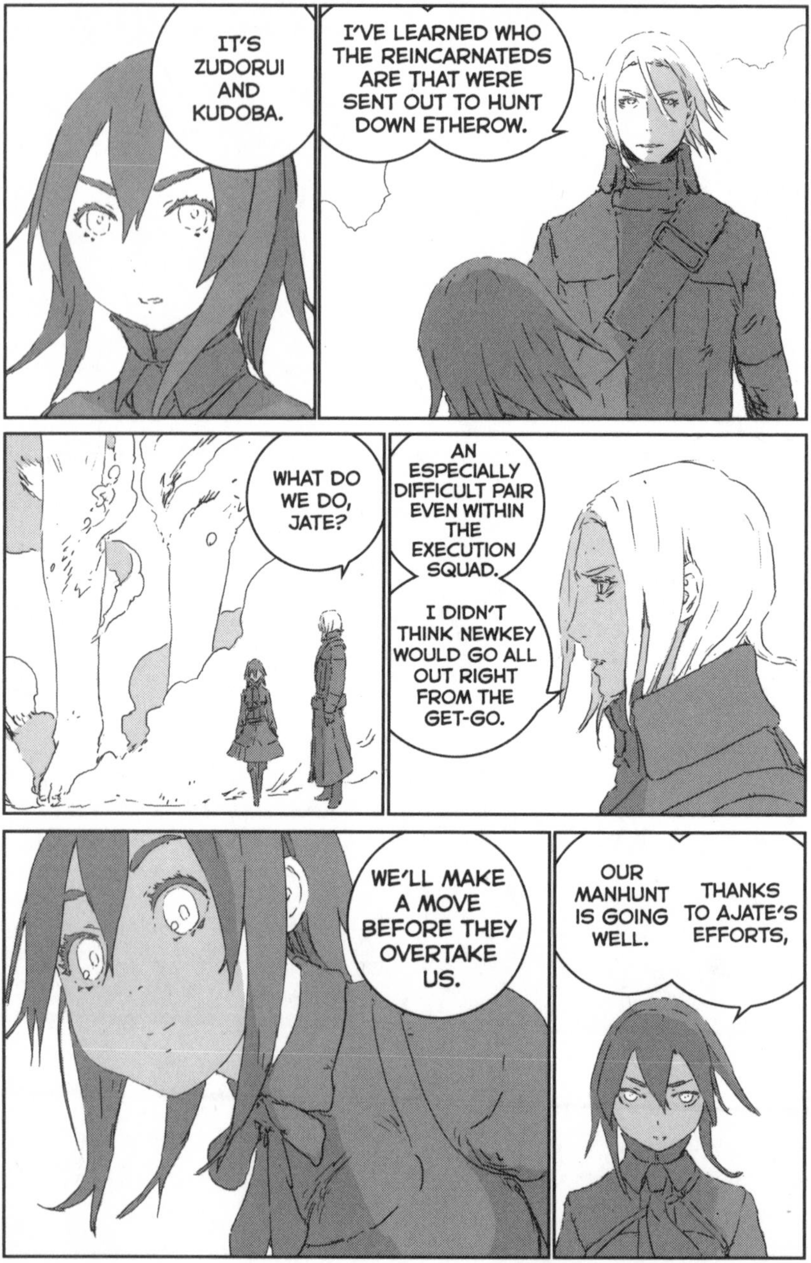
I'VE LEARNED WHO THE REINCARNATEDS ARE THAT WERE SENT OUT TO HUNT DOWN ETHEROW.
IT'S ZUDORUI AND KUDOBA.
AN ESPECIALLY DIFFICULT PAIR EVEN WITHIN THE EXECUTION SQUAD.
I DIDN'T THINK NEWKEY WOULD GO ALL OUT RIGHT FROM THE GET-GO.
WHAT DO WE DO, JATE?
THANKS TO AJATE'S EFFORTS,
OUR MANHUNT IS GOING WELL.
WE'LL MAKE A MOVE BEFORE THEY OVERTAKE US.

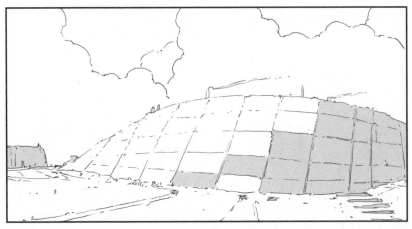

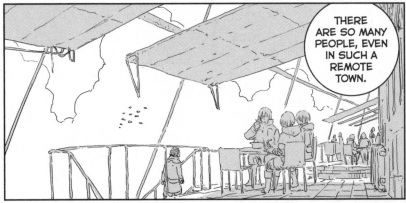

THERE ARE SO MANY PEOPLE, EVEN IN SUCH A REMOTE TOWN.

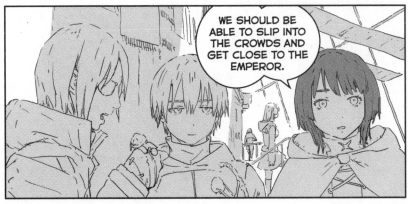

WE SHOULD BE ABLE TO SLIP INTO THE CROWDS AND GET CLOSE TO THE EMPEROR.

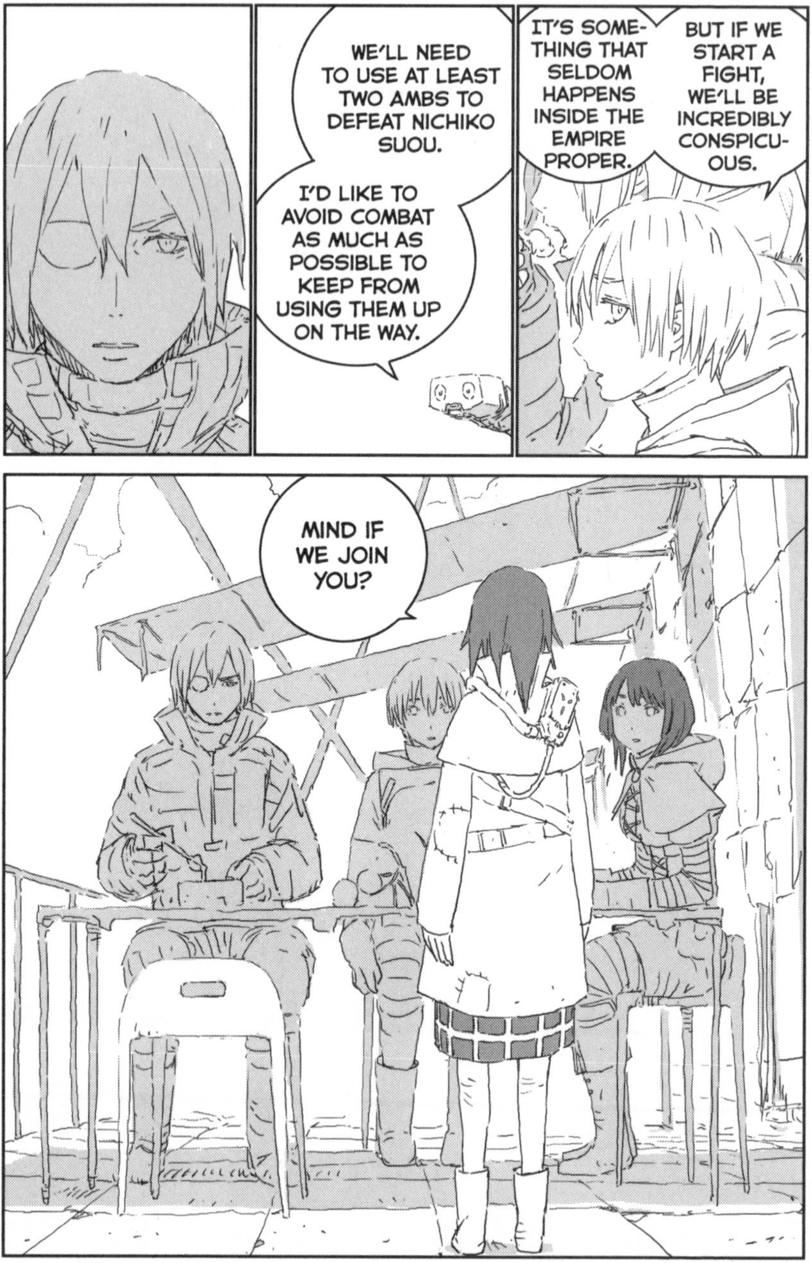
BUT IF WE START A FIGHT, WE'LL BE INCREDIBLY CONSPICU-OUS.
IT'S SOME-THING THAT SELDOM HAPPENS INSIDE THE EMPIRE PROPER.
WE'LL NEED TO USE AT LEAST TWO AMBS TO DEFEAT NICHIKO SUOU.
I'D LIKE TO AVOID COMBAT AS MUCH AS POSSIBLE TO KEEP FROM USING THEM UP ON THE WAY.
MIND IF WE JOIN YOU?

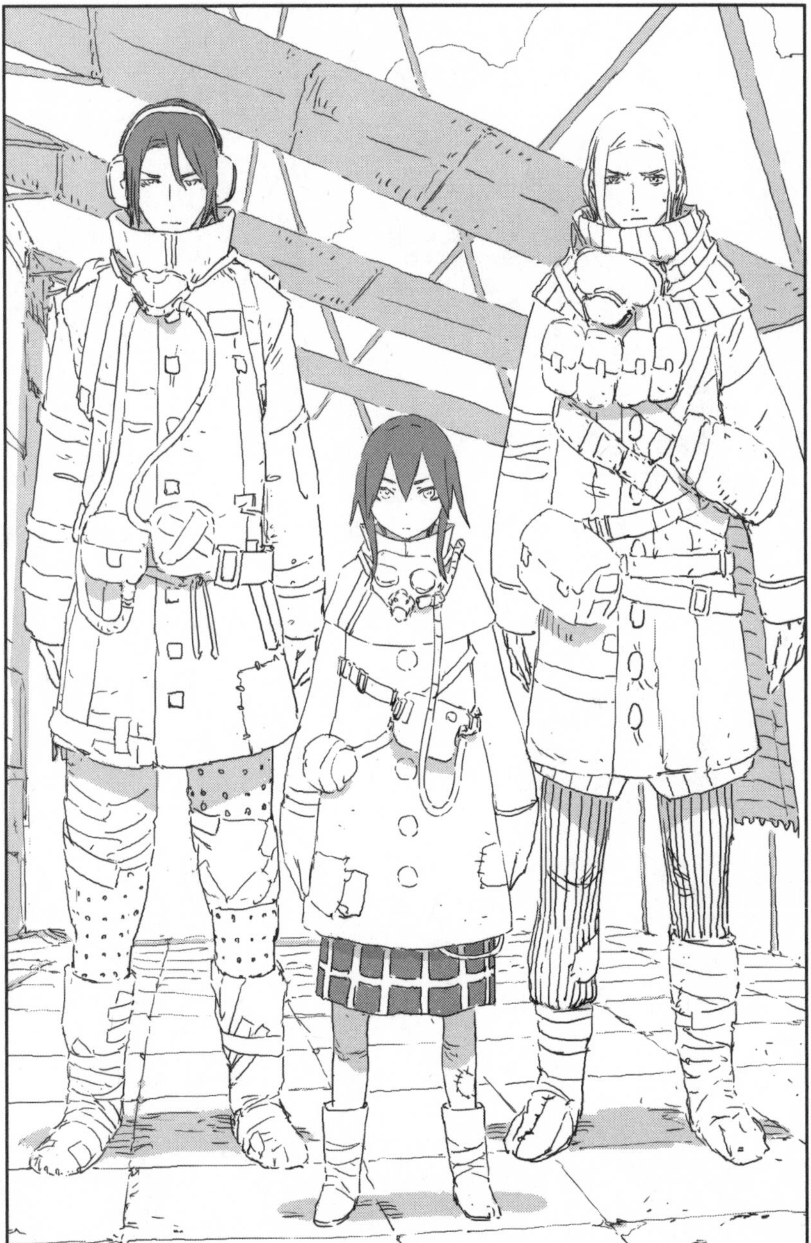

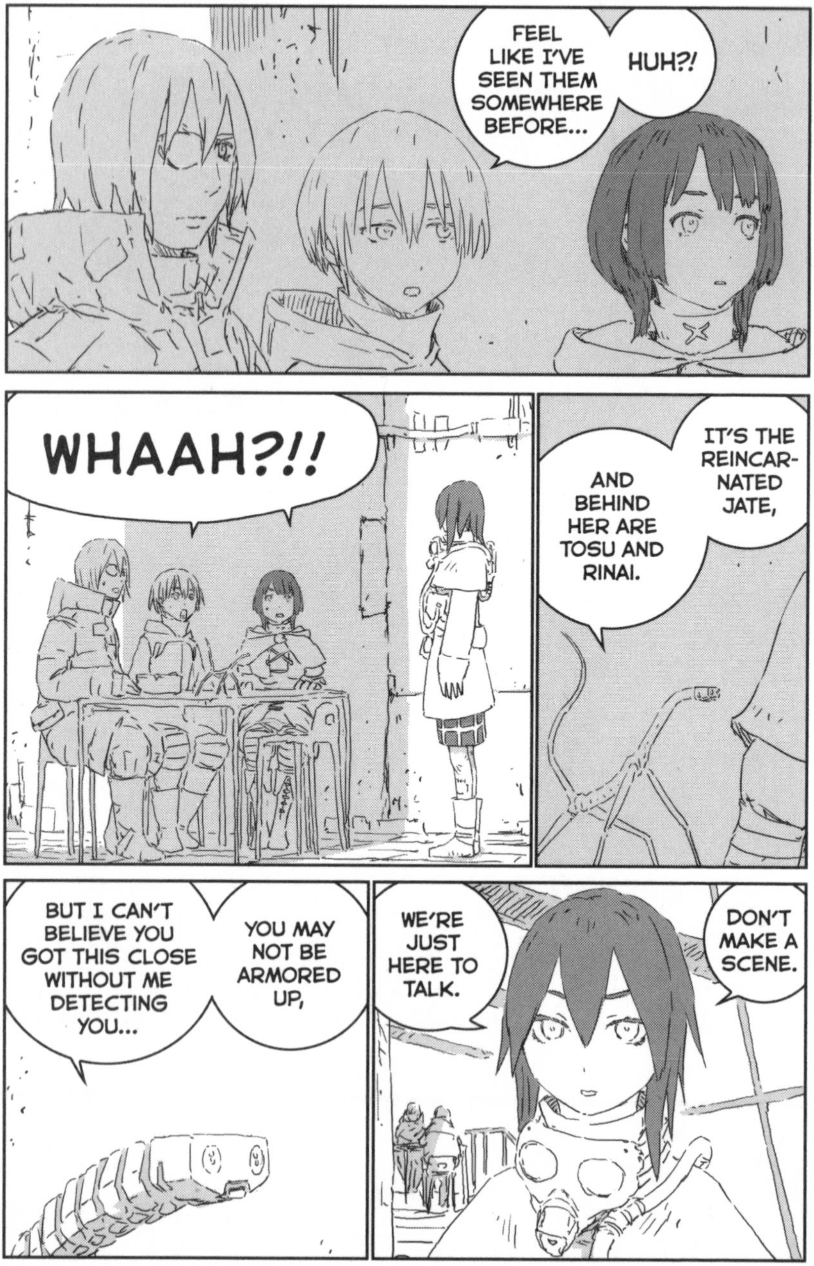
HUH?!
FEEL LIKE I'VE SEEN THEM SOMEWHERE BEFORE...
IT'S THE REINCAR-NATED JATE,
AND BEHIND HER ARE TOSU AND RINAI.
WHAAH?!!
DON'T MAKE A SCENE.
WE'RE JUST HERE TO TALK.
YOU MAY NOT BE ARMORED UP,
BUT I CAN'T BELIEVE YOU GOT THIS CLOSE WITHOUT ME DETECTING YOU...

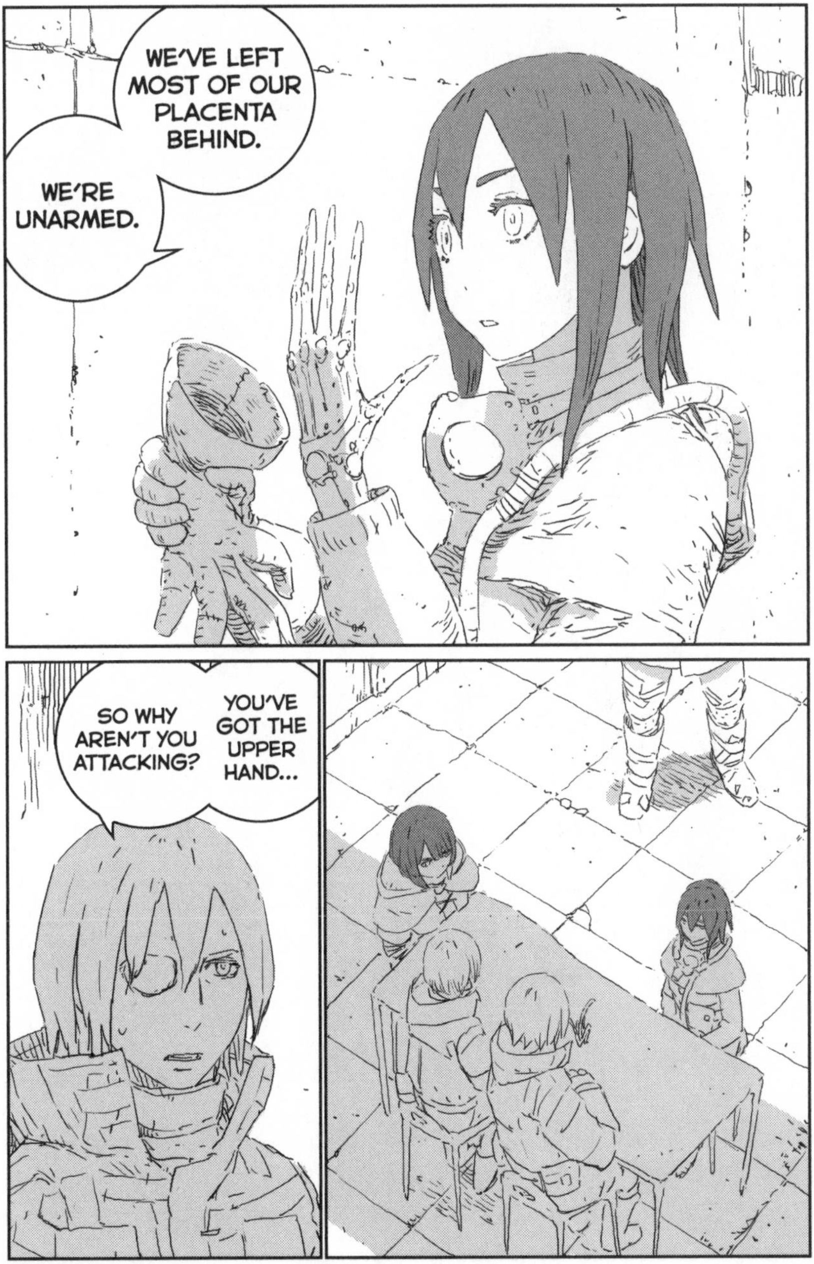
WE'VE LEFT MOST OF OUR PLACENTA BEHIND.
WE'RE UNARMED.
YOU'VE GOT THE UPPER HAND...
SO WHY AREN'T YOU ATTACKING?

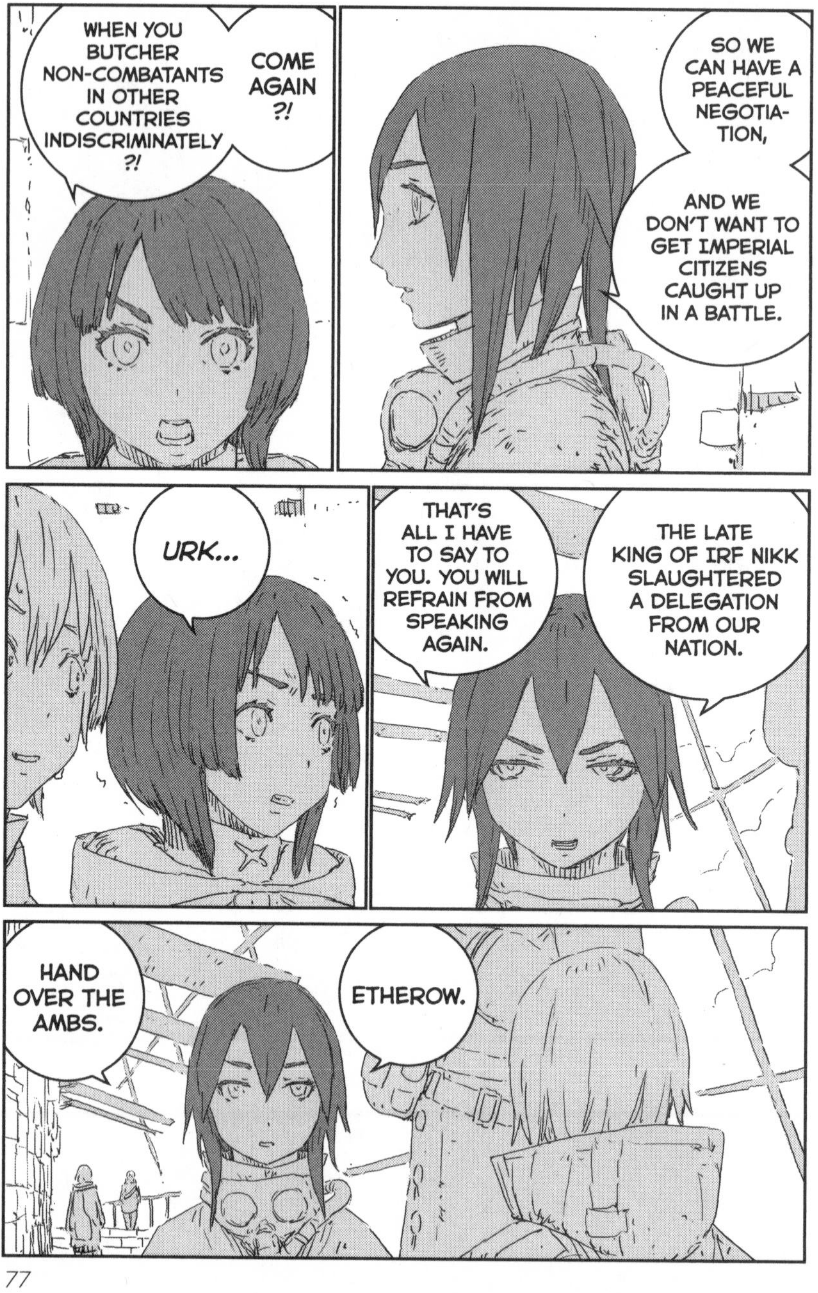
SO WE CAN HAVE A PEACEFUL NEGOTIA-TION,
AND WE DON'T WANT TO GET IMPERIAL CITIZENS CAUGHT UP IN A BATTLE.
COME AGAIN ?!
WHEN YOU BUTCHER NON-COMBATANTS IN OTHER COUNTRIES INDISCRIMINATELY ?!
THE LATE KING OF IRF NIKK SLAUGHTERED A DELEGATION FROM OUR NATION.
THAT'S ALL I HAVE TO SAY TO YOU. YOU WILL REFRAIN FROM SPEAKING AGAIN.
URK...
ETHEROW.
HAND OVER THE AMBS.

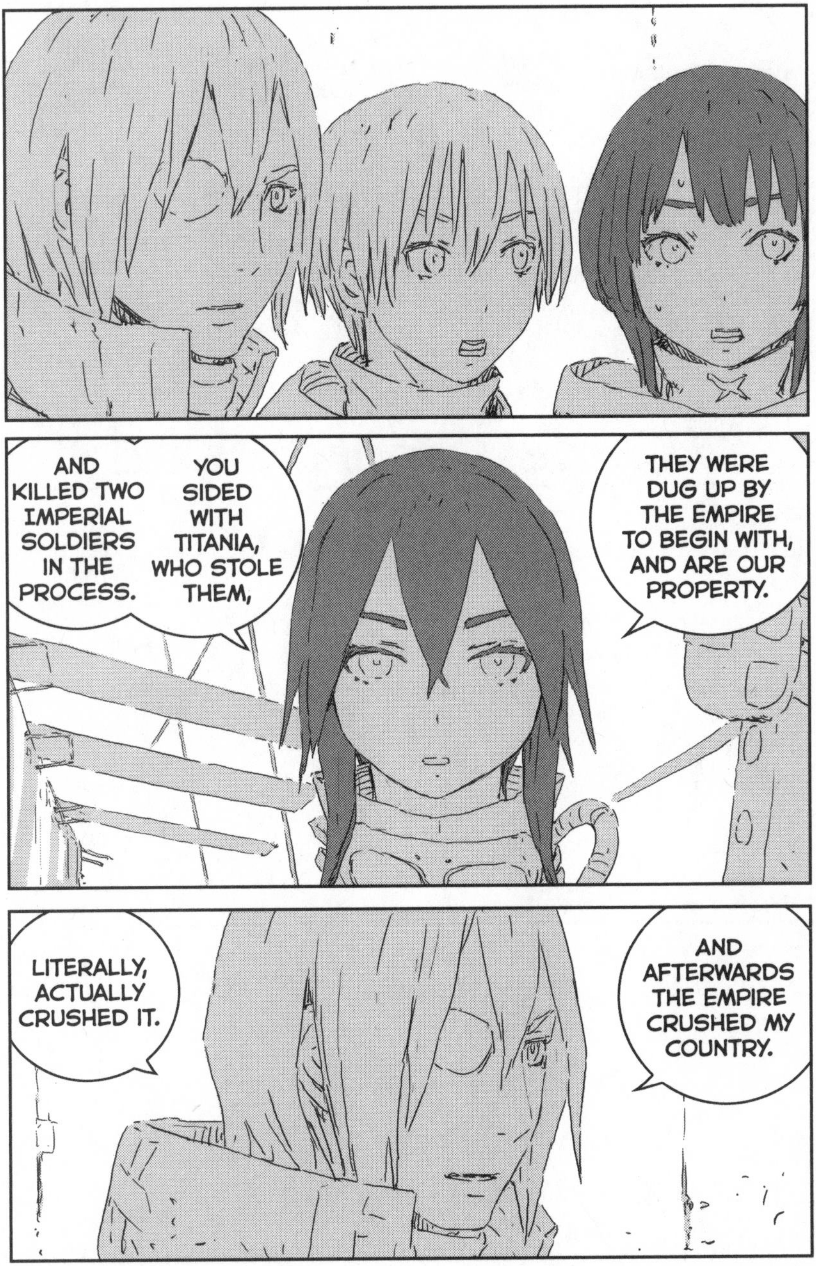
THEY WERE DUG UP BY THE EMPIRE TO BEGIN WITH, AND ARE OUR PROPERTY.
YOU SIDED WITH TITANIA, WHO STOLE THEM,
AND KILLED TWO IMPERIAL SOLDIERS IN THE PROCESS.
AND AFTERWARDS THE EMPIRE CRUSHED MY COUNTRY.
LITERALLY, ACTUALLY CRUSHED IT.

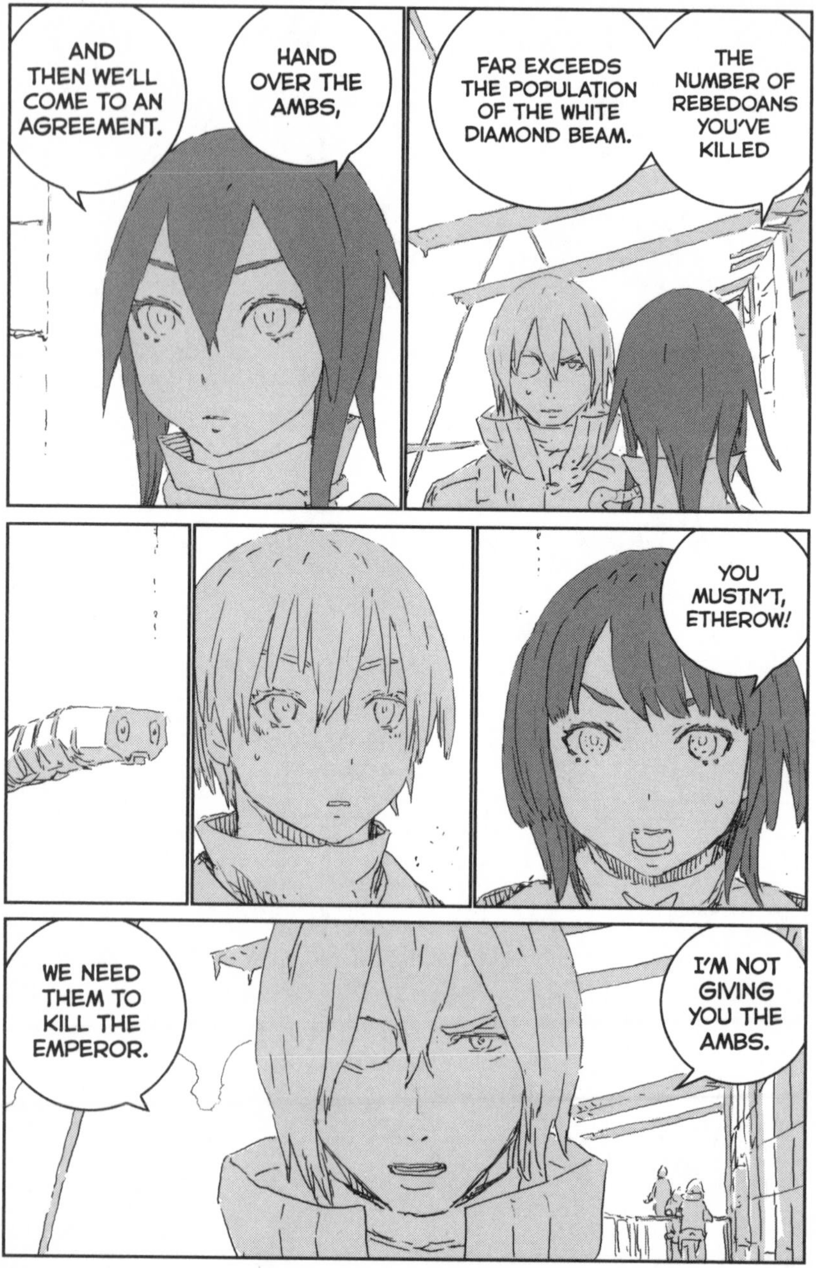
THE NUMBER OF REBEDOANS YOU'VE KILLED
FAR EXCEEDS THE POPULATION OF THE WHITE DIAMOND BEAM.
HAND OVER THE AMBS,
AND THEN WE'LL COME TO AN AGREEMENT.
YOU MUSTN'T, ETHEROW!
I'M NOT GIVING YOU THE AMBS.
WE NEED THEM TO KILL THE EMPEROR.

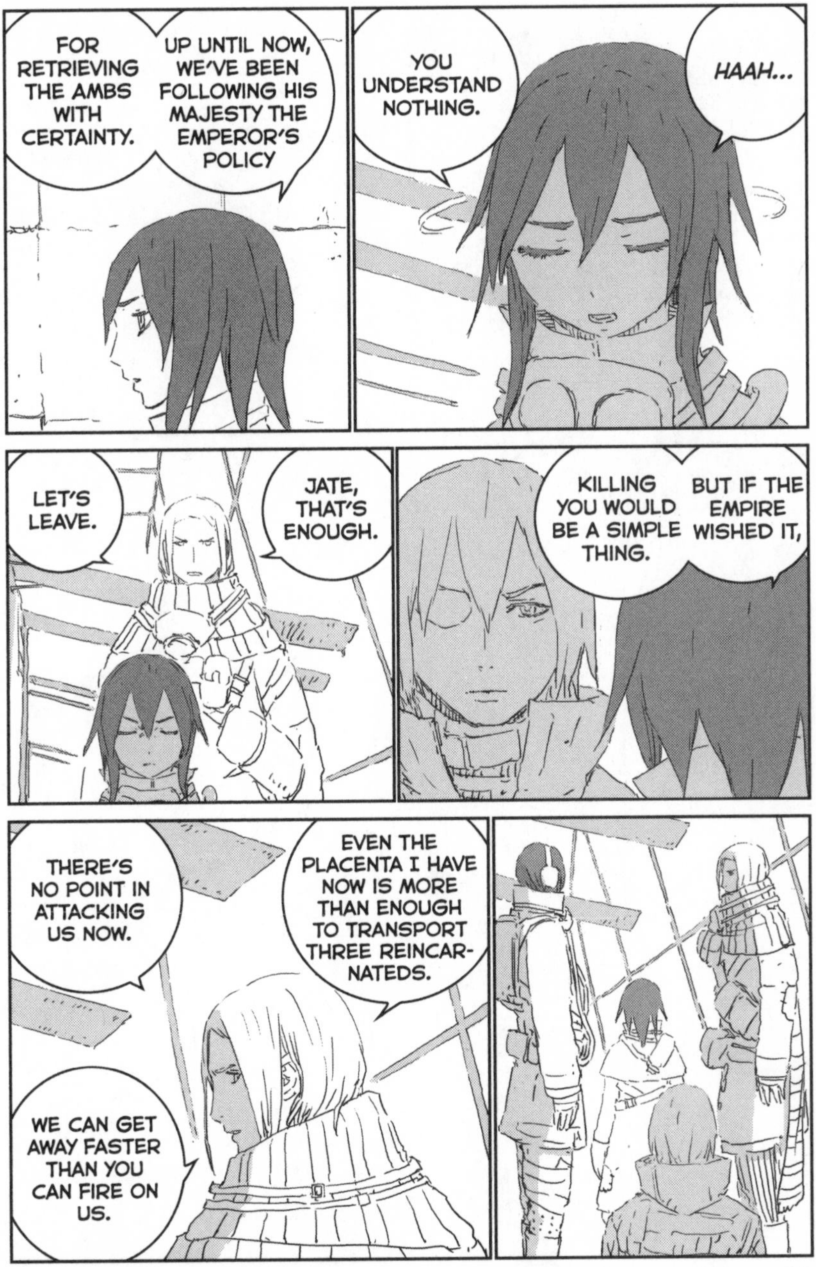
HAAH...
YOU UNDERSTAND NOTHING.
UP UNTIL NOW, WE'VE BEEN FOLLOWING HIS MAJESTY THE EMPEROR'S POLICY
FOR RETRIEVING THE AMBS WITH CERTAINTY.
BUT IF THE EMPIRE WISHED IT,
KILLING YOU WOULD BE A SIMPLE THING.
JATE, THAT'S ENOUGH.
LET'S LEAVE.
EVEN THE PLACENTA I HAVE NOW IS MORE THAN ENOUGH TO TRANSPORT THREE REINCAR-NATEDS.
THERE'S NO POINT IN ATTACKING US NOW.
WE CAN GET AWAY FASTER THAN YOU CAN FIRE ON US.

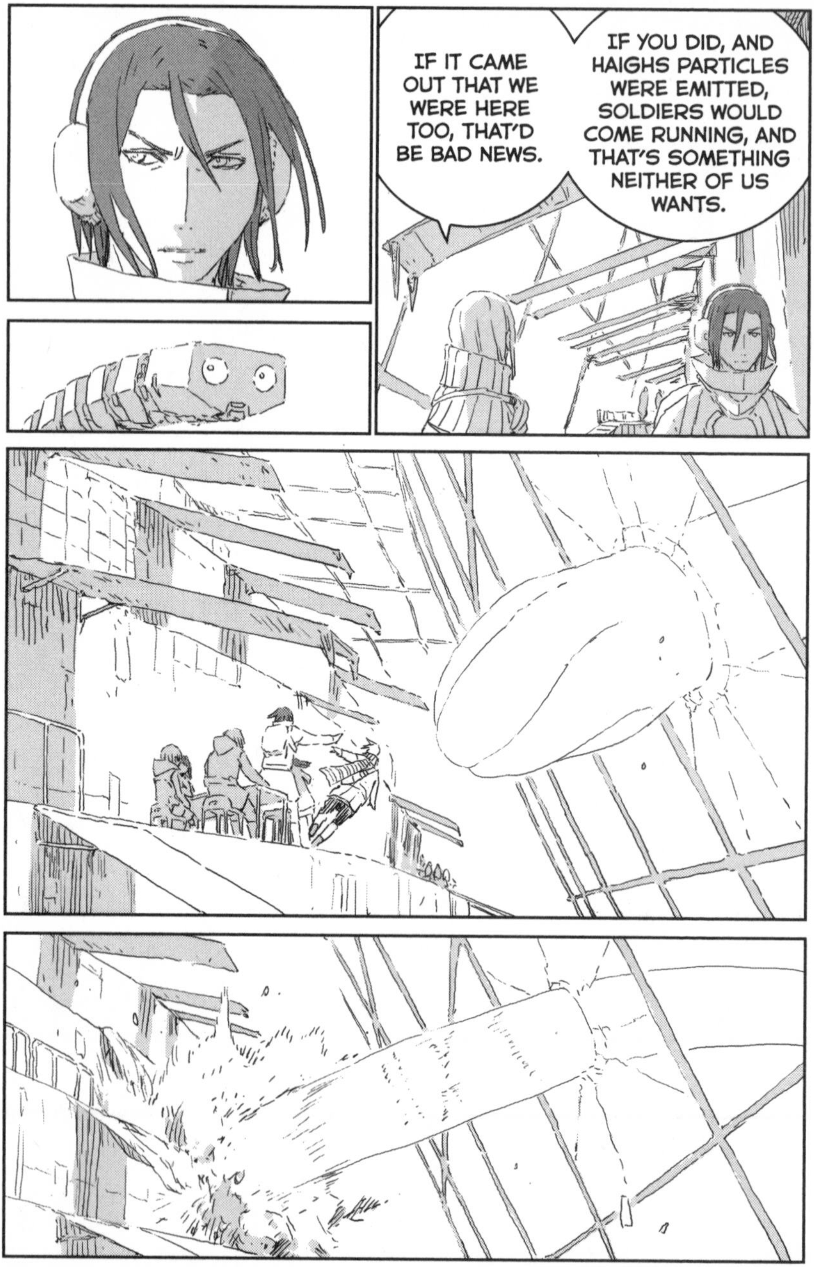
IF YOU DID, AND HAIGHS PARTICLES WERE EMITTED, SOLDIERS WOULD COME RUNNING, AND THAT'S SOMETHING NEITHER OF US WANTS.
IF IT CAME OUT THAT WE WERE HERE TOO, THAT'D BE BAD NEWS.

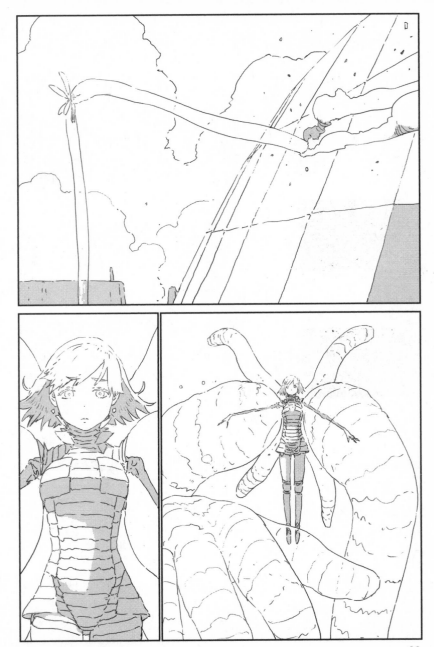

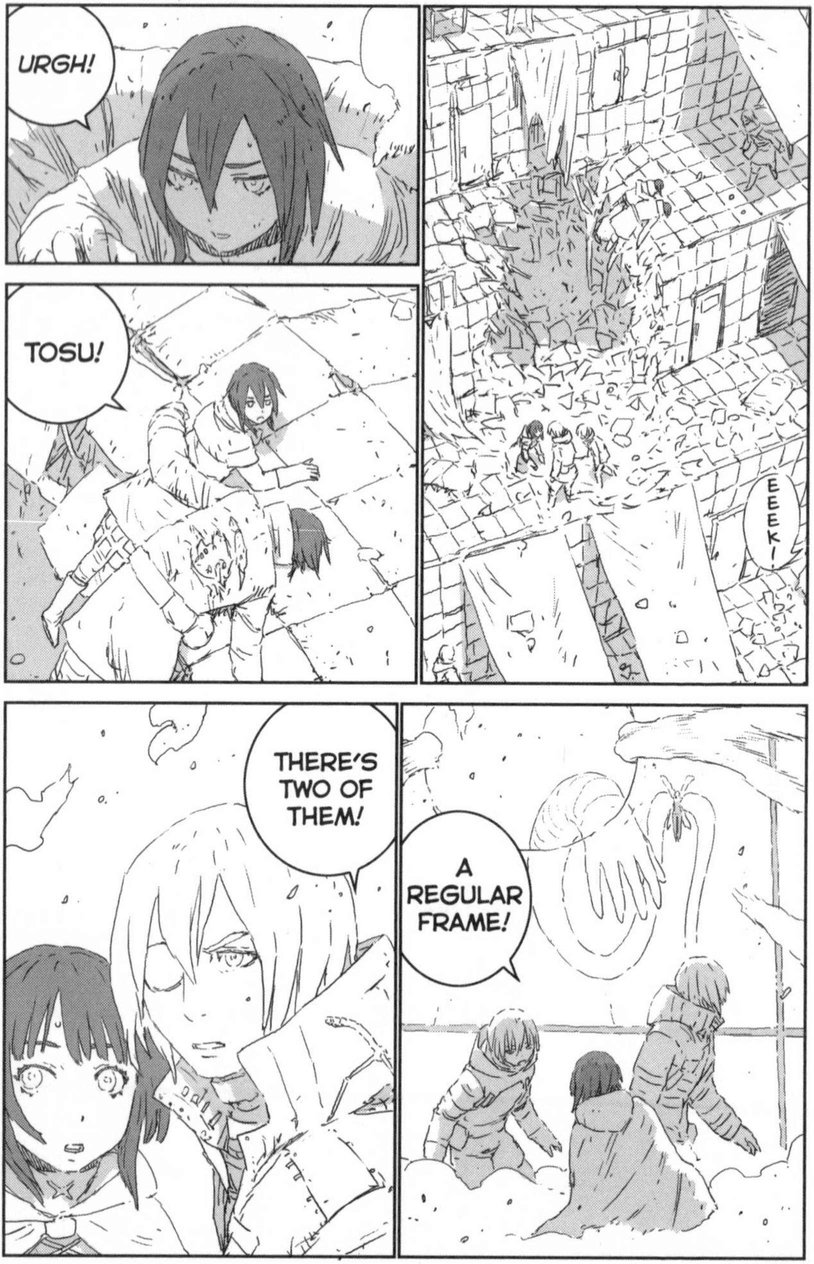
EEEK!
URGH!
TOSU!
A REGULAR FRAME!
THERE'S TWO OF THEM!

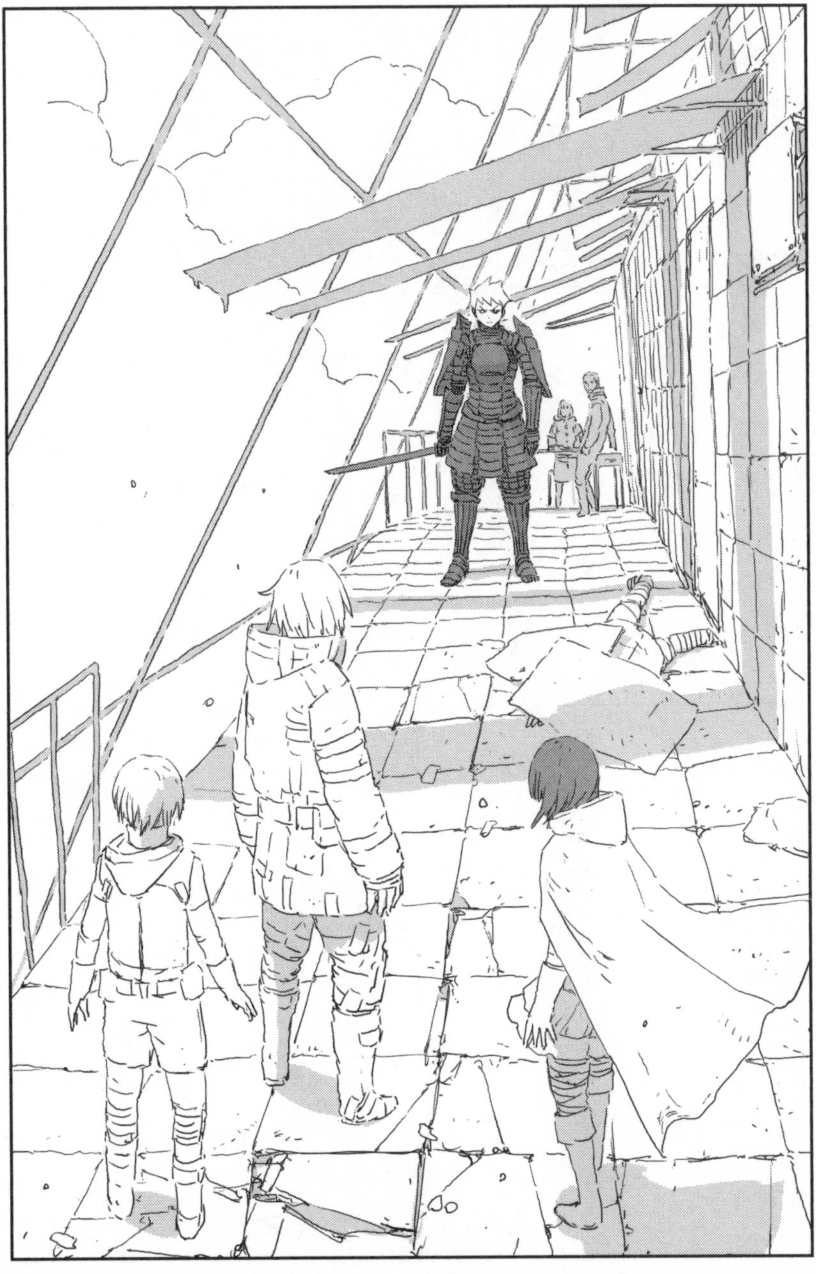

CHAPTER 39 END

APOSIMZ

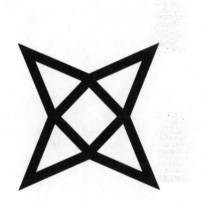

CHAPTER 40

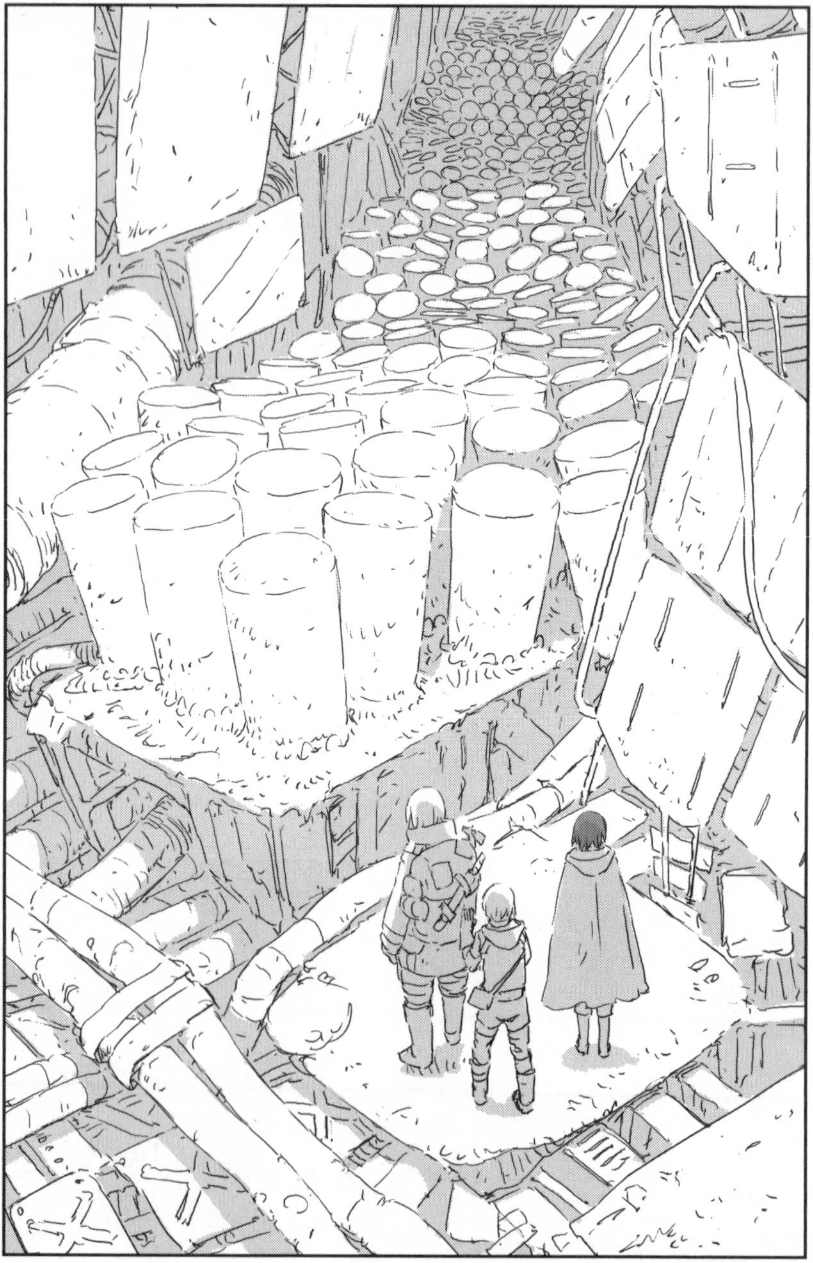

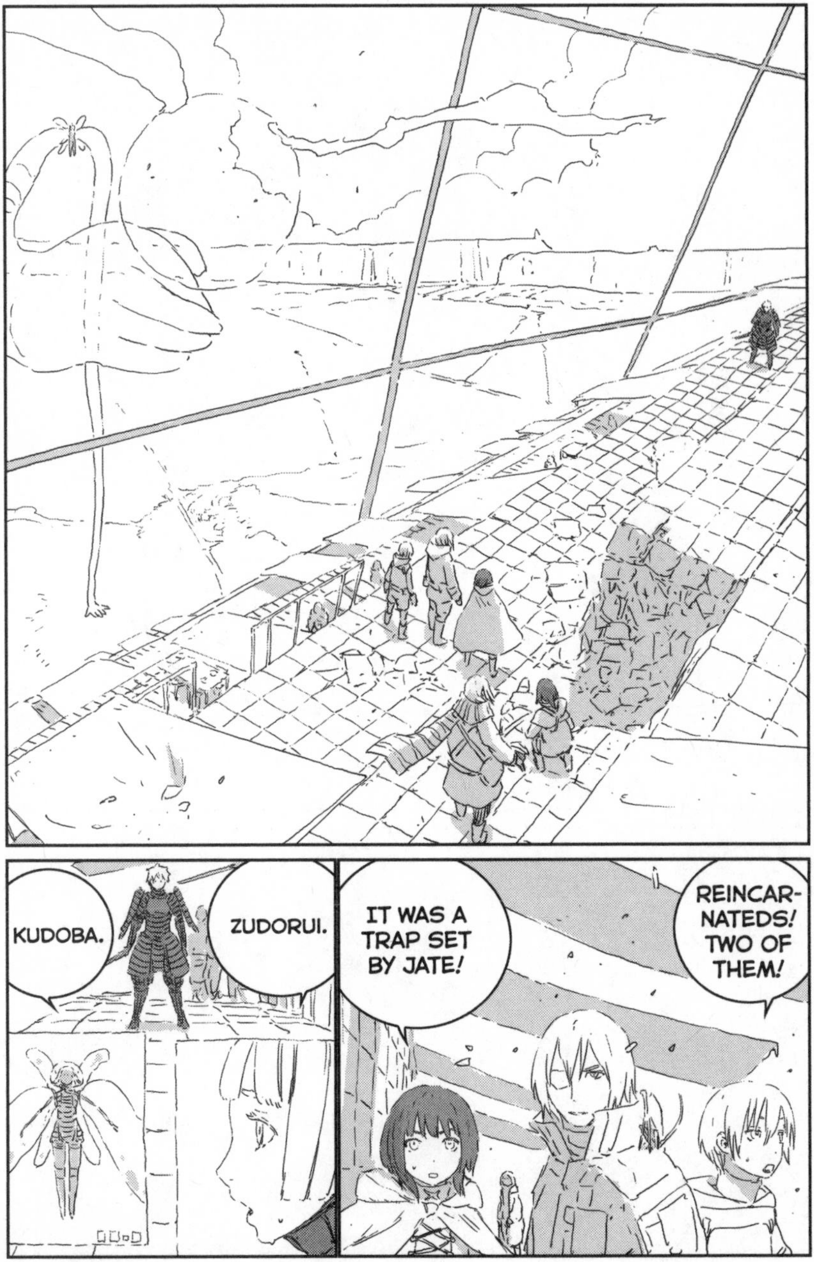
REINCAR-
NATEDS!
TWO OF
THEM!
IT WAS A
TRAP SET
BY JATE!
ZUDORUI.
KUDOBA.

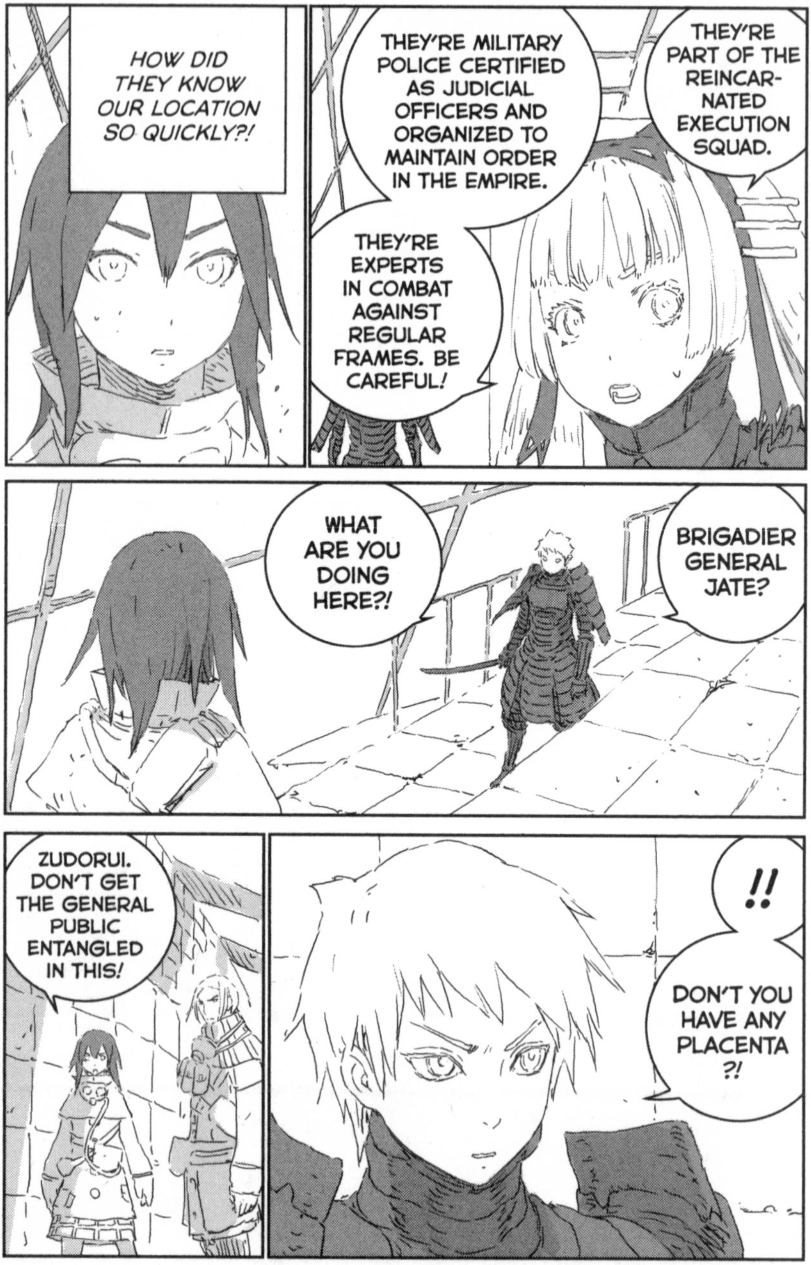
THEY'RE PART OF THE REINCARNATED EXECUTION SQUAD.
THEY'RE MILITARY POLICE CERTIFIED AS JUDICIAL OFFICERS AND ORGANIZED TO MAINTAIN ORDER IN THE EMPIRE.
THEY'RE EXPERTS IN COMBAT AGAINST REGULAR FRAMES. BE CAREFUL!
HOW DID THEY KNOW OUR LOCATION SO QUICKLY?!
BRIGADIER GENERAL JATE?
WHAT ARE YOU DOING HERE?!
!!
DON'T YOU HAVE ANY PLACENTA?!
ZUDORUI. DON'T GET THE GENERAL PUBLIC ENTANGLED IN THIS!

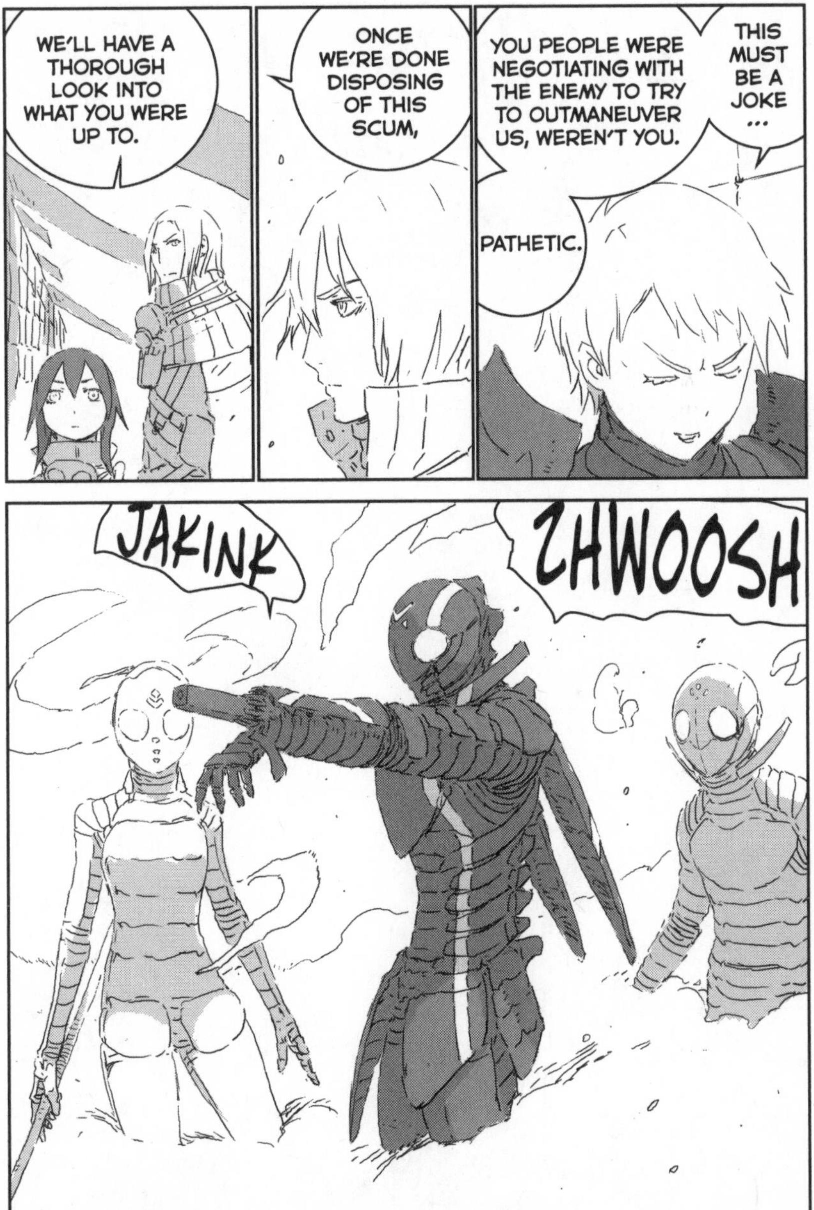
THIS MUST BE A JOKE ...
YOU PEOPLE WERE NEGOTIATING WITH THE ENEMY TO TRY TO OUTMANEUVER US, WEREN'T YOU.
PATHETIC.
ONCE WE'RE DONE DISPOSING OF THIS SCUM,
WE'LL HAVE A THOROUGH LOOK INTO WHAT YOU WERE UP TO.
ZHWOOSH
JAKINK

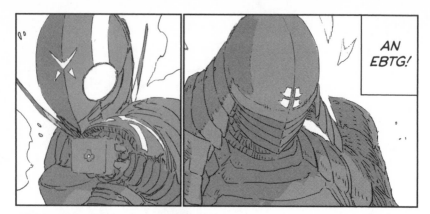

AN
EBTG!

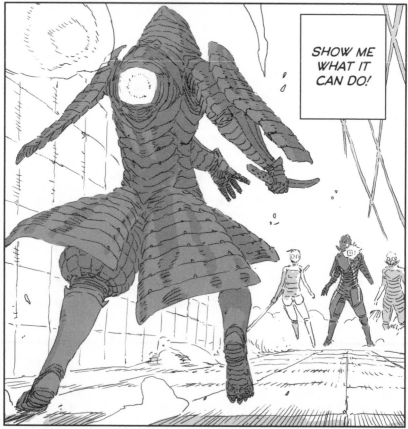

SHOW ME
WHAT IT
CAN DO!

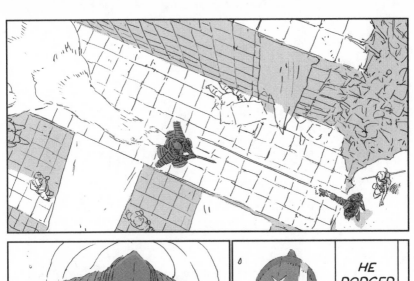

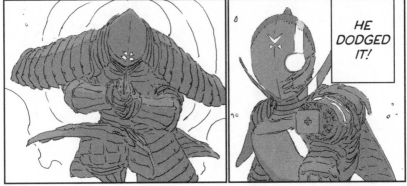

HE
DODGED
IT!

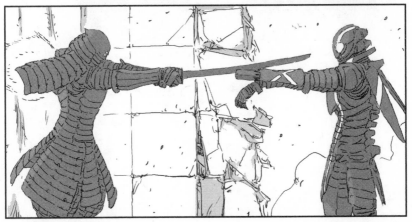

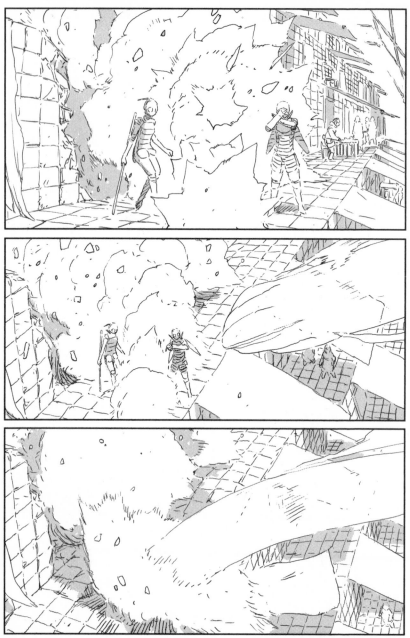

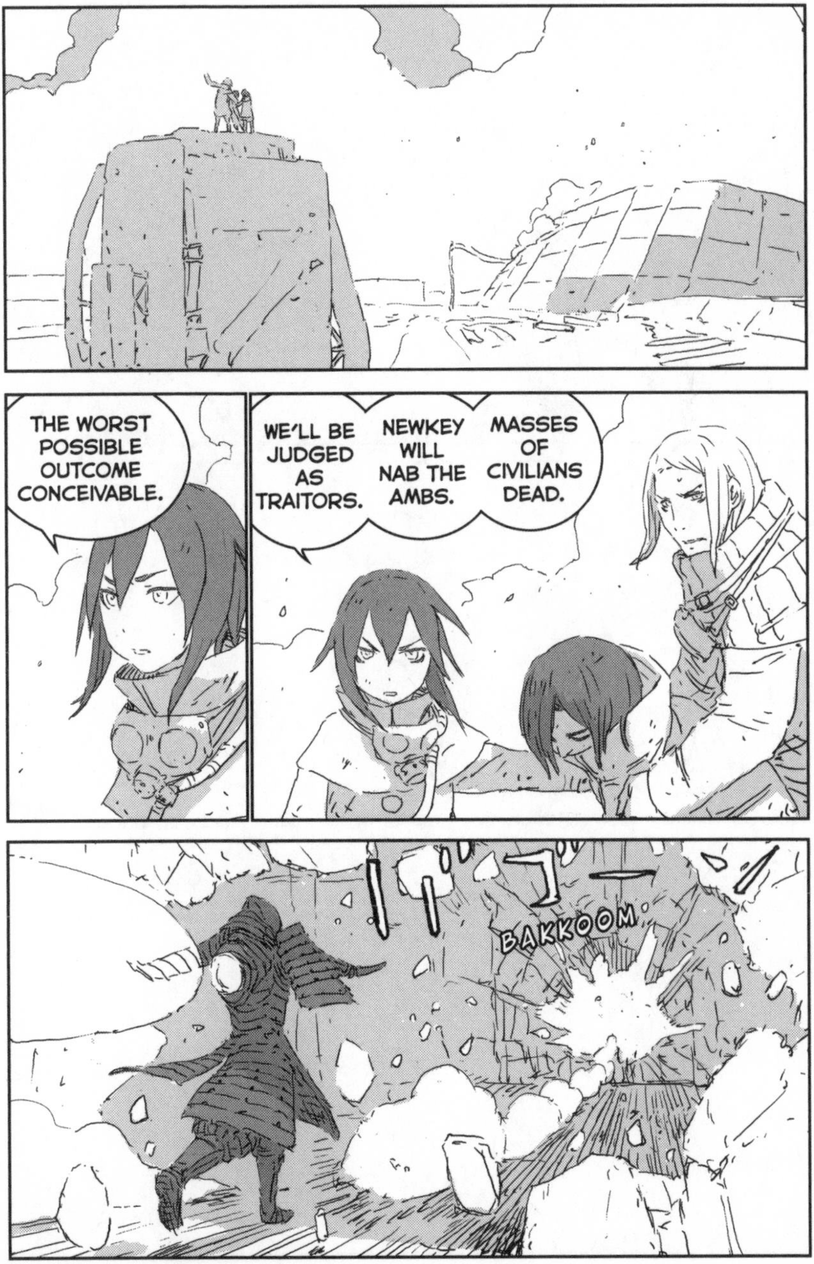
MASSES OF CIVILIANS DEAD.
NEWKEY WILL NAB THE AMBS.
WE'LL BE JUDGED AS TRAITORS.
THE WORST POSSIBLE OUTCOME CONCEIVABLE.
BAKKOOM

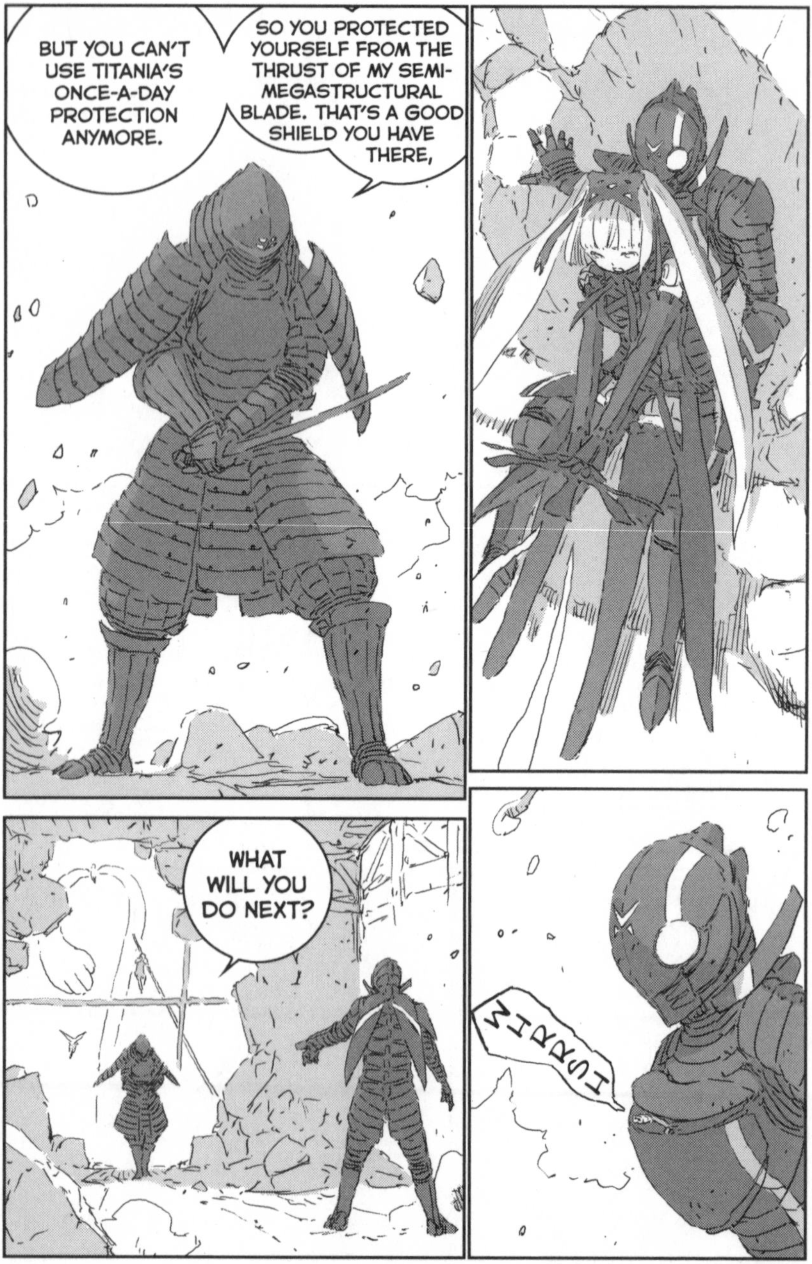
SO YOU PROTECTED YOURSELF FROM THE THRUST OF MY SEMI-MEGASTRUCTURAL BLADE. THAT'S A GOOD SHIELD YOU HAVE THERE,
BUT YOU CAN'T USE TITANIA'S ONCE-A-DAY PROTECTION ANYMORE.
WHAT WILL YOU DO NEXT?

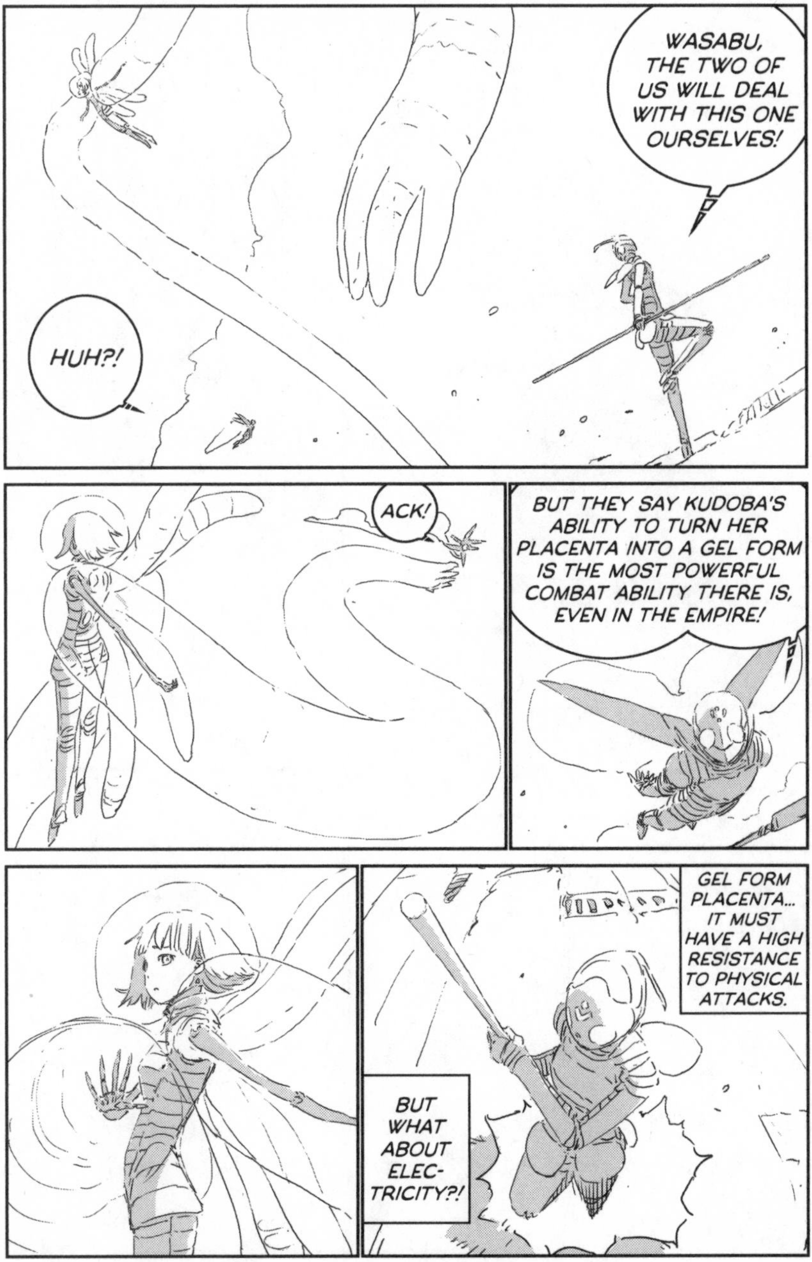

WASABU, THE TWO OF US WILL DEAL WITH THIS ONE OURSELVES!
HUH?!
BUT THEY SAY KUDOBA'S ABILITY TO TURN HER PLACENTA INTO A GEL FORM IS THE MOST POWERFUL COMBAT ABILITY THERE IS, EVEN IN THE EMPIRE!
ACK!
GEL FORM PLACENTA... IT MUST HAVE A HIGH RESISTANCE TO PHYSICAL ATTACKS.
BUT WHAT ABOUT ELEC-TRICITY?!

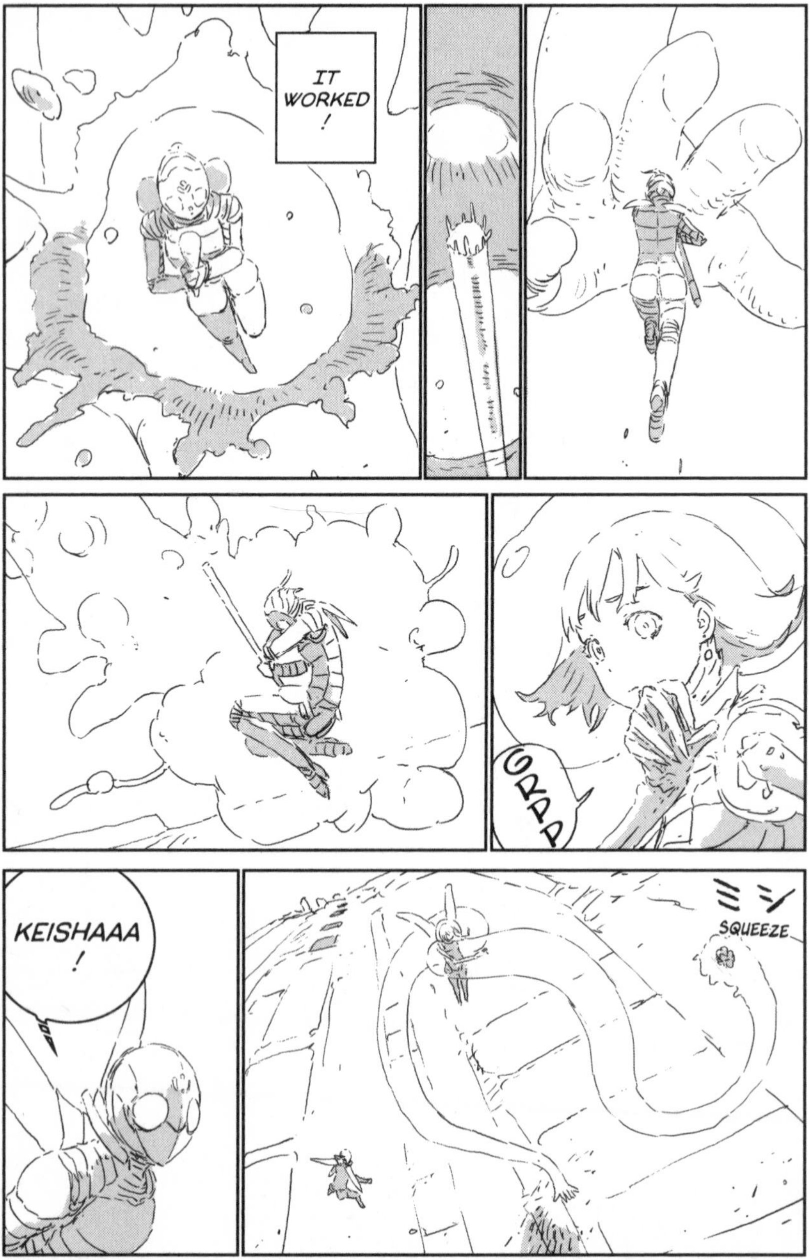
IT WORKED !
GRPP
ミシ
SQUEEZE
KEISHAAA !

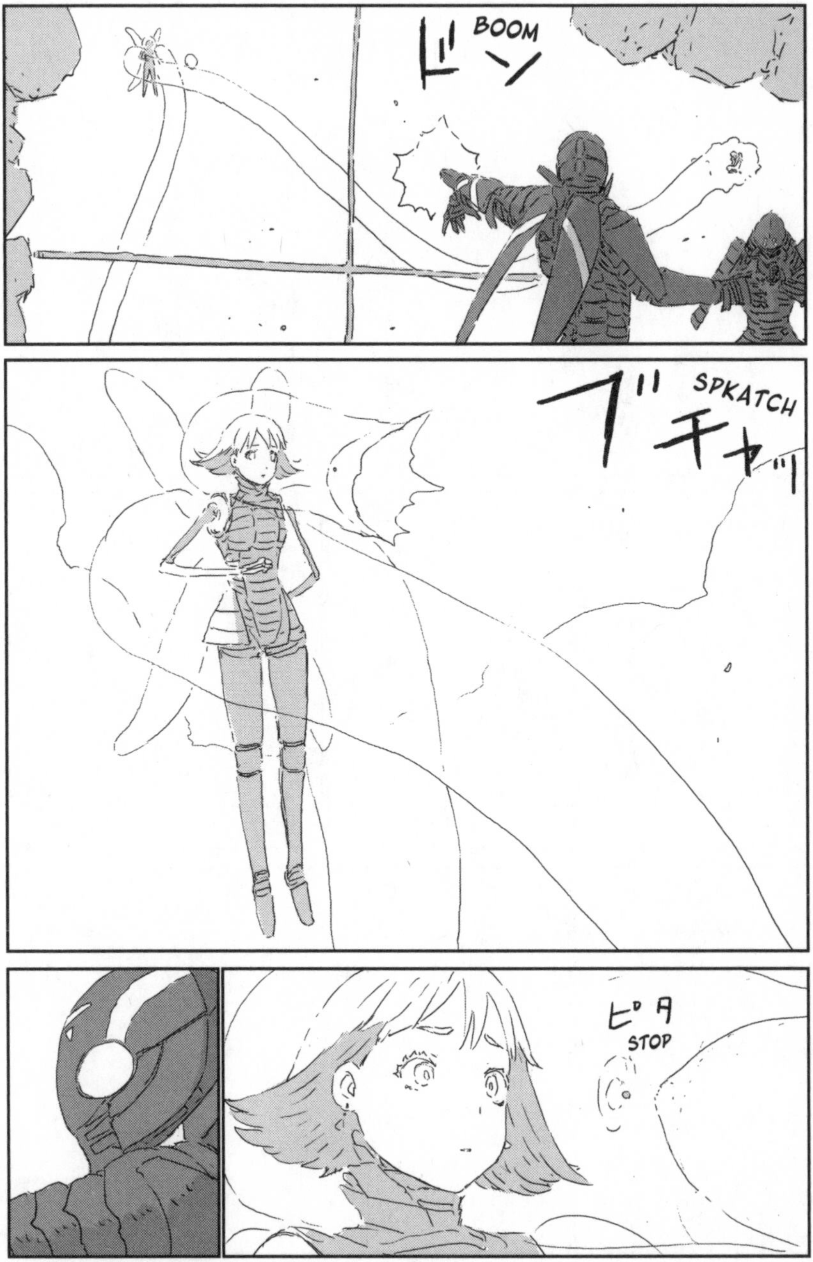
ドン
BOOM
ブチャッ
SPKATCH
ピタ
STOP

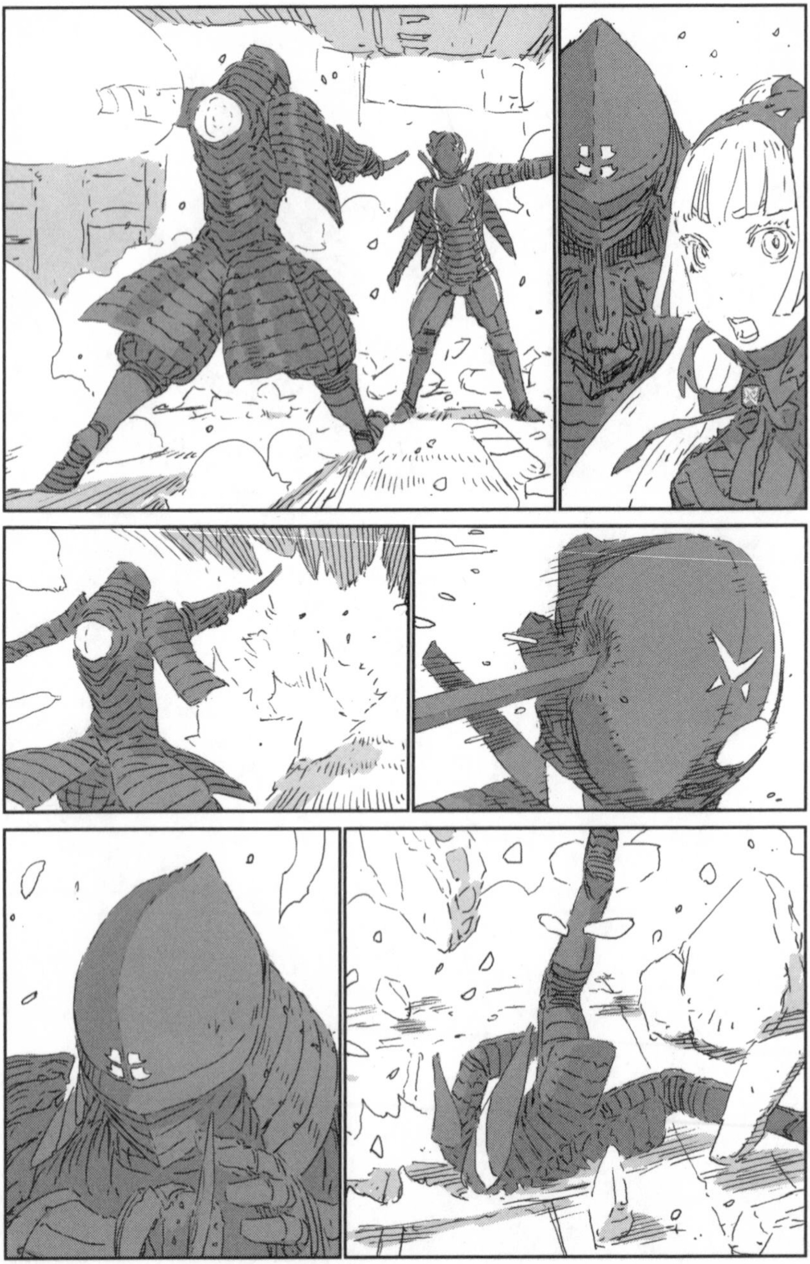

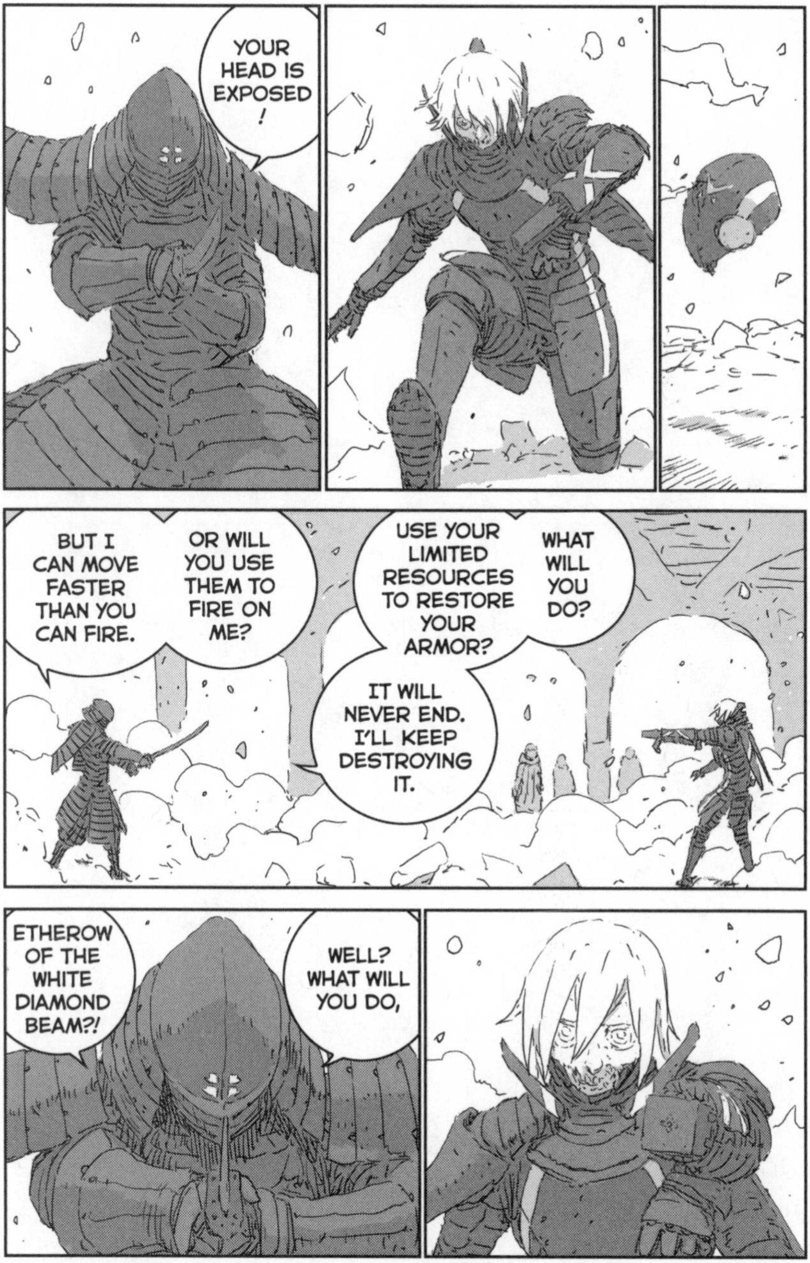
YOUR HEAD IS EXPOSED!
WHAT WILL YOU DO?
USE YOUR LIMITED RESOURCES TO RESTORE YOUR ARMOR?
OR WILL YOU USE THEM TO FIRE ON ME?
BUT I CAN MOVE FASTER THAN YOU CAN FIRE.
IT WILL NEVER END. I'LL KEEP DESTROYING IT.
WELL? WHAT WILL YOU DO,
ETHEROW OF THE WHITE DIAMOND BEAM?!

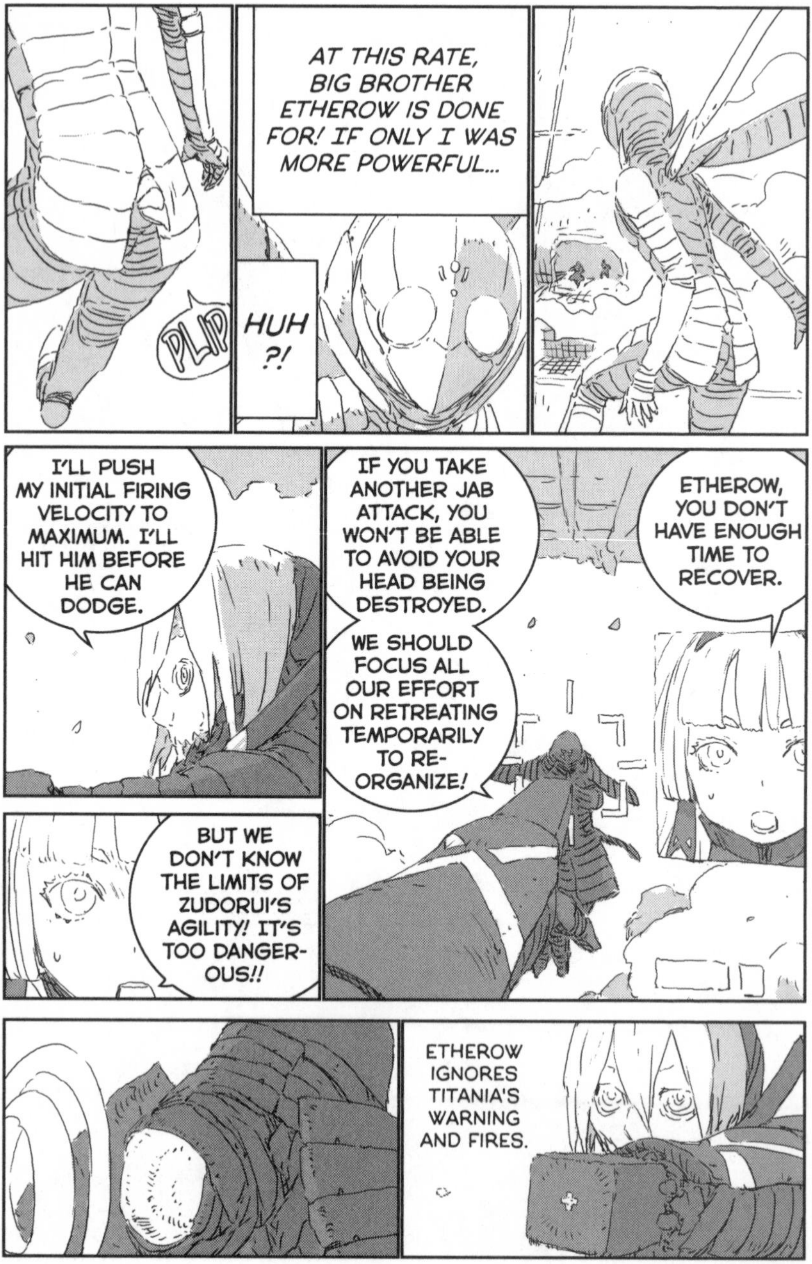
AT THIS RATE, BIG BROTHER ETHEROW IS DONE FOR! IF ONLY I WAS MORE POWERFUL...
HUH ?!
PLIP
ETHEROW, YOU DON'T HAVE ENOUGH TIME TO RECOVER.
IF YOU TAKE ANOTHER JAB ATTACK, YOU WON'T BE ABLE TO AVOID YOUR HEAD BEING DESTROYED.
WE SHOULD FOCUS ALL OUR EFFORT ON RETREATING TEMPORARILY TO RE-ORGANIZE!
I'LL PUSH MY INITIAL FIRING VELOCITY TO MAXIMUM. I'LL HIT HIM BEFORE HE CAN DODGE.
BUT WE DON'T KNOW THE LIMITS OF ZUDORUI'S AGILITY! IT'S TOO DANGER-OUS!!
ETHEROW IGNORES TITANIA'S WARNING AND FIRES.

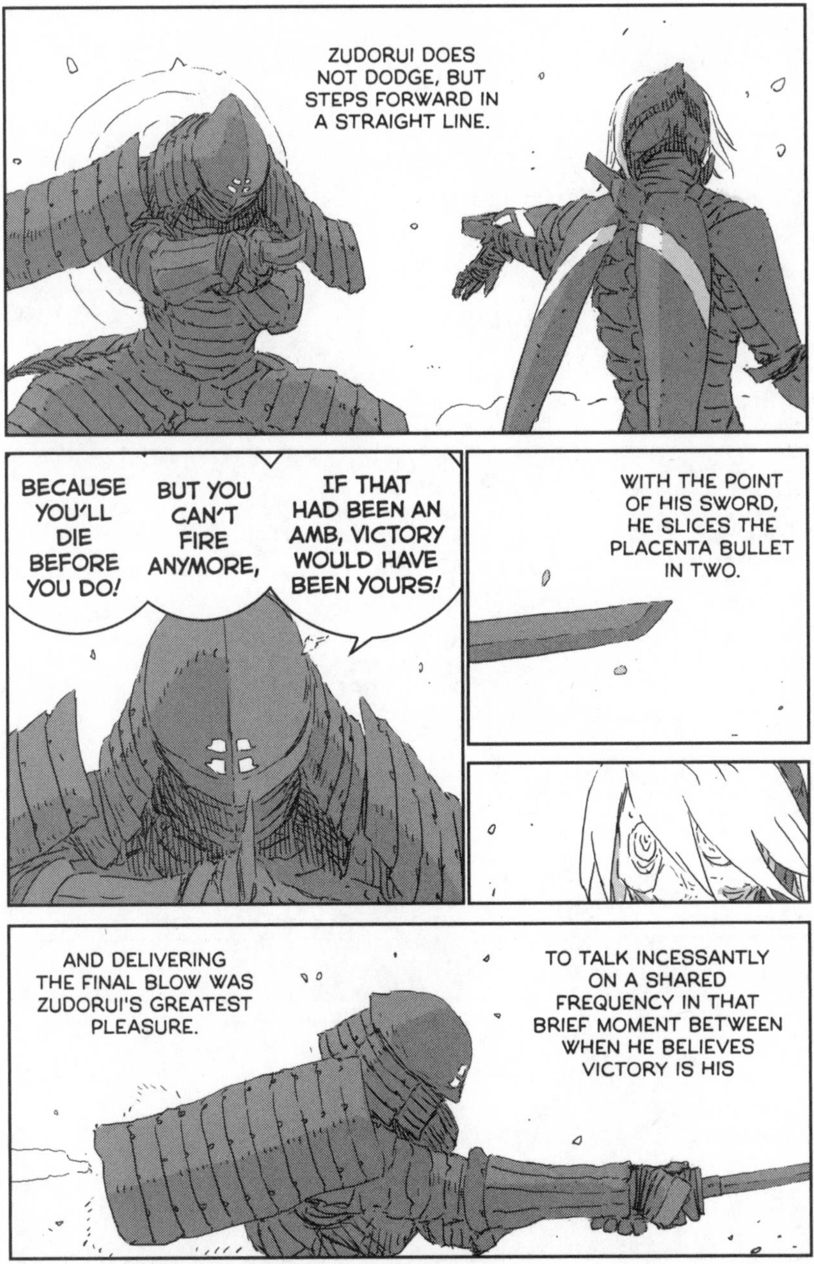
ZUDORUI DOES NOT DODGE, BUT STEPS FORWARD IN A STRAIGHT LINE.
WITH THE POINT OF HIS SWORD, HE SLICES THE PLACENTA BULLET IN TWO.
IF THAT HAD BEEN AN AMB, VICTORY WOULD HAVE BEEN YOURS!
BUT YOU CAN'T FIRE ANYMORE,
BECAUSE YOU'LL DIE BEFORE YOU DO!
TO TALK INCESSANTLY ON A SHARED FREQUENCY IN THAT BRIEF MOMENT BETWEEN WHEN HE BELIEVES VICTORY IS HIS
AND DELIVERING THE FINAL BLOW WAS ZUDORUI'S GREATEST PLEASURE.

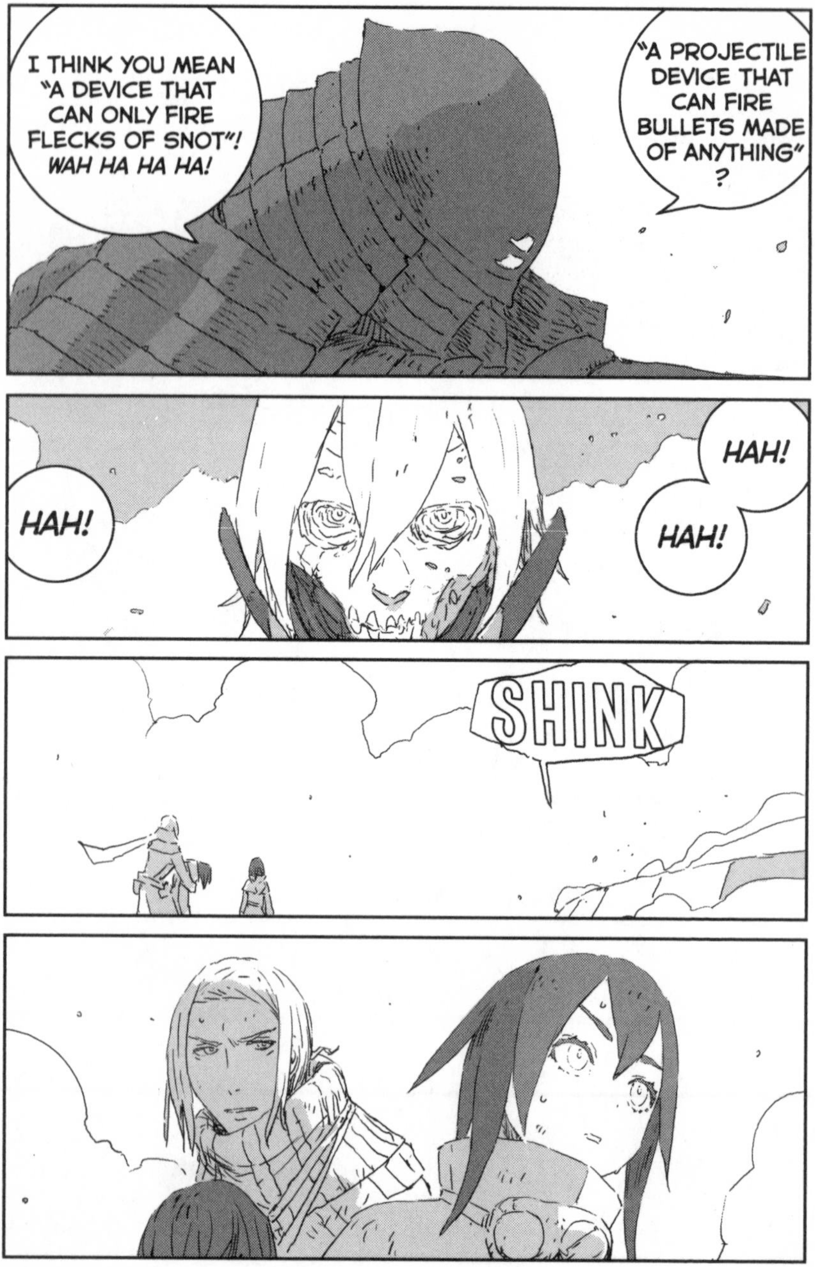
"A PROJECTILE DEVICE THAT CAN FIRE BULLETS MADE OF ANYTHING"?
I THINK YOU MEAN "A DEVICE THAT CAN ONLY FIRE FLECKS OF SNOT"! *WAH HA HA HA!*
HAH!
HAH!
HAH!
SHINK

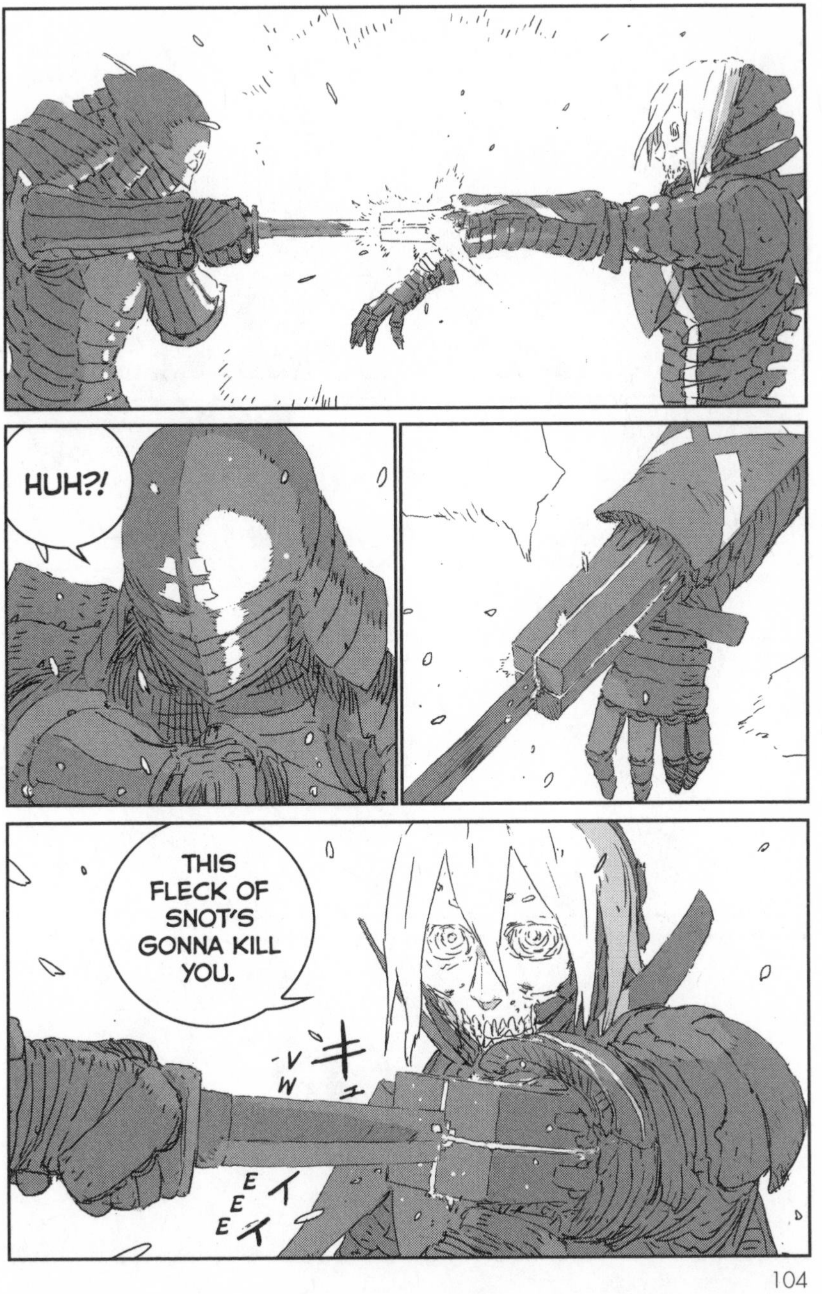
HUH?!
THIS FLECK OF SNOT'S GONNA KILL YOU.
VWEEE

NO...
CHOOM
W–
BÀKAM

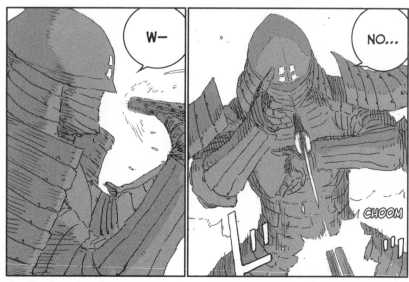

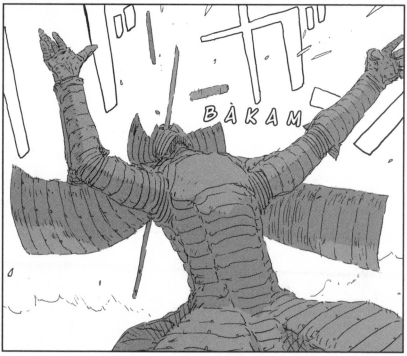

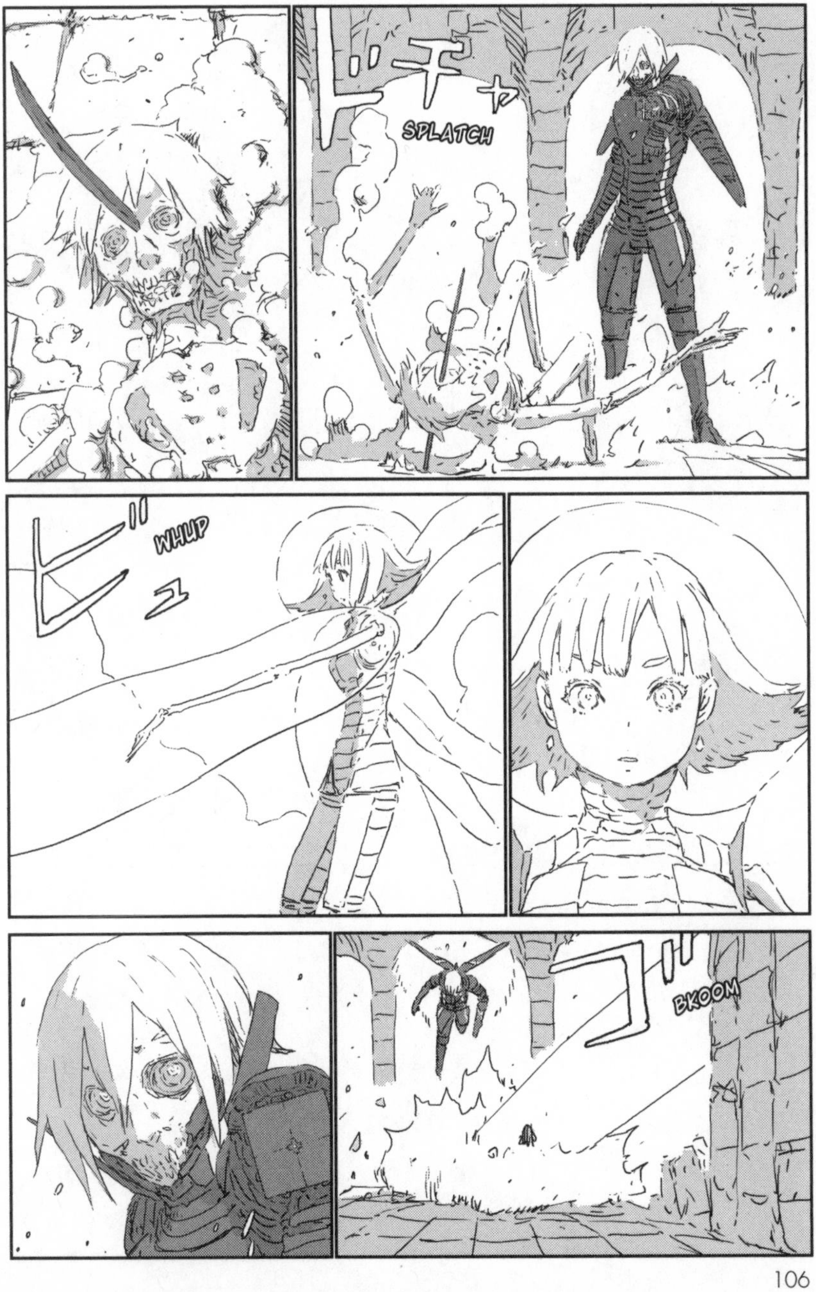
SPLATCH
WHUP
BKOOM

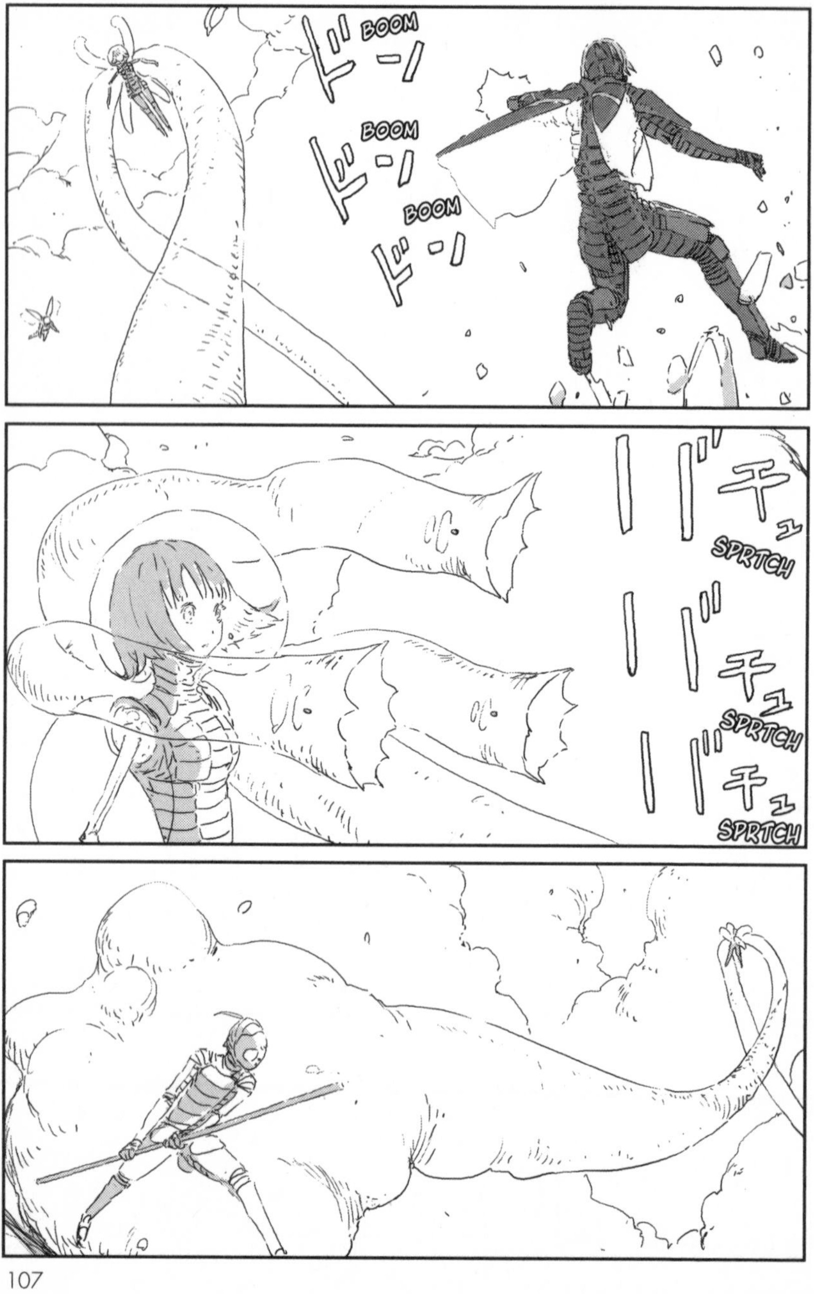
BOOM
BOOM
BOOM
SPRTCH
SPRTCH
SPRTCH

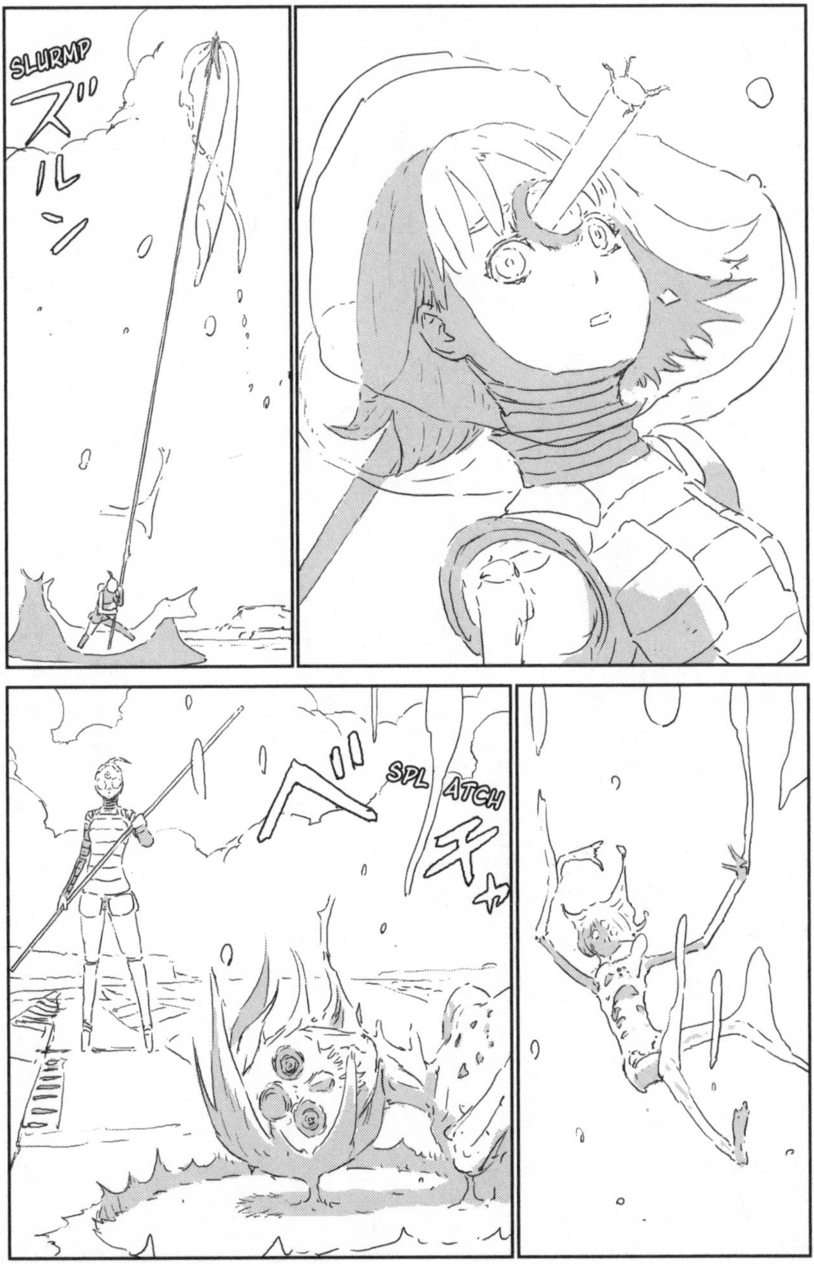
SLURMP
ズルン
SPL ATCH
ベチャ

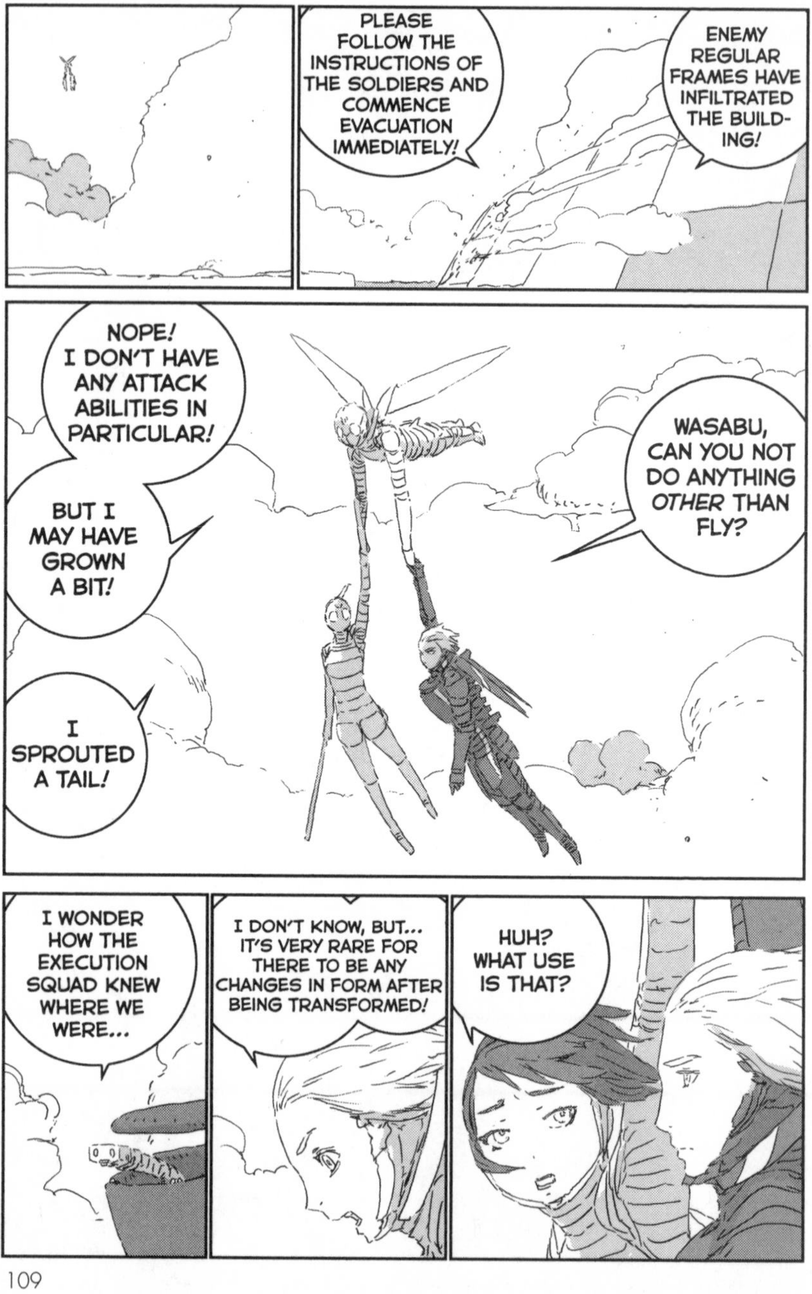
ENEMY REGULAR FRAMES HAVE INFILTRATED THE BUILD-ING!
PLEASE FOLLOW THE INSTRUCTIONS OF THE SOLDIERS AND COMMENCE EVACUATION IMMEDIATELY!
WASABU, CAN YOU NOT DO ANYTHING *OTHER* THAN FLY?
NOPE! I DON'T HAVE ANY ATTACK ABILITIES IN PARTICULAR!
BUT I MAY HAVE GROWN A BIT!
I SPROUTED A TAIL!
HUH? WHAT USE IS THAT?
I DON'T KNOW, BUT... IT'S VERY RARE FOR THERE TO BE ANY CHANGES IN FORM AFTER BEING TRANSFORMED!
I WONDER HOW THE EXECUTION SQUAD KNEW WHERE WE WERE...

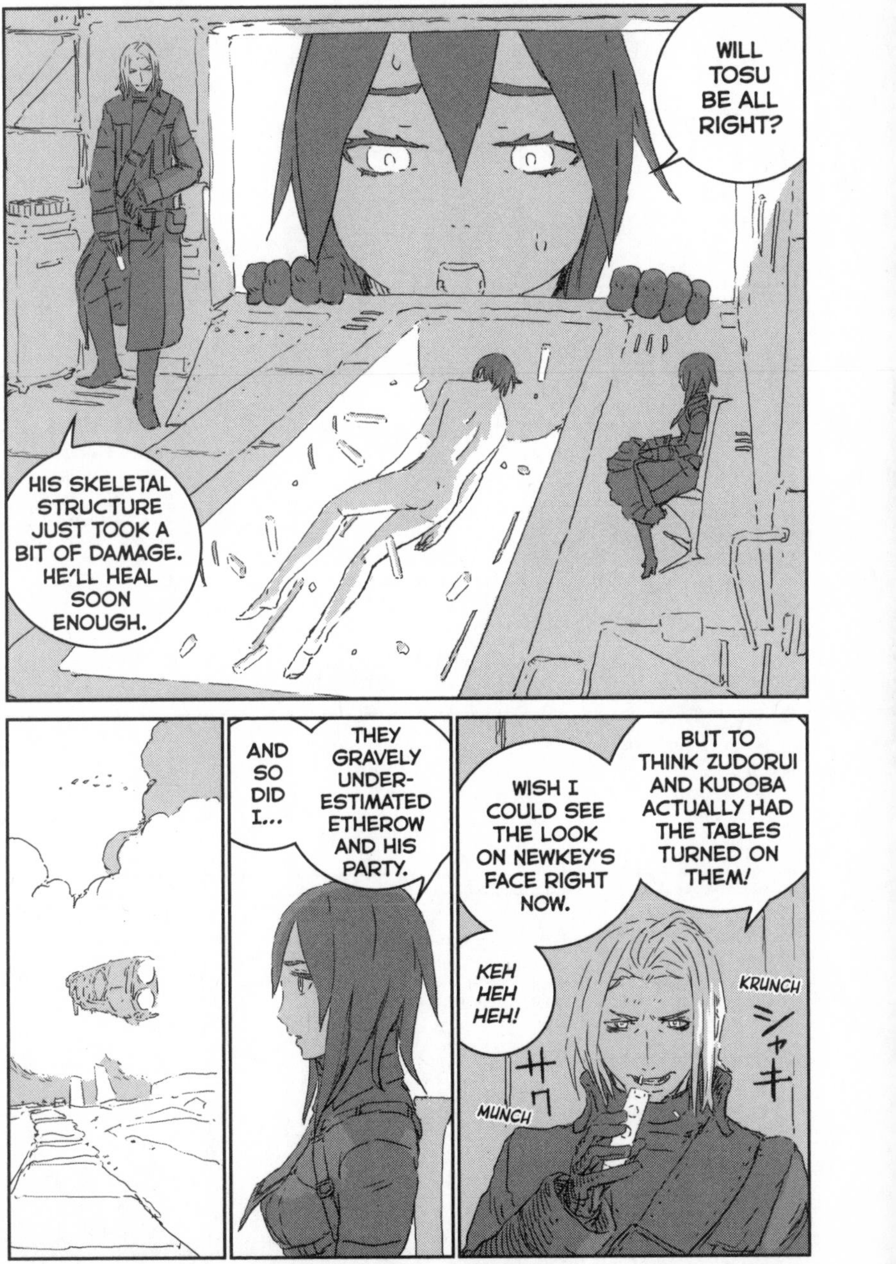
WILL TOSU BE ALL RIGHT?
HIS SKELETAL STRUCTURE JUST TOOK A BIT OF DAMAGE. HE'LL HEAL SOON ENOUGH.
BUT TO THINK ZUDORUI AND KUDOBA ACTUALLY HAD THE TABLES TURNED ON THEM!
WISH I COULD SEE THE LOOK ON NEWKEY'S FACE RIGHT NOW.
KEH HEH HEH!
KRUNCH
シャキ
サク
MUNCH
THEY GRAVELY UNDER-ESTIMATED ETHEROW AND HIS PARTY.
AND SO DID I...

CHAPTER 40 END

APOSIMZ

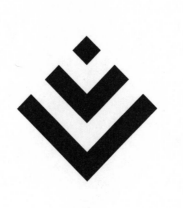

CHAPTER 41

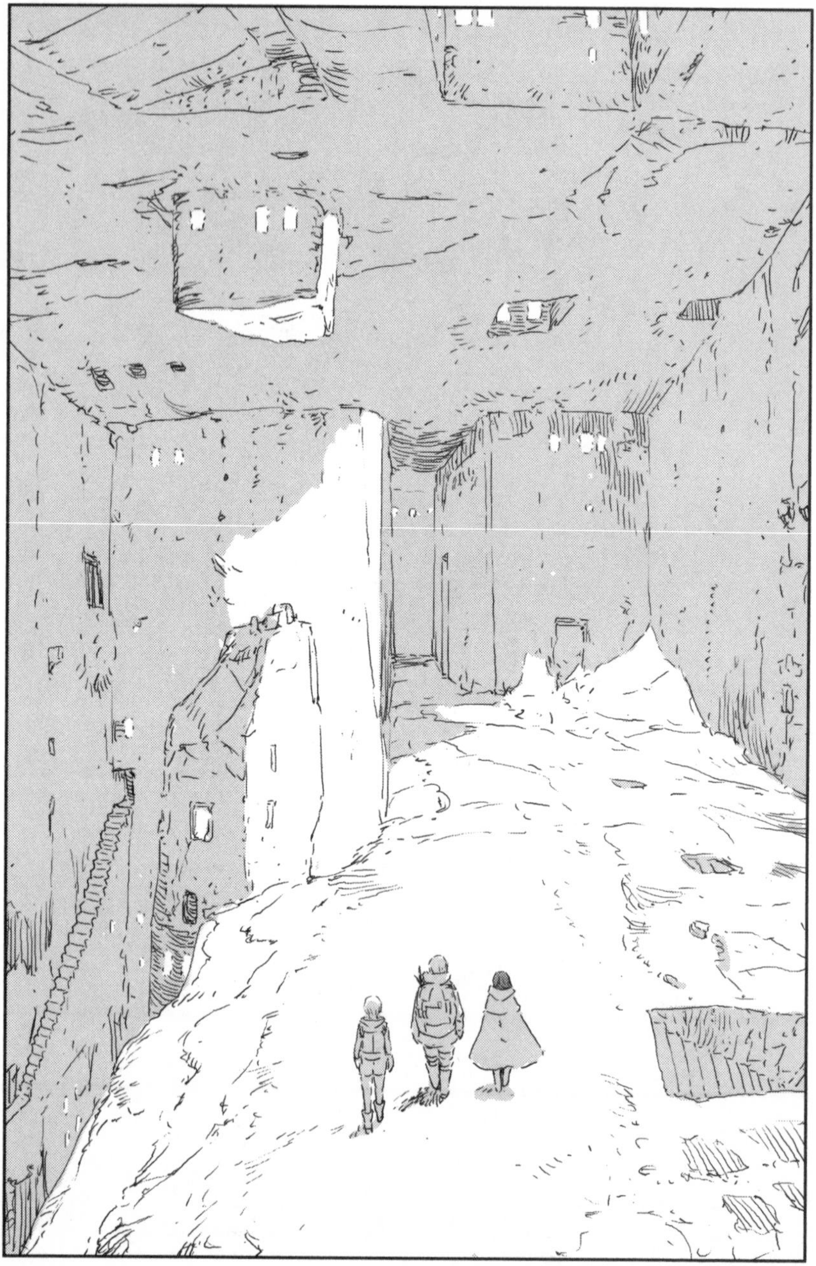

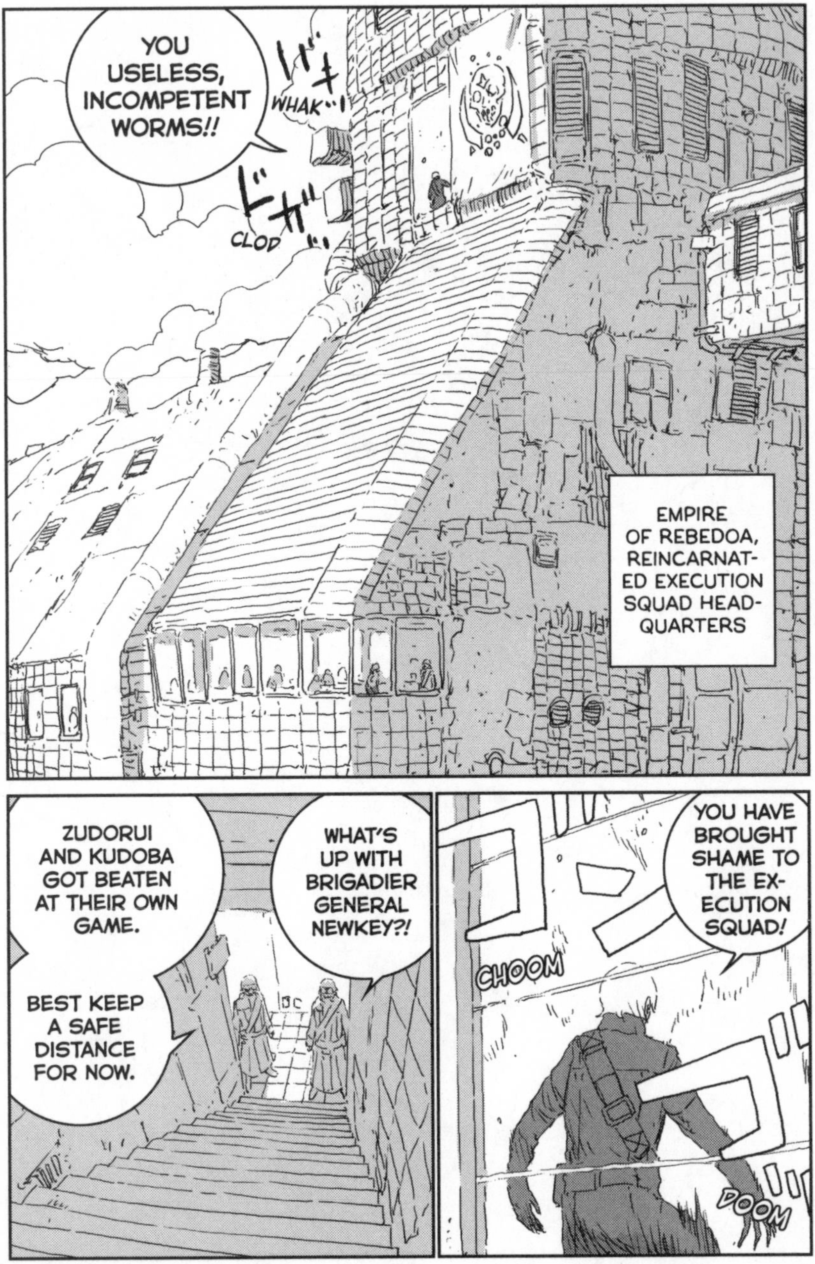

YOU USELESS, INCOMPETENT WORMS!!
WHAK
CLOD
EMPIRE OF REBEDOA, REINCARNATED EXECUTION SQUAD HEADQUARTERS
YOU HAVE BROUGHT SHAME TO THE EXECUTION SQUAD!
CHOOM
DOOM
WHAT'S UP WITH BRIGADIER GENERAL NEWKEY?!
ZUDORUI AND KUDOBA GOT BEATEN AT THEIR OWN GAME.
BEST KEEP A SAFE DISTANCE FOR NOW.

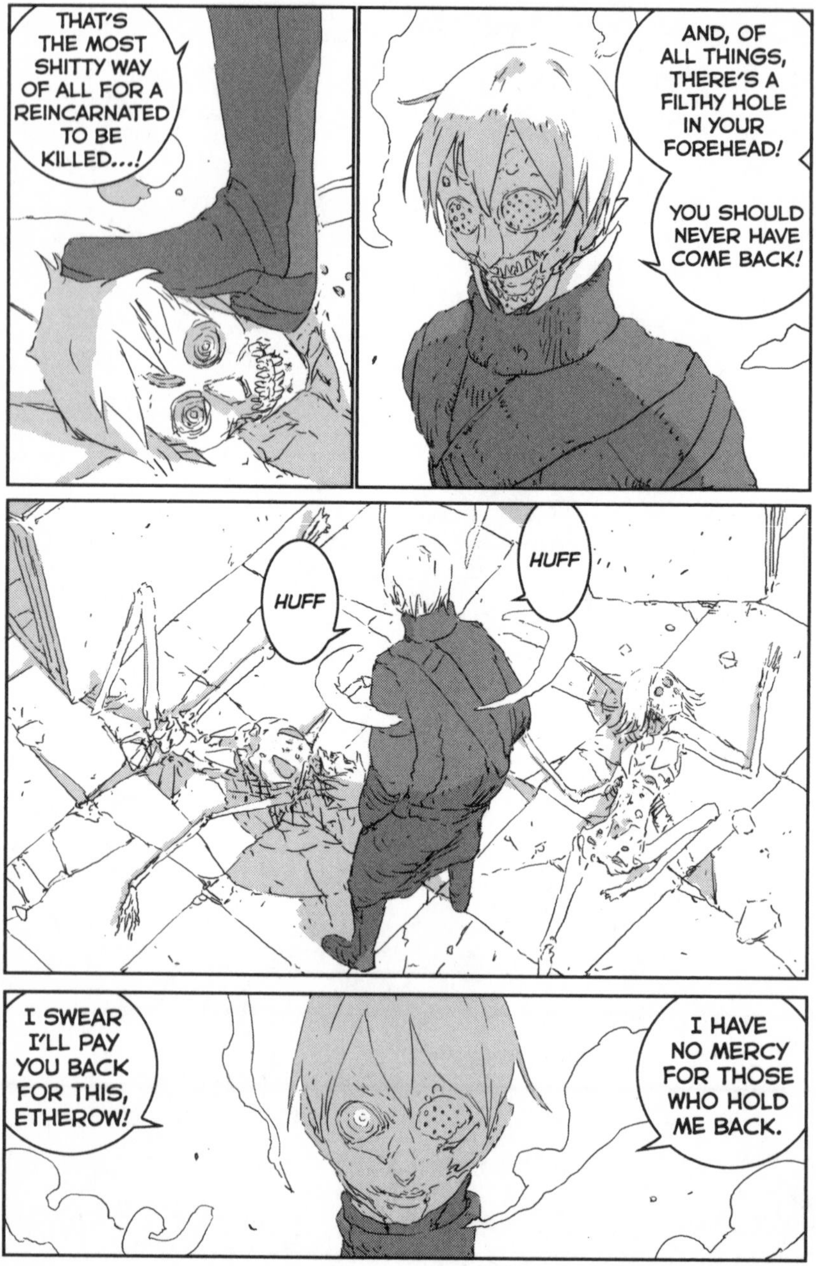
AND, OF ALL THINGS, THERE'S A FILTHY HOLE IN YOUR FOREHEAD!
YOU SHOULD NEVER HAVE COME BACK!
THAT'S THE MOST SHITTY WAY OF ALL FOR A REINCARNATED TO BE KILLED...!
HUFF
HUFF
I HAVE NO MERCY FOR THOSE WHO HOLD ME BACK.
I SWEAR I'LL PAY YOU BACK FOR THIS, ETHEROW!

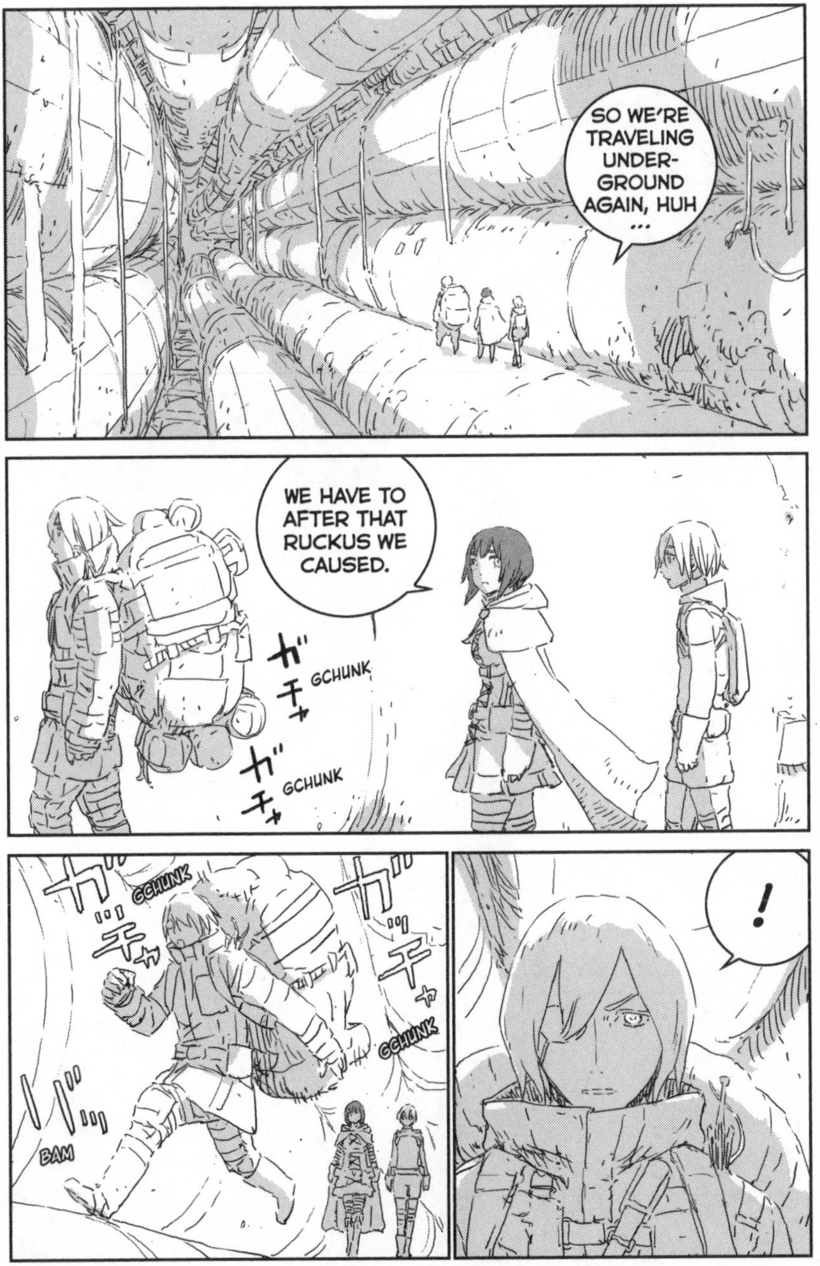
SO WE'RE TRAVELING UNDER-GROUND AGAIN, HUH ...
WE HAVE TO AFTER THAT RUCKUS WE CAUSED.
ガチャ
GCHUNK
ガチャ
GCHUNK
!
GCHUNK
GCHUNK
BAM

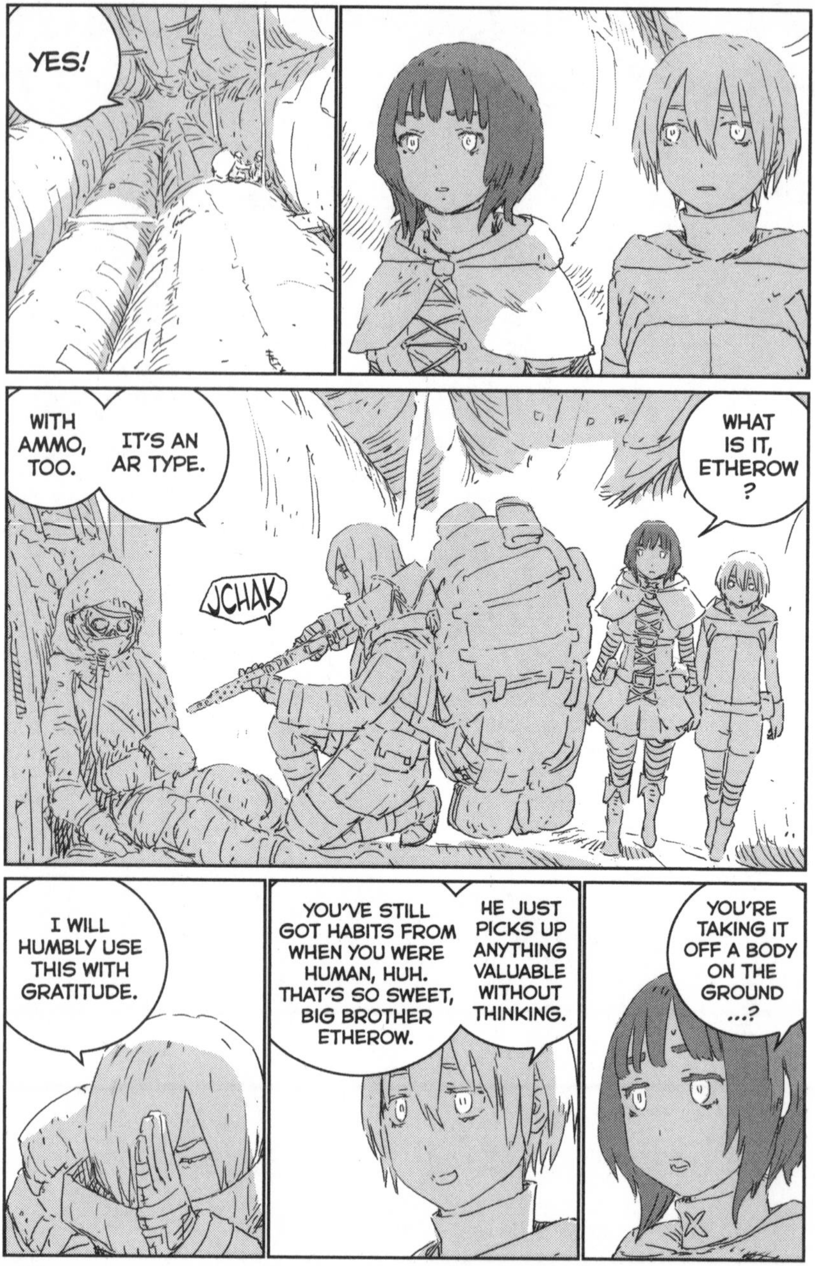
YES!
WHAT IS IT, ETHEROW?
IT'S AN AR TYPE.
WITH AMMO, TOO.
JCHAK
YOU'RE TAKING IT OFF A BODY ON THE GROUND...?
HE JUST PICKS UP ANYTHING VALUABLE WITHOUT THINKING.
YOU'VE STILL GOT HABITS FROM WHEN YOU WERE HUMAN, HUH. THAT'S SO SWEET, BIG BROTHER ETHEROW.
I WILL HUMBLY USE THIS WITH GRATITUDE.

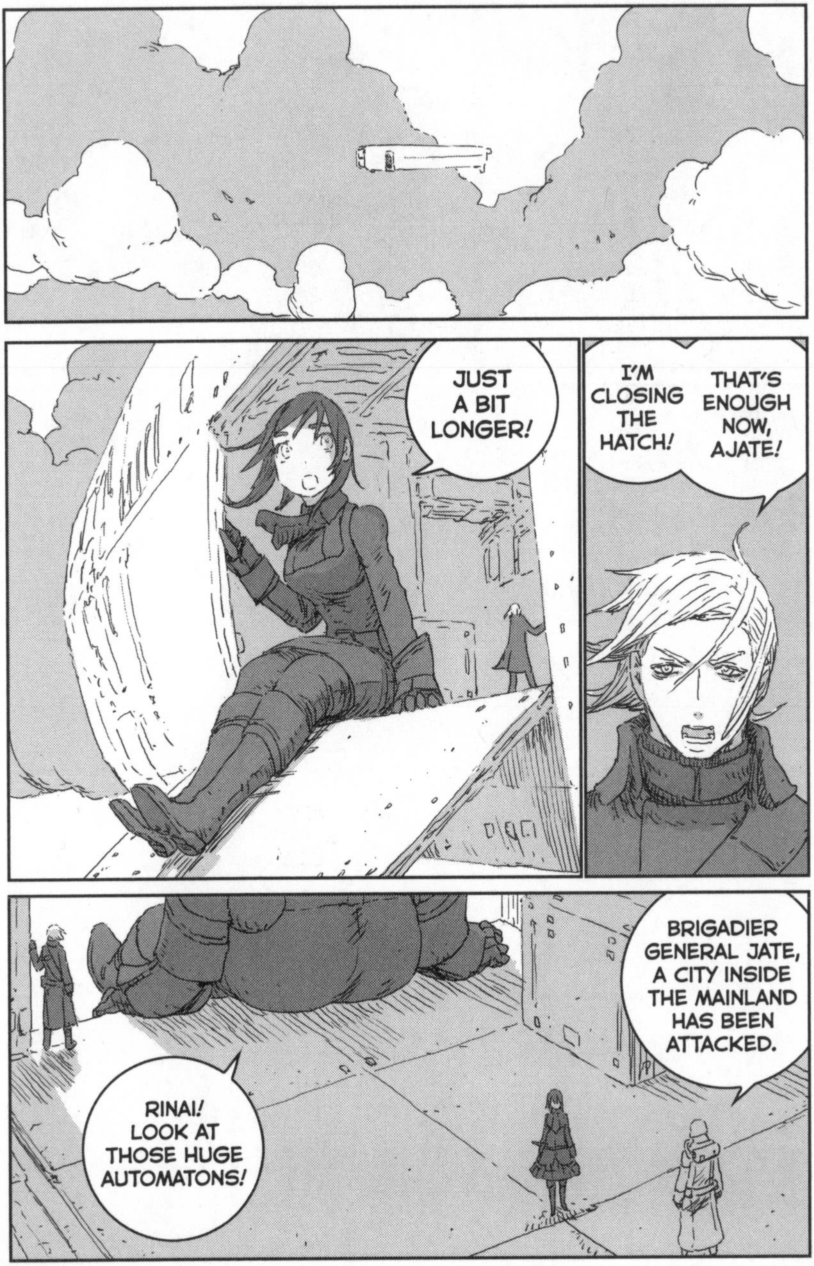
THAT'S ENOUGH NOW, AJATE!
I'M CLOSING THE HATCH!
JUST A BIT LONGER!
BRIGADIER GENERAL JATE, A CITY INSIDE THE MAINLAND HAS BEEN ATTACKED.
RINAI! LOOK AT THOSE HUGE AUTOMATONS!

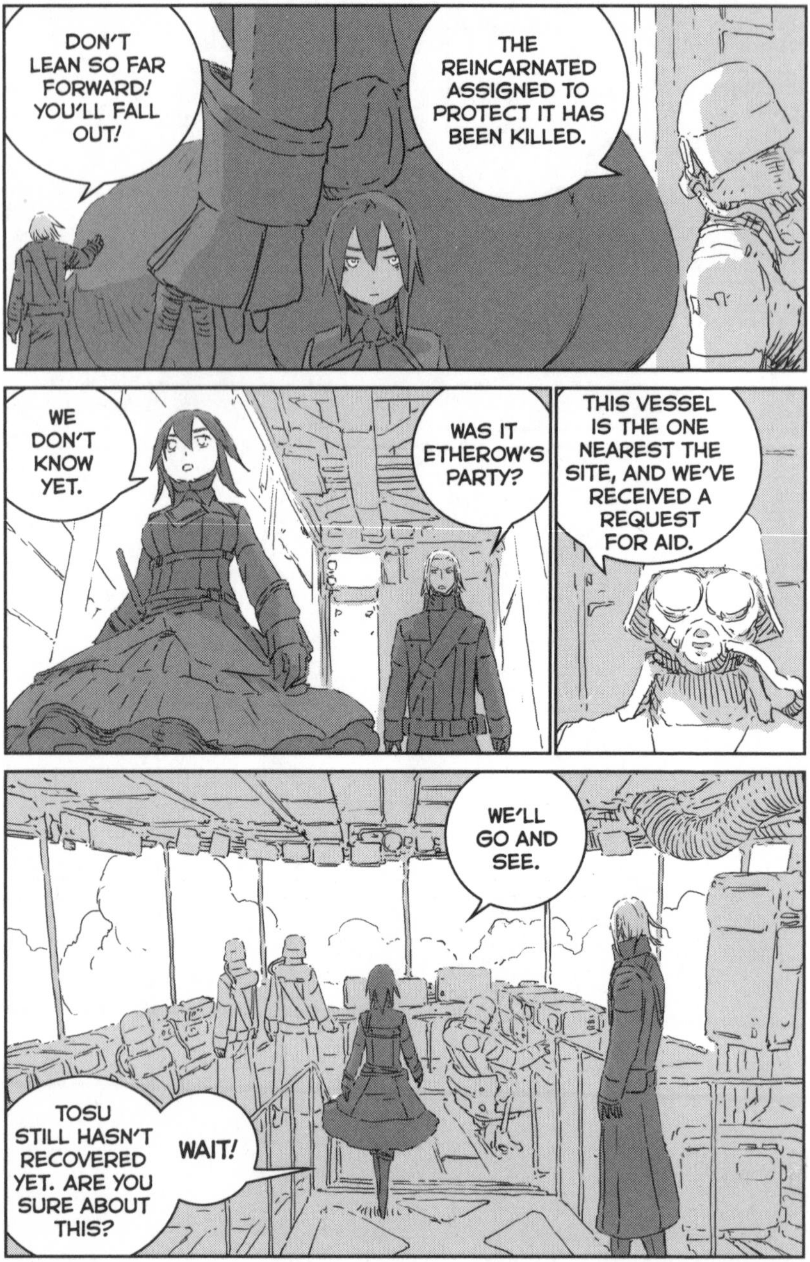
THE REINCARNATED ASSIGNED TO PROTECT IT HAS BEEN KILLED.
DON'T LEAN SO FAR FORWARD! YOU'LL FALL OUT!
THIS VESSEL IS THE ONE NEAREST THE SITE, AND WE'VE RECEIVED A REQUEST FOR AID.
WAS IT ETHEROW'S PARTY?
WE DON'T KNOW YET.
WE'LL GO AND SEE.
WAIT!
TOSU STILL HASN'T RECOVERED YET. ARE YOU SURE ABOUT THIS?

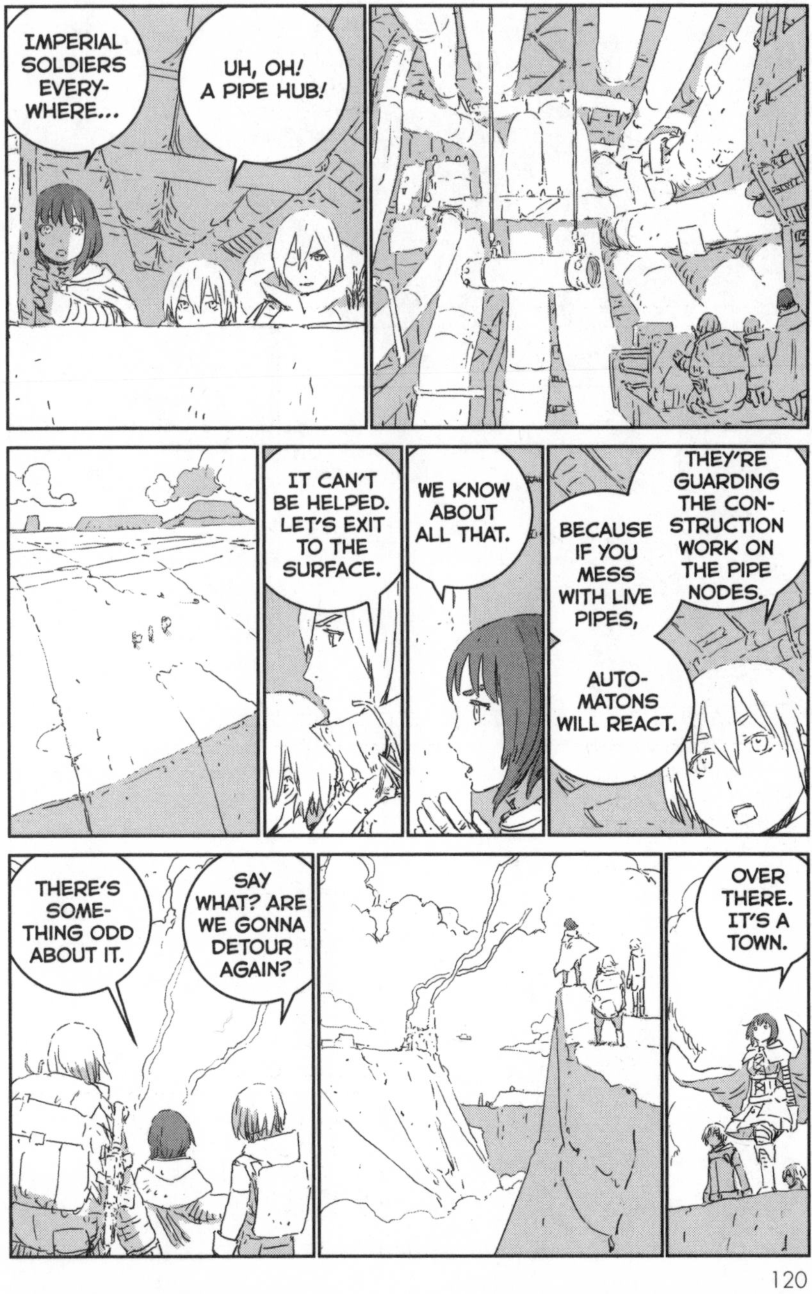
UH, OH! A PIPE HUB!
IMPERIAL SOLDIERS EVERYWHERE...
THEY'RE GUARDING THE CONSTRUCTION WORK ON THE PIPE NODES.
BECAUSE IF YOU MESS WITH LIVE PIPES,
AUTOMATONS WILL REACT.
WE KNOW ABOUT ALL THAT.
IT CAN'T BE HELPED. LET'S EXIT TO THE SURFACE.
OVER THERE. IT'S A TOWN.
SAY WHAT? ARE WE GONNA DETOUR AGAIN?
THERE'S SOMETHING ODD ABOUT IT.

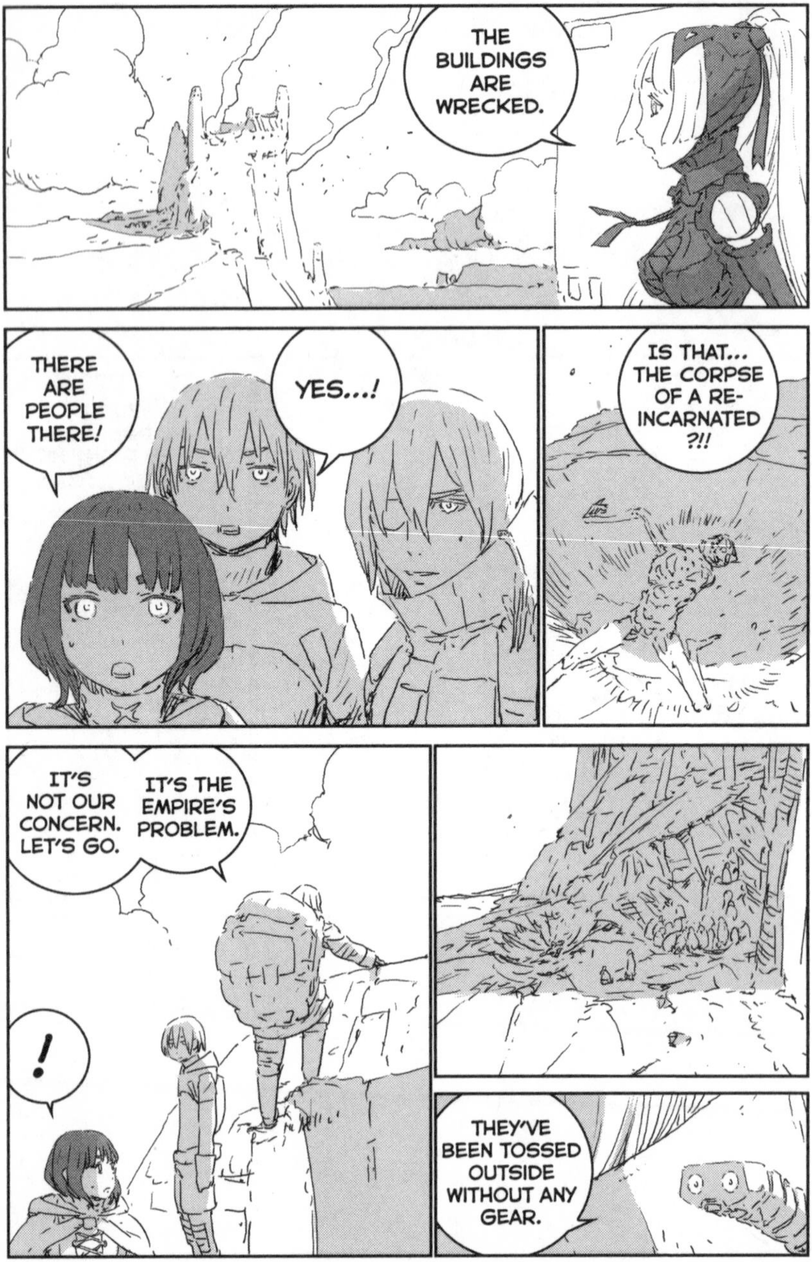
THE BUILDINGS ARE WRECKED.
IS THAT... THE CORPSE OF A RE-INCARNATED ?!!
YES...!
THERE ARE PEOPLE THERE!
THEY'VE BEEN TOSSED OUTSIDE WITHOUT ANY GEAR.
IT'S THE EMPIRE'S PROBLEM.
IT'S NOT OUR CONCERN. LET'S GO.
!

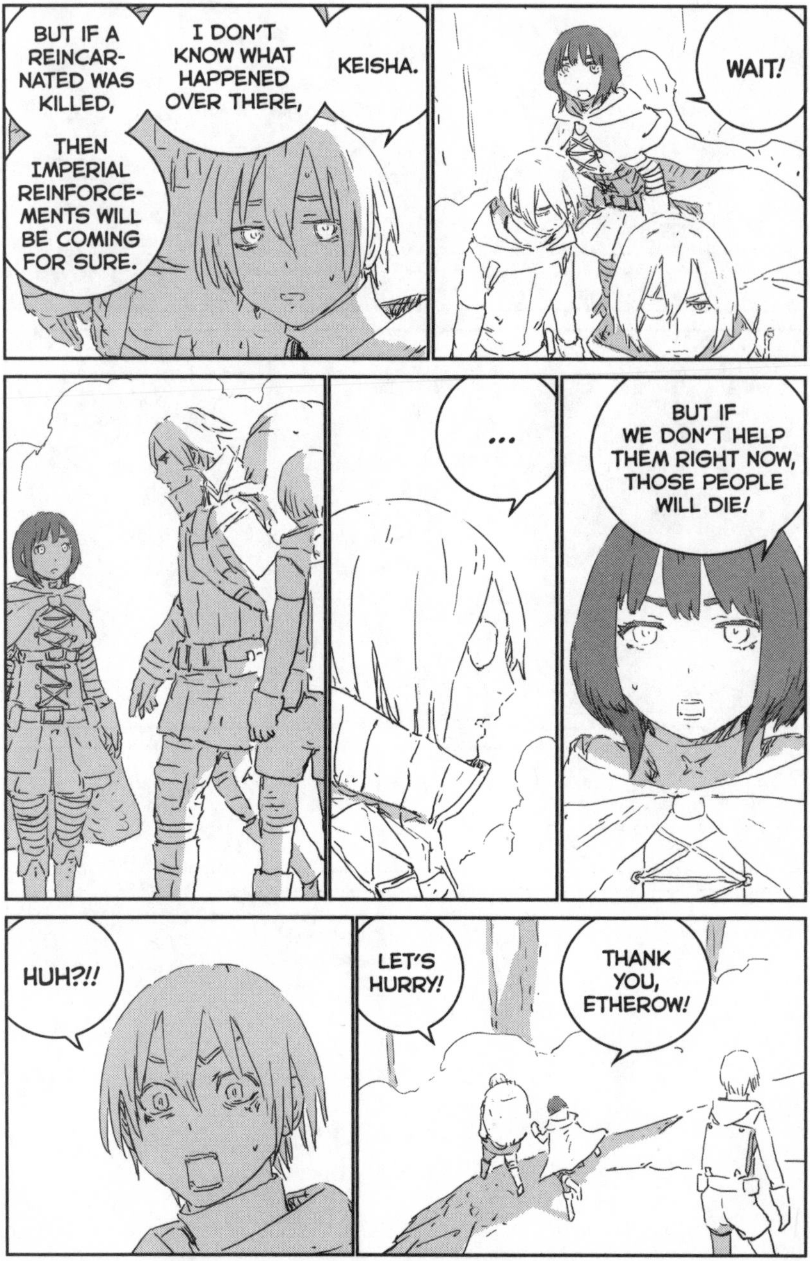
WAIT!
KEISHA.
I DON'T KNOW WHAT HAPPENED OVER THERE,
BUT IF A REINCAR-NATED WAS KILLED,
THEN IMPERIAL REINFORCE-MENTS WILL BE COMING FOR SURE.
BUT IF WE DON'T HELP THEM RIGHT NOW, THOSE PEOPLE WILL DIE!
...
THANK YOU, ETHEROW!
LET'S HURRY!
HUH?!!

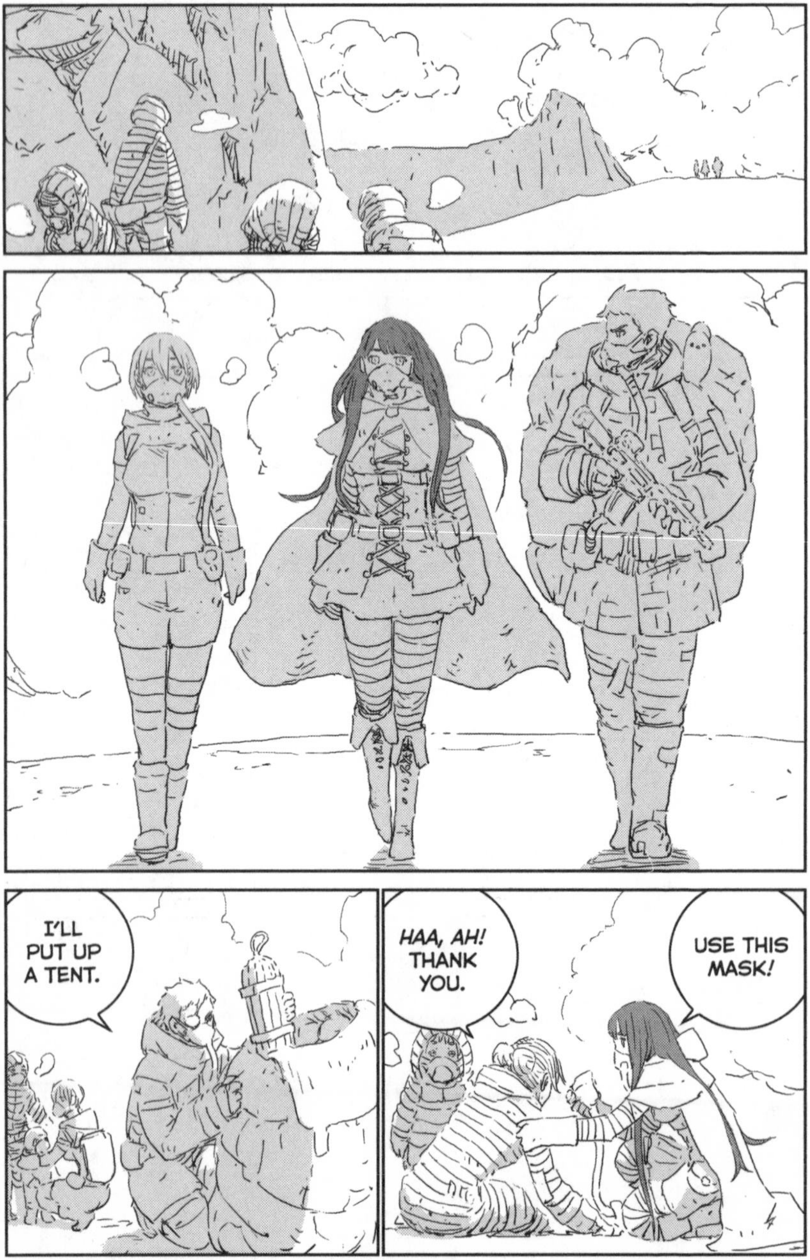

USE THIS MASK!
HAA, AH! THANK YOU.
I'LL PUT UP A TENT.

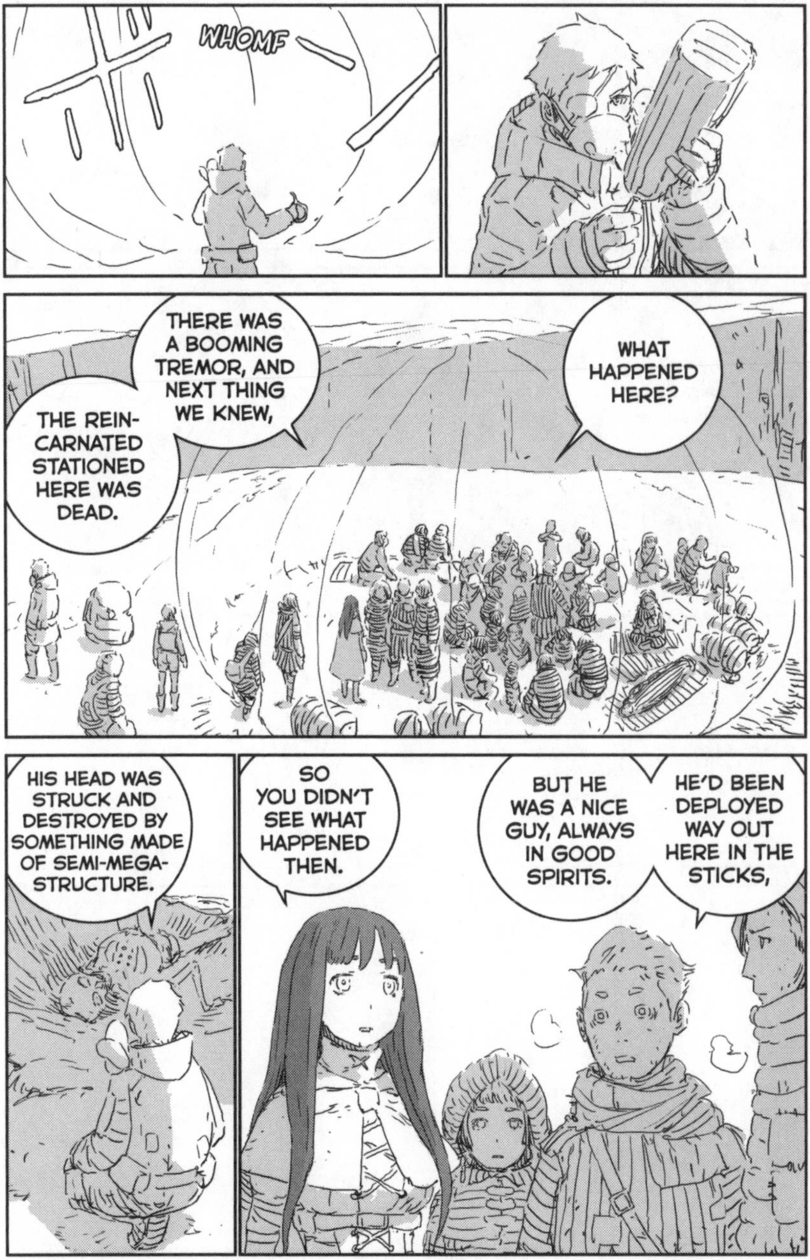
WHOMF
WHAT HAPPENED HERE?
THERE WAS A BOOMING TREMOR, AND NEXT THING WE KNEW,
THE REIN-CARNATED STATIONED HERE WAS DEAD.
HE'D BEEN DEPLOYED WAY OUT HERE IN THE STICKS,
BUT HE WAS A NICE GUY, ALWAYS IN GOOD SPIRITS.
SO YOU DIDN'T SEE WHAT HAPPENED THEN.
HIS HEAD WAS STRUCK AND DESTROYED BY SOMETHING MADE OF SEMI-MEGA-STRUCTURE.

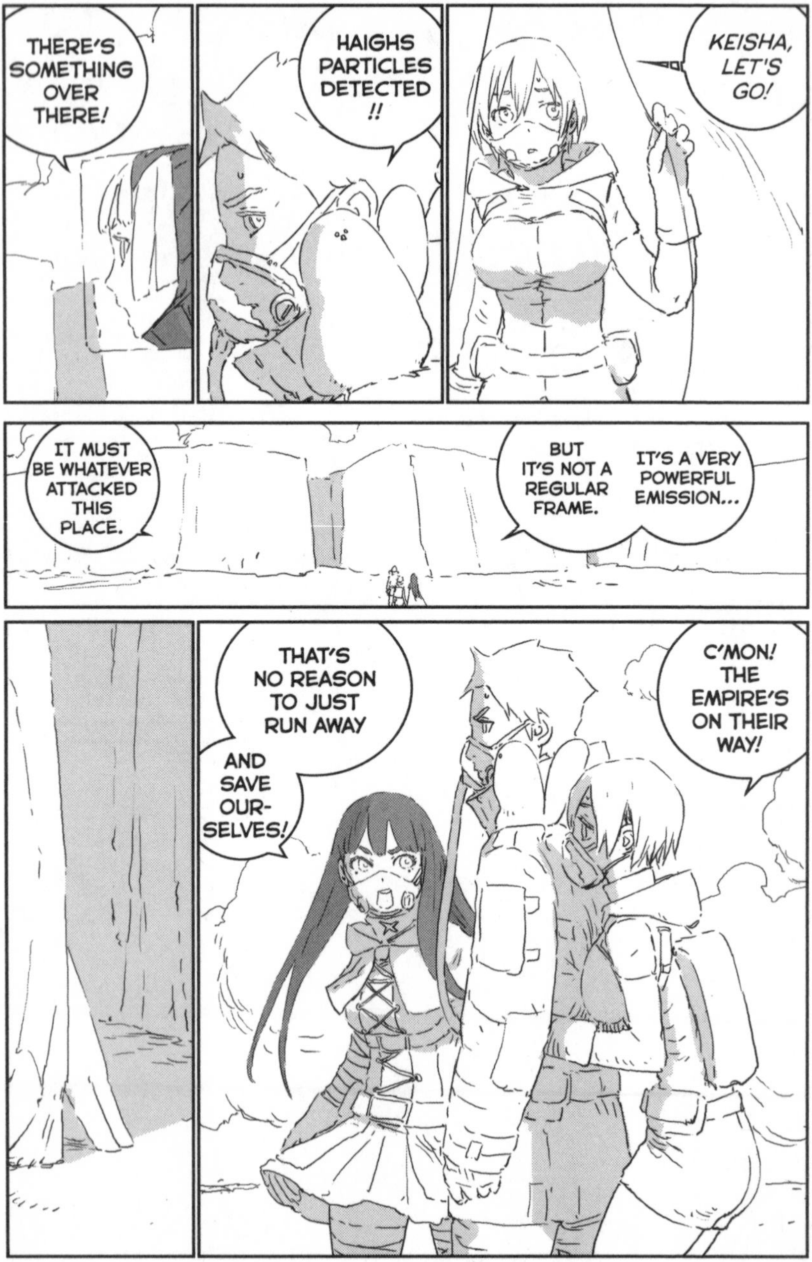
KEISHA, LET'S GO!
HAIGHS PARTICLES DETECTED !!
THERE'S SOMETHING OVER THERE!
IT'S A VERY POWERFUL EMISSION...
BUT IT'S NOT A REGULAR FRAME.
IT MUST BE WHATEVER ATTACKED THIS PLACE.
C'MON! THE EMPIRE'S ON THEIR WAY!
THAT'S NO REASON TO JUST RUN AWAY
AND SAVE OUR-SELVES!

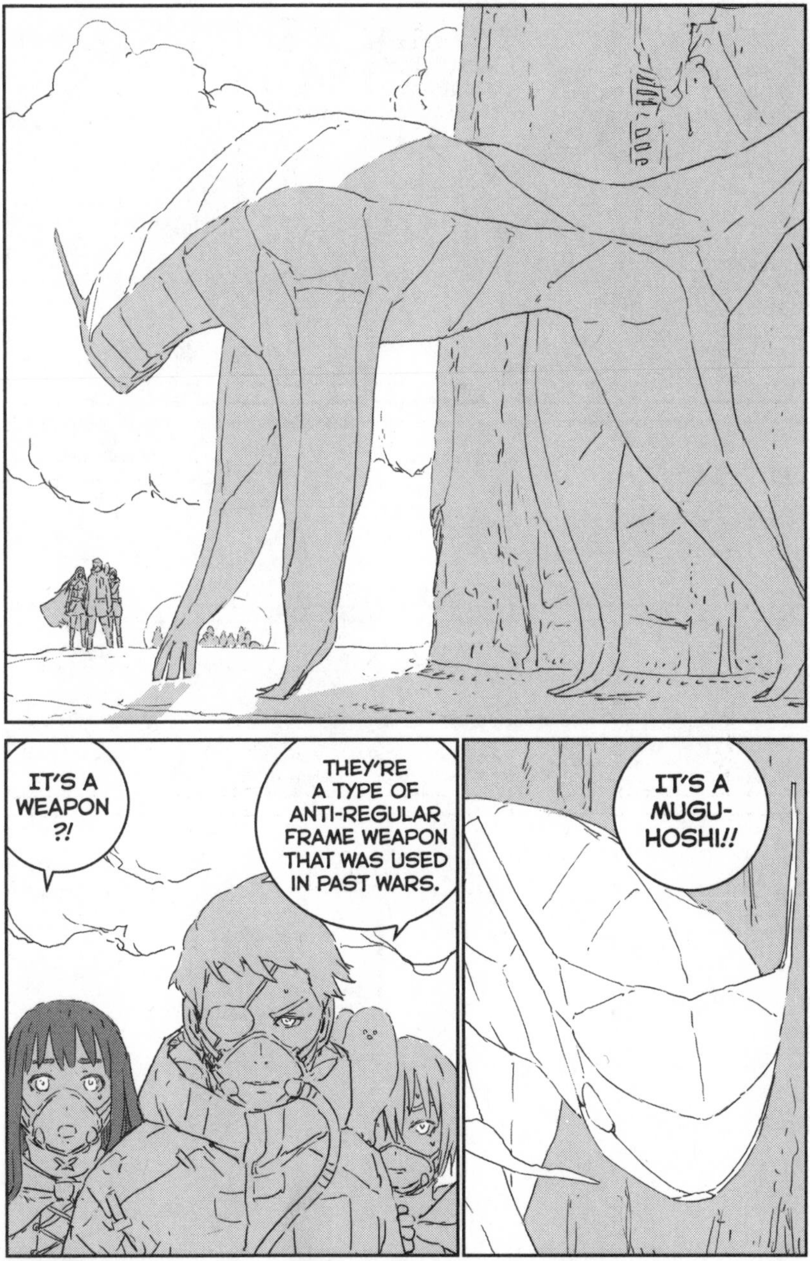
IT'S A MUGU-HOSHI!!
IT'S A WEAPON ?!
THEY'RE A TYPE OF ANTI-REGULAR FRAME WEAPON THAT WAS USED IN PAST WARS.

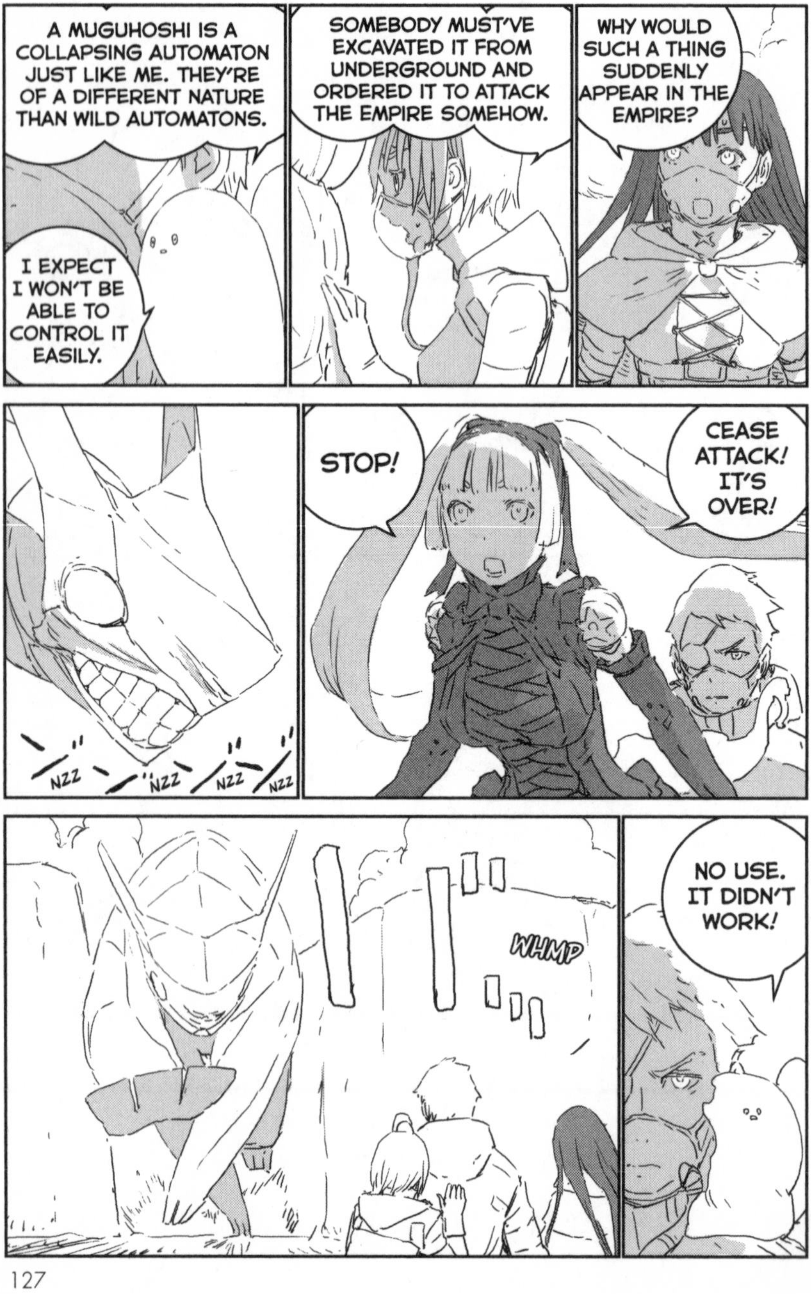
WHY WOULD SUCH A THING SUDDENLY APPEAR IN THE EMPIRE?
SOMEBODY MUST'VE EXCAVATED IT FROM UNDERGROUND AND ORDERED IT TO ATTACK THE EMPIRE SOMEHOW.
A MUGUHOSHI IS A COLLAPSING AUTOMATON JUST LIKE ME. THEY'RE OF A DIFFERENT NATURE THAN WILD AUTOMATONS.
I EXPECT I WON'T BE ABLE TO CONTROL IT EASILY.
CEASE ATTACK! IT'S OVER!
STOP!
NZZ NZZ NZZ NZZ
NO USE. IT DIDN'T WORK!
WHMP

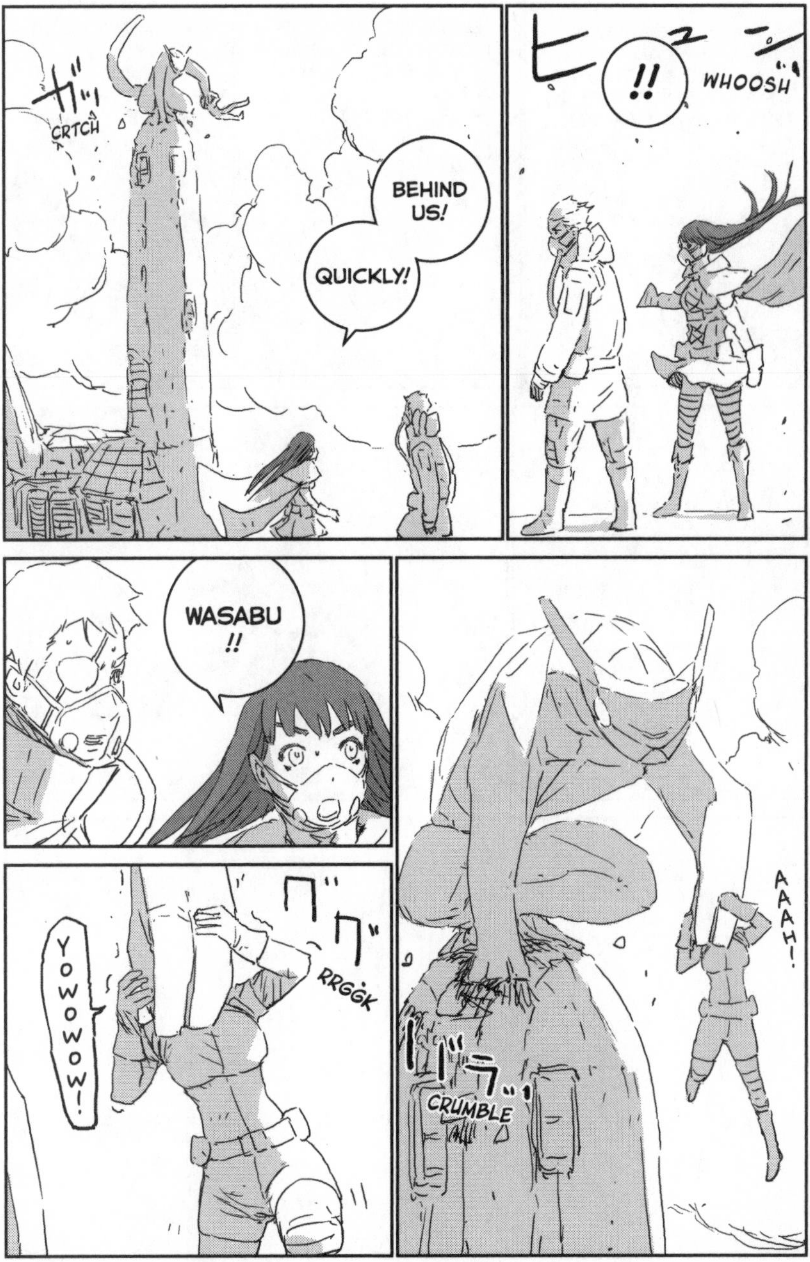
!!
WHOOSH
BEHIND US!
QUICKLY!
CRTCH
AAAH!
CRUMBLE
WASABU !!
RRGGK
YOWOWOW!

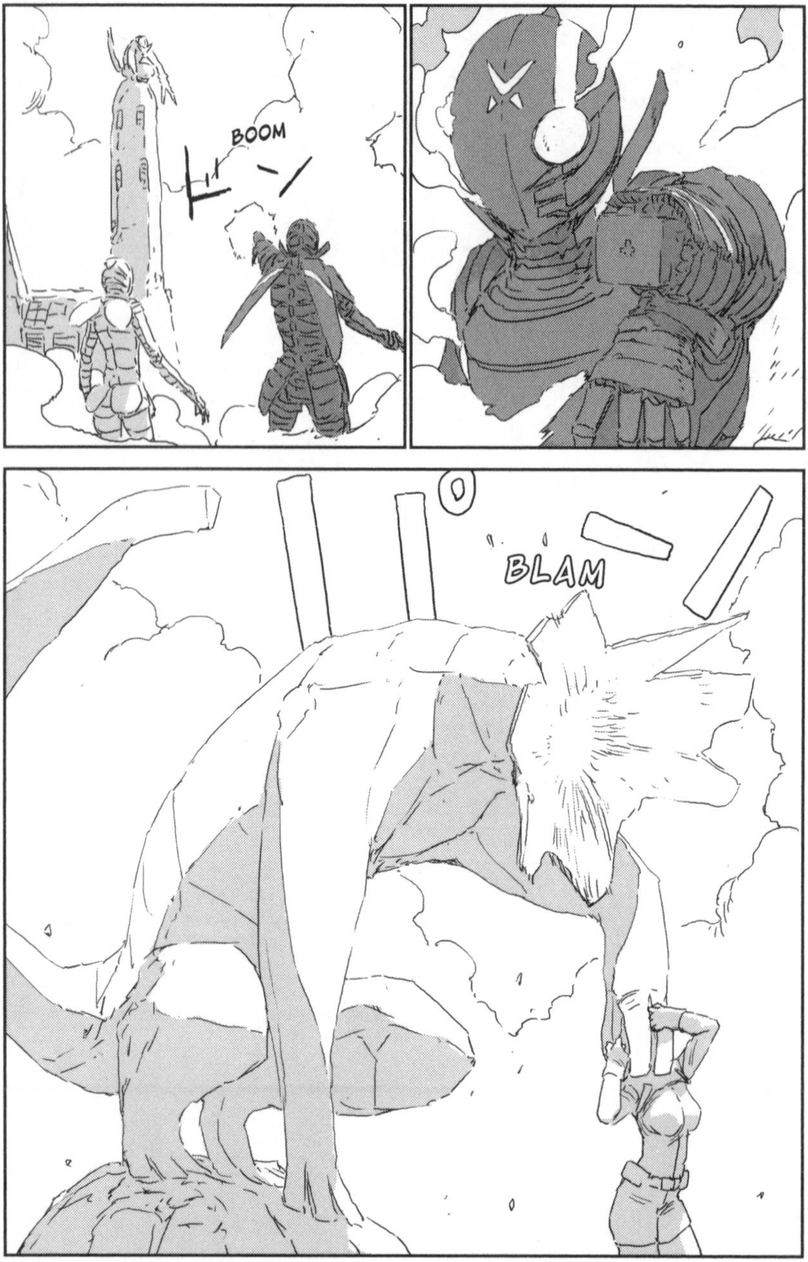
BOOM
BLAM

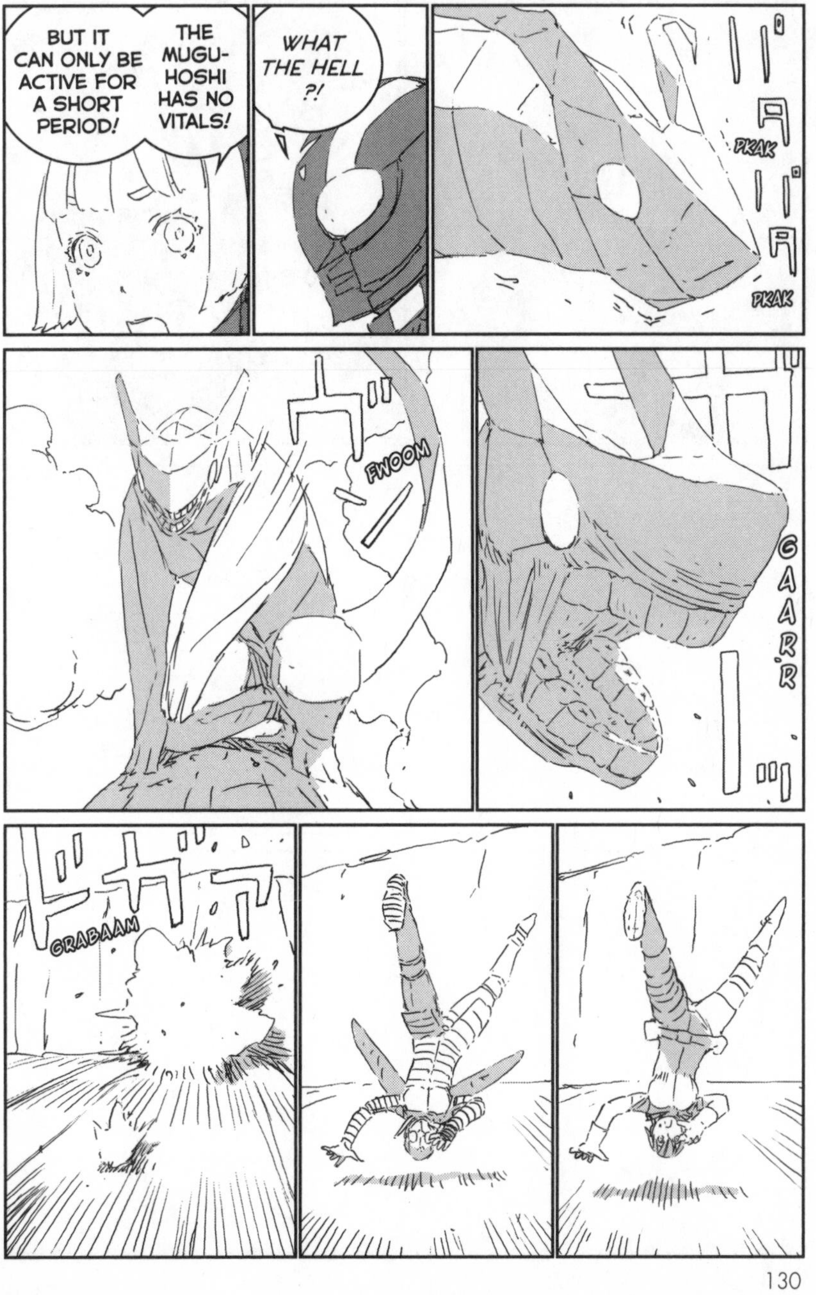
PKAK
PKAK
WHAT THE HELL ?!
THE MUGU-HOSHI HAS NO VITALS!
BUT IT CAN ONLY BE ACTIVE FOR A SHORT PERIOD!
GAARR
FWOOM
GRABAAM

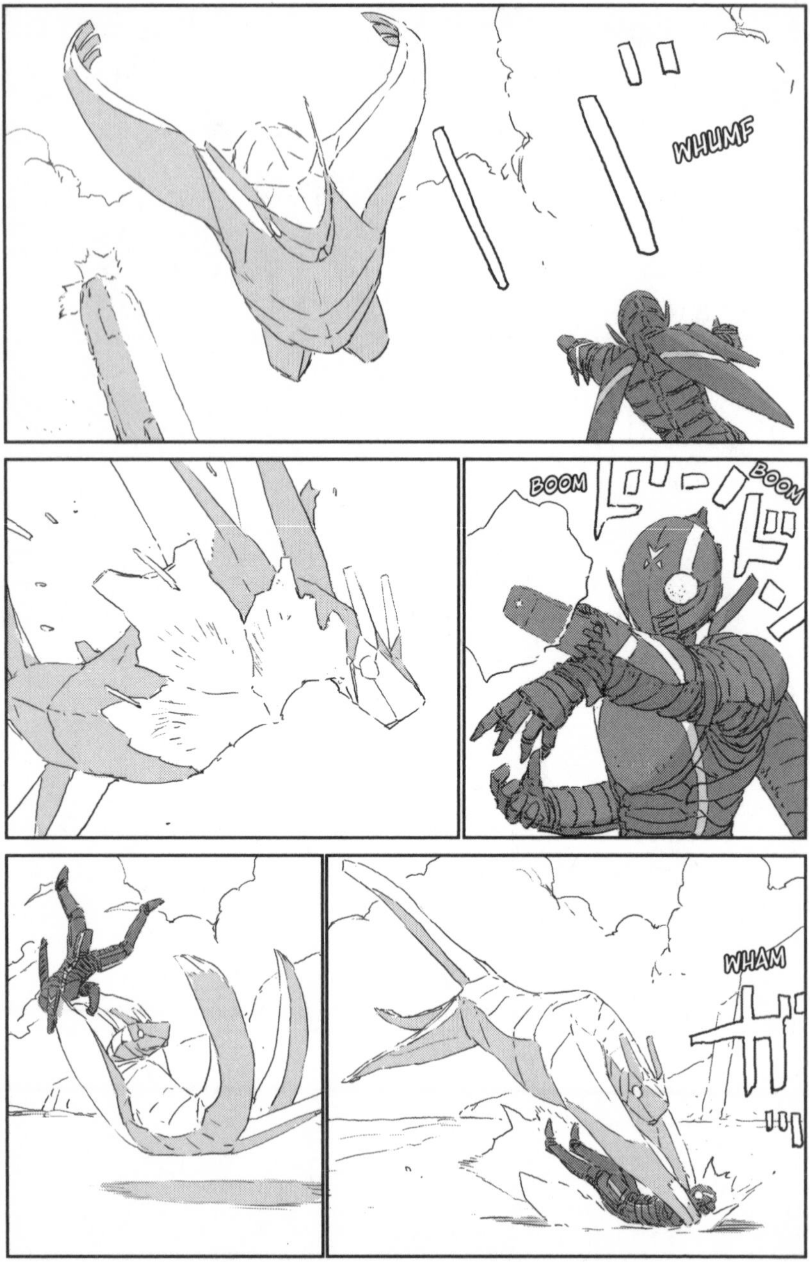
WHUMF
BOOM
BOOM
WHAM

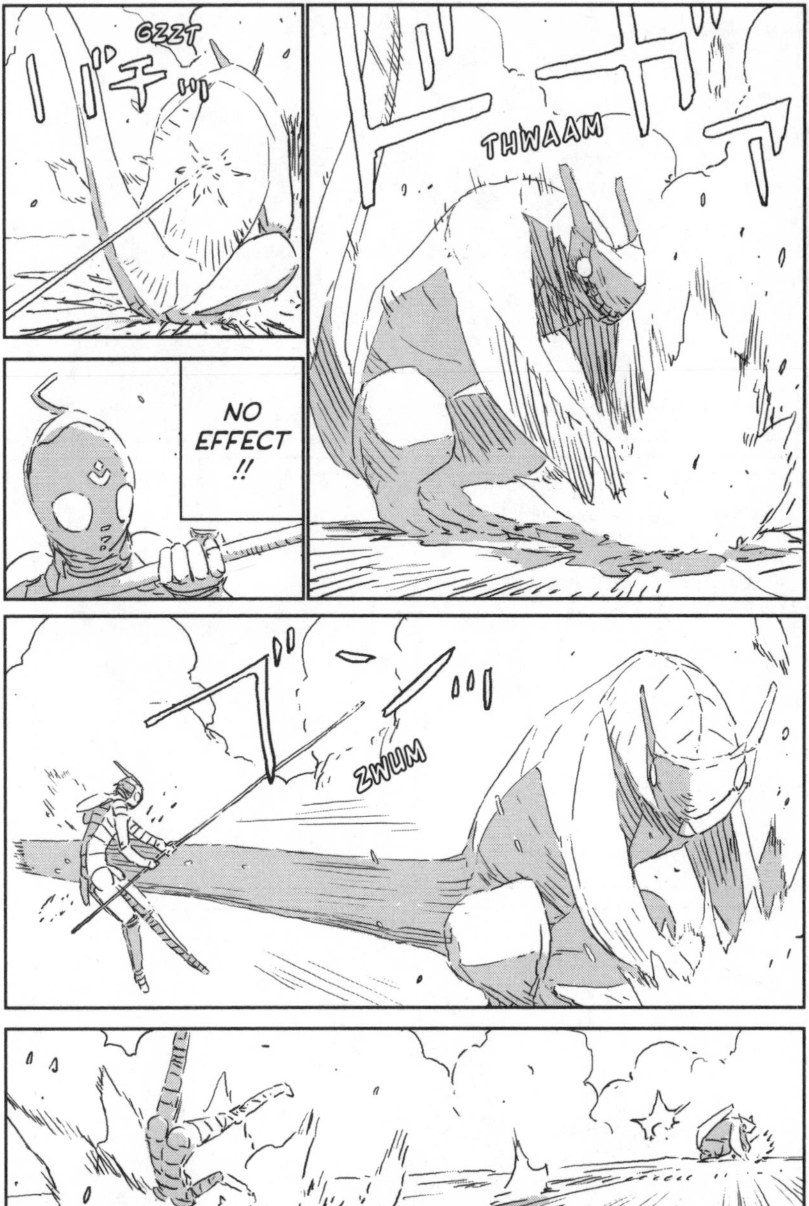
THWAAM
GZZT
NO EFFECT !!
ZWUM

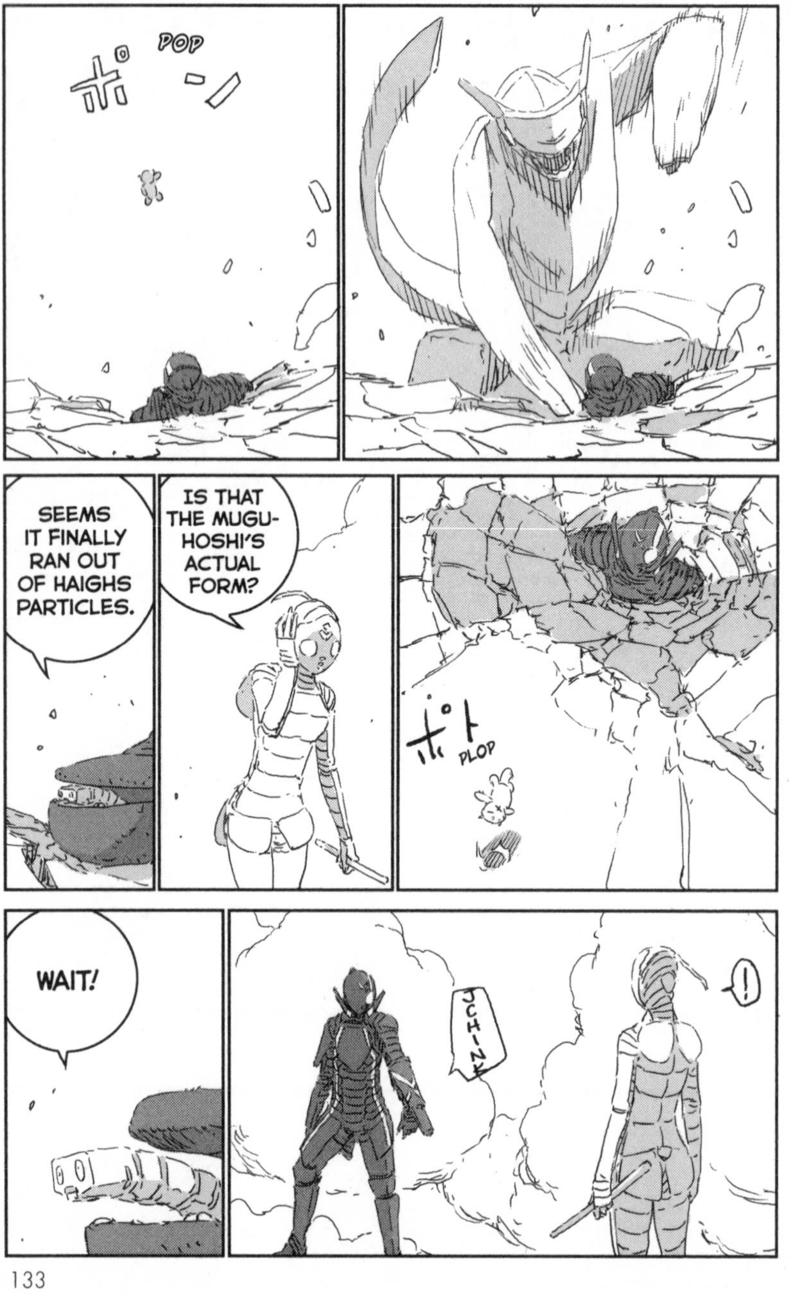
POP
ポト
PLOP
IS THAT THE MUGU-HOSHI'S ACTUAL FORM?
SEEMS IT FINALLY RAN OUT OF HAIGHS PARTICLES.
!
JCHINK
WAIT!

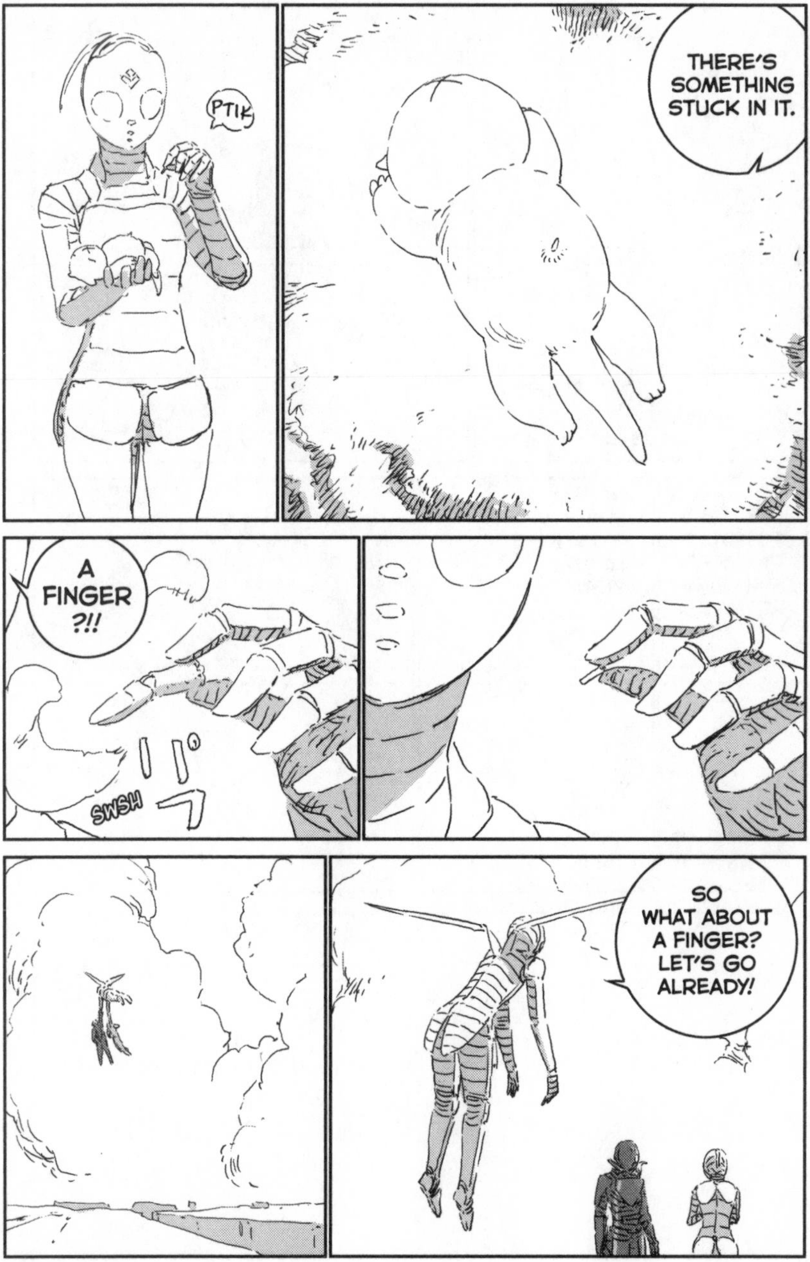
THERE'S SOMETHING STUCK IN IT.
PTIK
A FINGER ?!!
SWSH
SO WHAT ABOUT A FINGER? LET'S GO ALREADY!

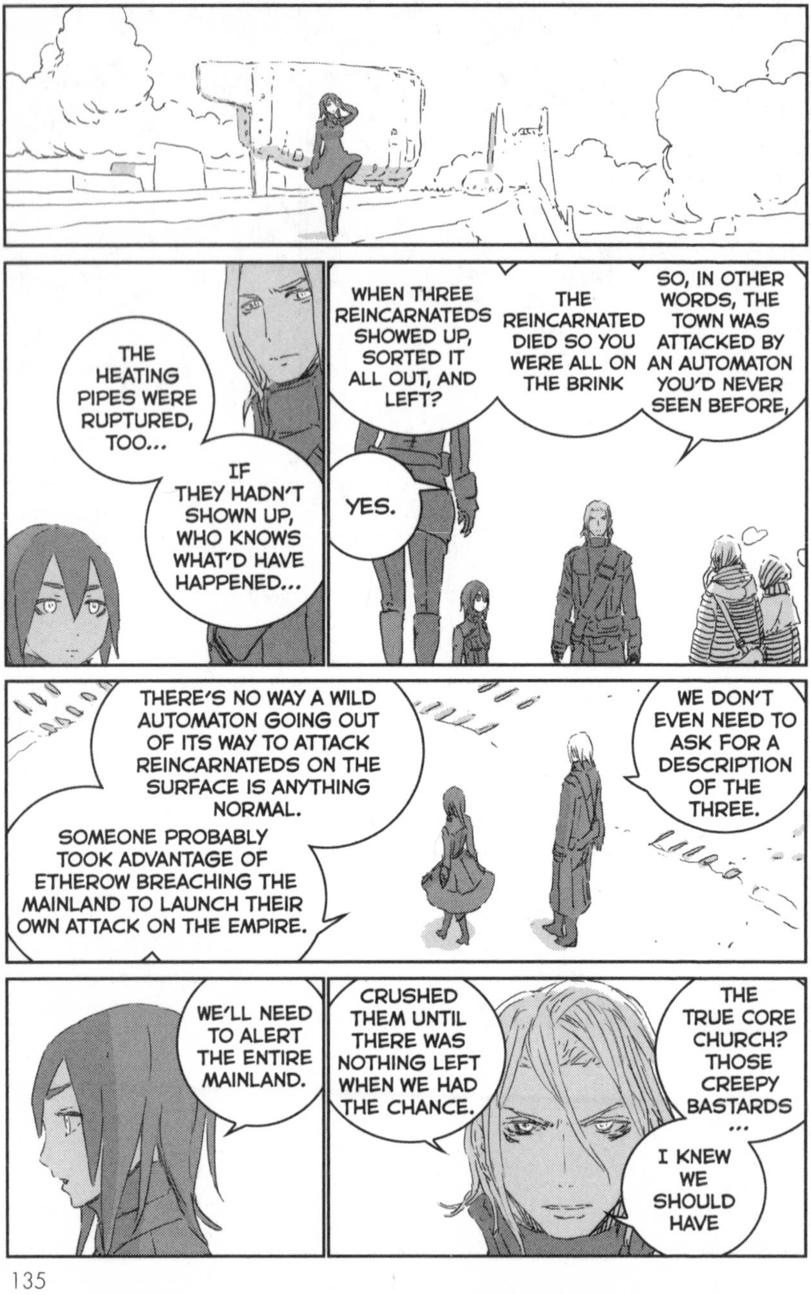
SO, IN OTHER WORDS, THE TOWN WAS ATTACKED BY AN AUTOMATON YOU'D NEVER SEEN BEFORE,
THE REINCARNATED DIED SO YOU WERE ALL ON THE BRINK
WHEN THREE REINCARNATEDS SHOWED UP, SORTED IT ALL OUT, AND LEFT?
YES.
THE HEATING PIPES WERE RUPTURED, TOO...
IF THEY HADN'T SHOWN UP, WHO KNOWS WHAT'D HAVE HAPPENED...
WE DON'T EVEN NEED TO ASK FOR A DESCRIPTION OF THE THREE.
THERE'S NO WAY A WILD AUTOMATON GOING OUT OF ITS WAY TO ATTACK REINCARNATEDS ON THE SURFACE IS ANYTHING NORMAL.
SOMEONE PROBABLY TOOK ADVANTAGE OF ETHEROW BREACHING THE MAINLAND TO LAUNCH THEIR OWN ATTACK ON THE EMPIRE.
THE TRUE CORE CHURCH? THOSE CREEPY BASTARDS ...
I KNEW WE SHOULD HAVE
CRUSHED THEM UNTIL THERE WAS NOTHING LEFT WHEN WE HAD THE CHANCE.
WE'LL NEED TO ALERT THE ENTIRE MAINLAND.

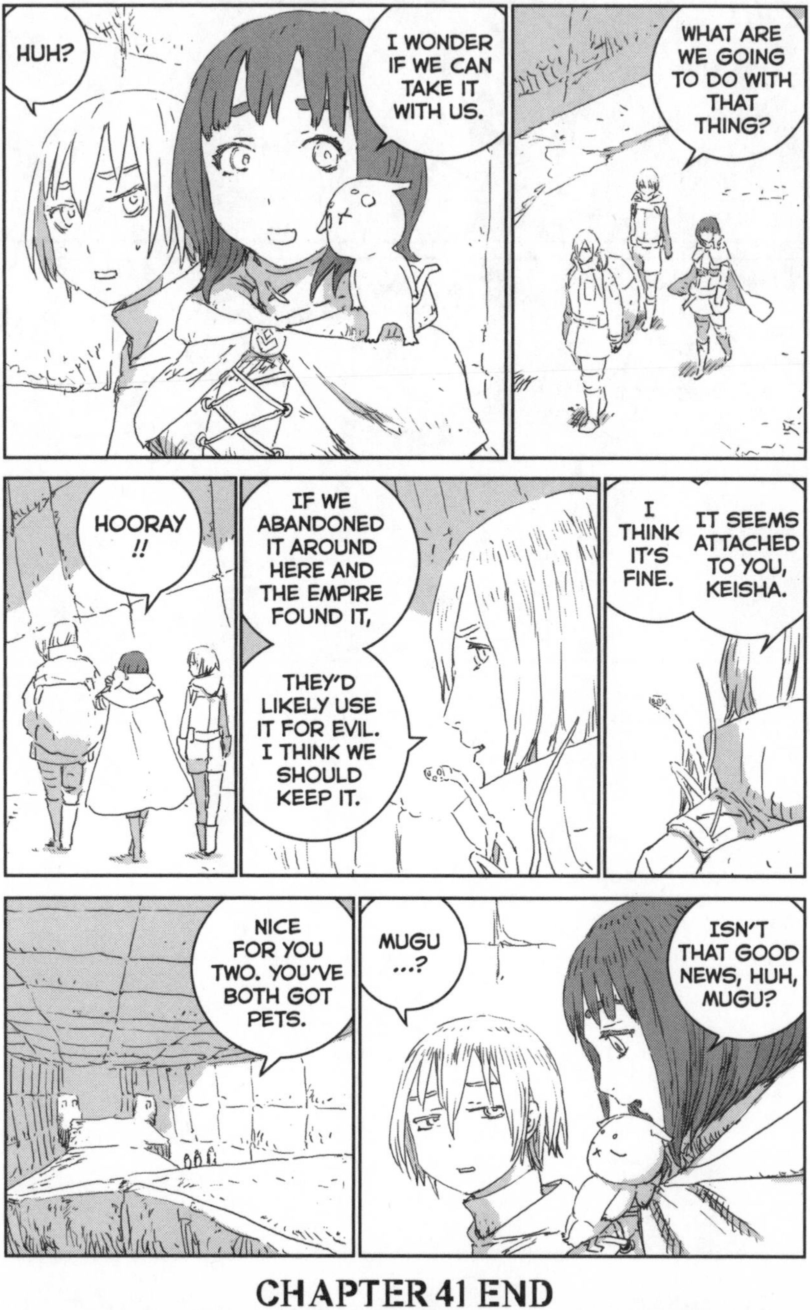
WHAT ARE WE GOING TO DO WITH THAT THING?
I WONDER IF WE CAN TAKE IT WITH US.
HUH?
IT SEEMS ATTACHED TO YOU, KEISHA.
I THINK IT'S FINE.
IF WE ABANDONED IT AROUND HERE AND THE EMPIRE FOUND IT,
THEY'D LIKELY USE IT FOR EVIL. I THINK WE SHOULD KEEP IT.
HOORAY !!
ISN'T THAT GOOD NEWS, HUH, MUGU?
MUGU ...?
NICE FOR YOU TWO. YOU'VE BOTH GOT PETS.

CHAPTER 41 END

APOSIMZ

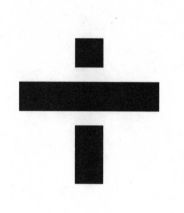

CHAPTER 42

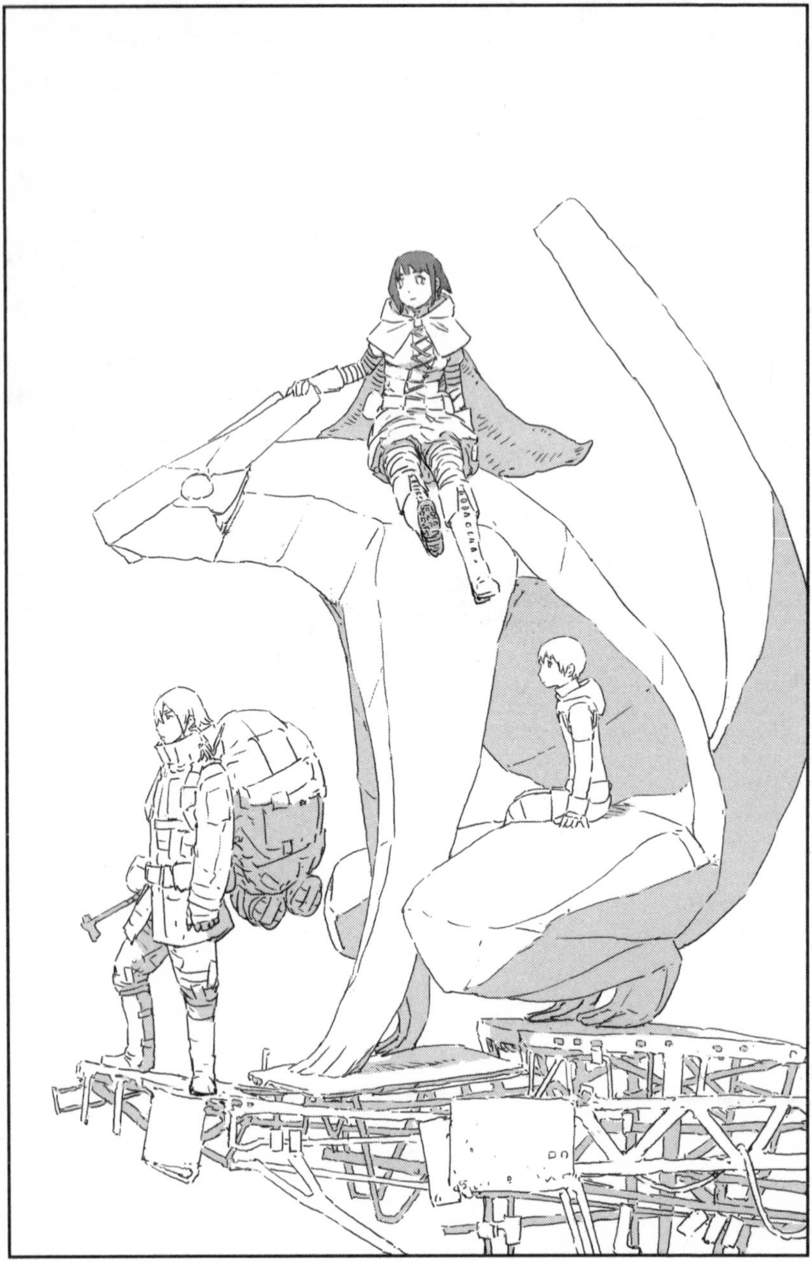

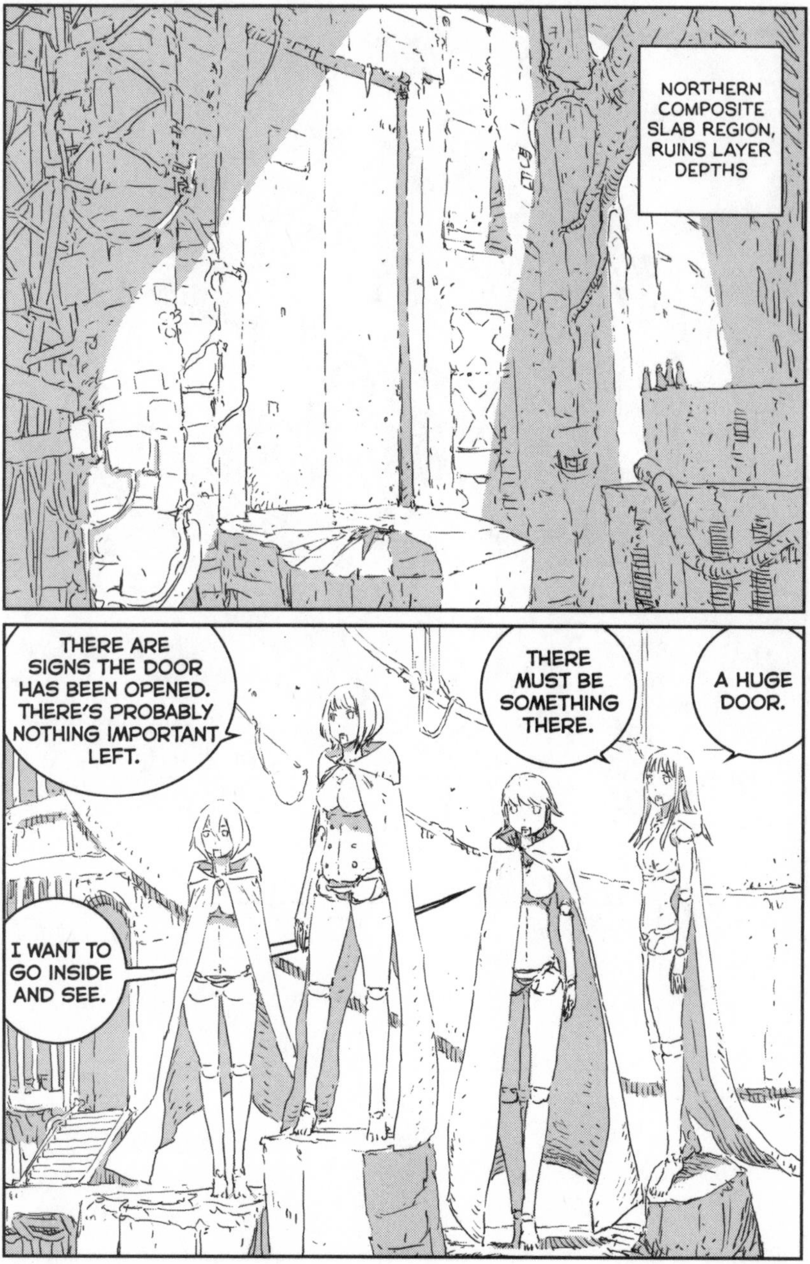
NORTHERN COMPOSITE SLAB REGION, RUINS LAYER DEPTHS
A HUGE DOOR.
THERE MUST BE SOMETHING THERE.
THERE ARE SIGNS THE DOOR HAS BEEN OPENED. THERE'S PROBABLY NOTHING IMPORTANT LEFT.
I WANT TO GO INSIDE AND SEE.

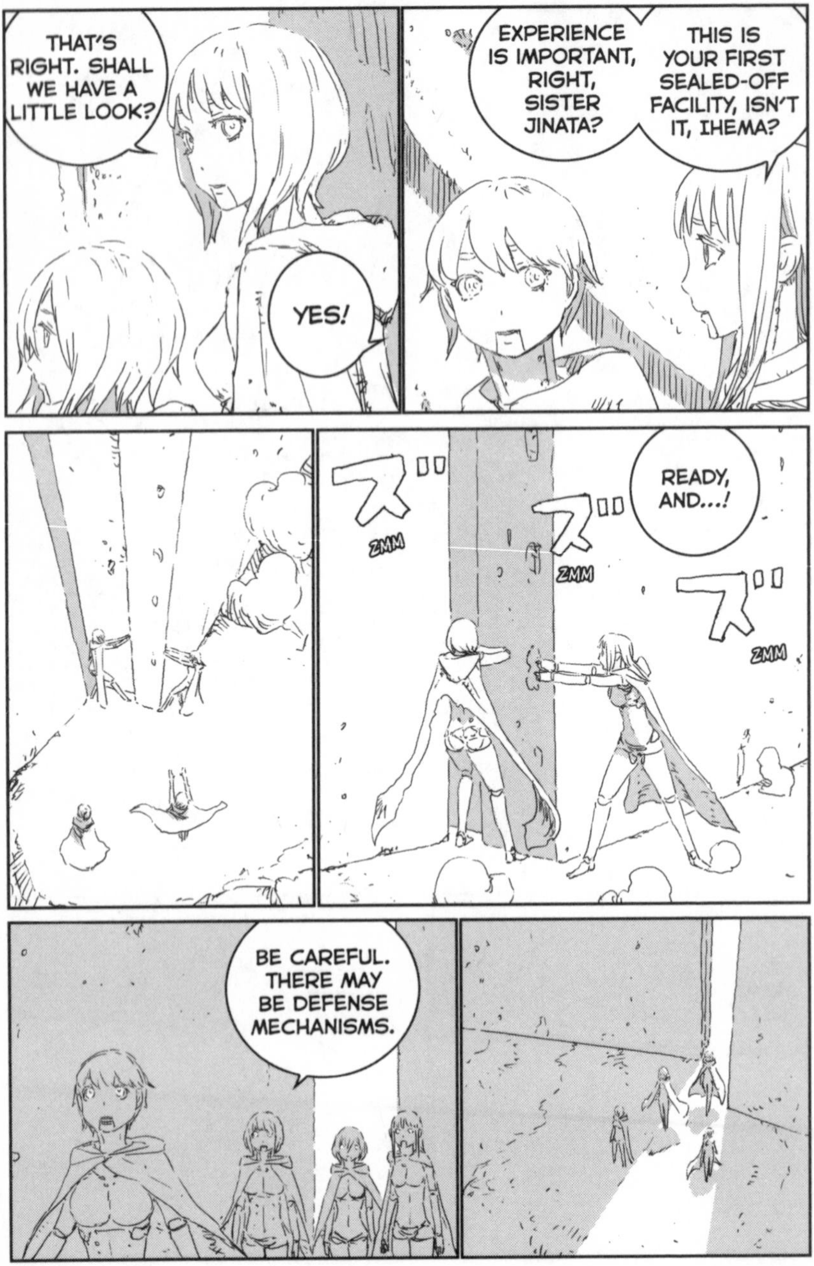
THIS IS YOUR FIRST SEALED-OFF FACILITY, ISN'T IT, IHEMA?
EXPERIENCE IS IMPORTANT, RIGHT, SISTER JINATA?
THAT'S RIGHT. SHALL WE HAVE A LITTLE LOOK?
YES!
READY, AND...!
ズッ
ZMM
ズッ
ZMM
ズッ
ZMM
BE CAREFUL. THERE MAY BE DEFENSE MECHANISMS.

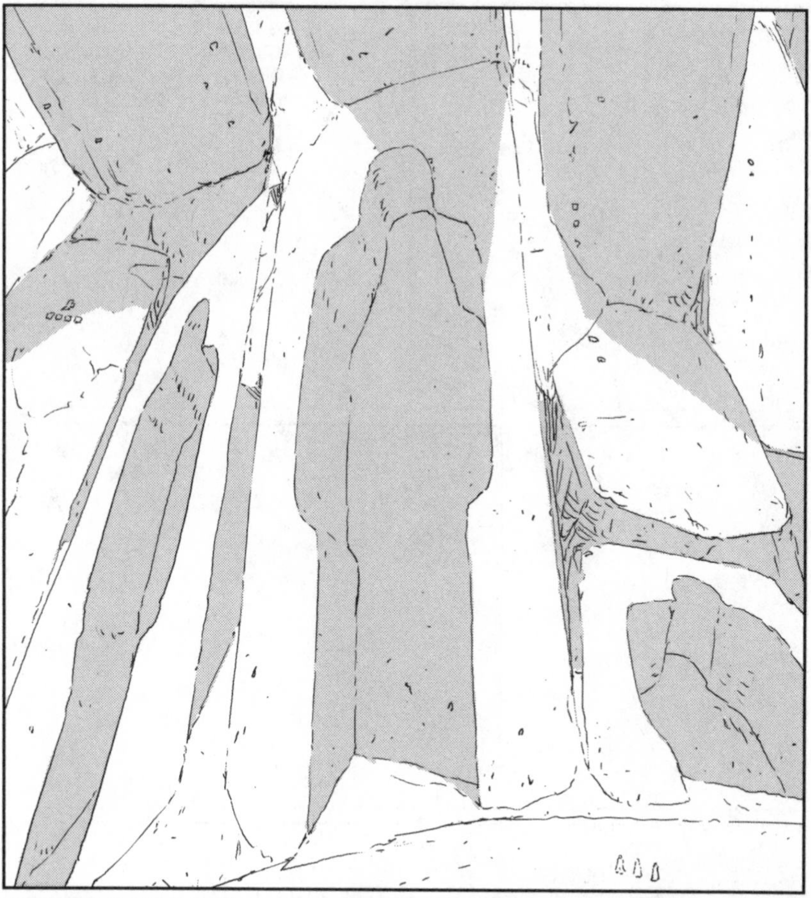

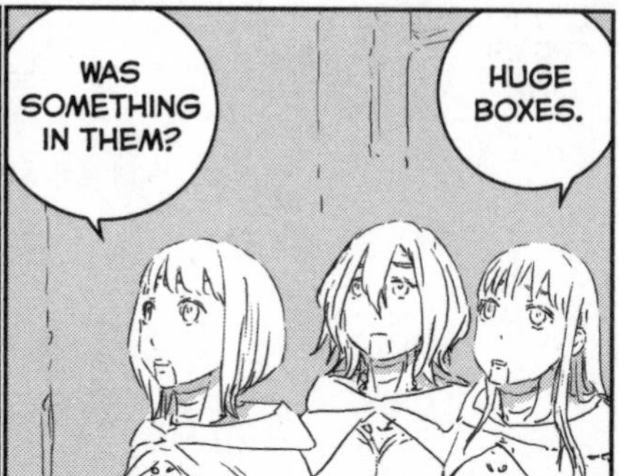
HUGE BOXES.
WAS SOMETHING IN THEM?

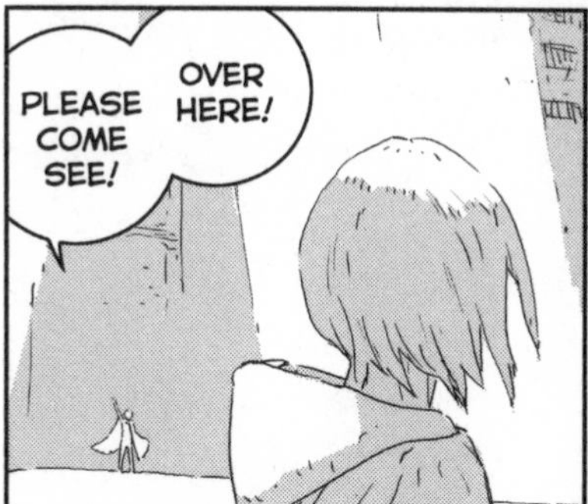
OVER HERE!
PLEASE COME SEE!

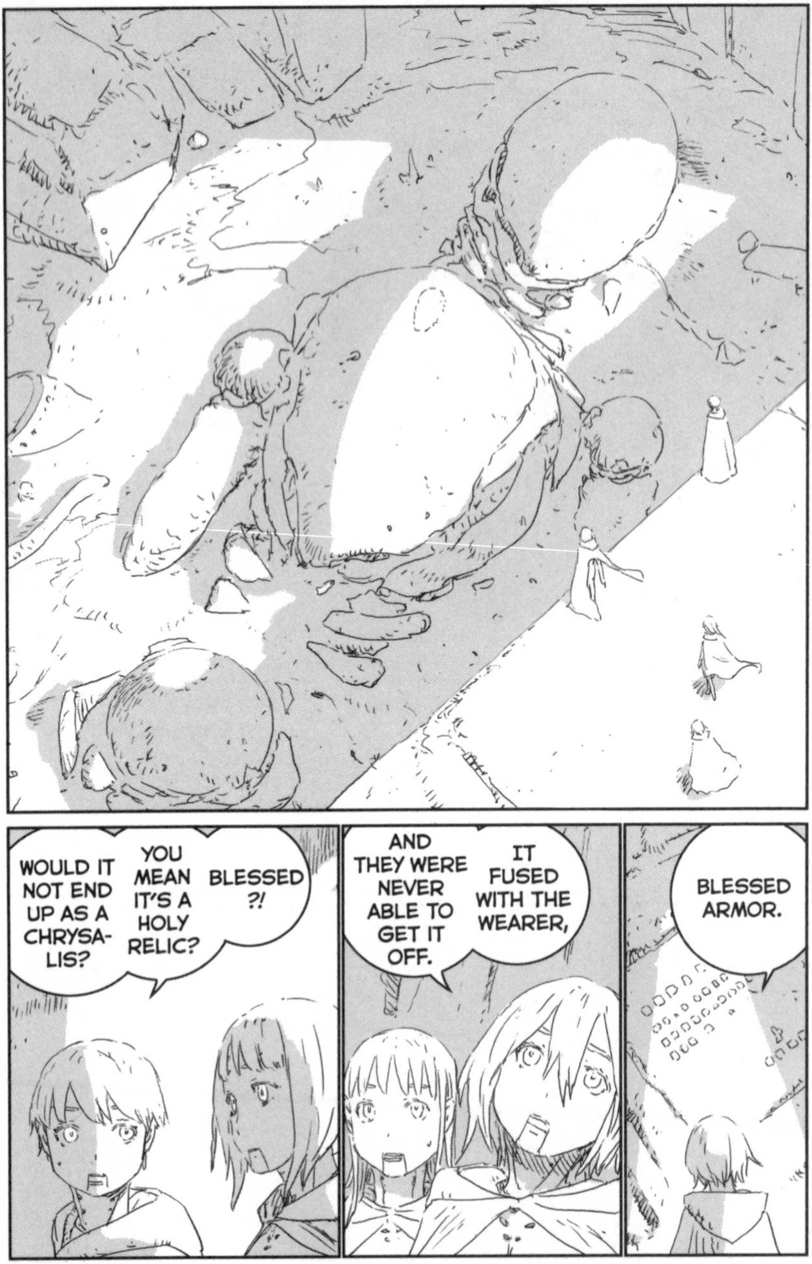
BLESSED ARMOR.
IT FUSED WITH THE WEARER,
AND THEY WERE NEVER ABLE TO GET IT OFF.
BLESSED ?!
YOU MEAN IT'S A HOLY RELIC?
WOULD IT NOT END UP AS A CHRYSA-LIS?

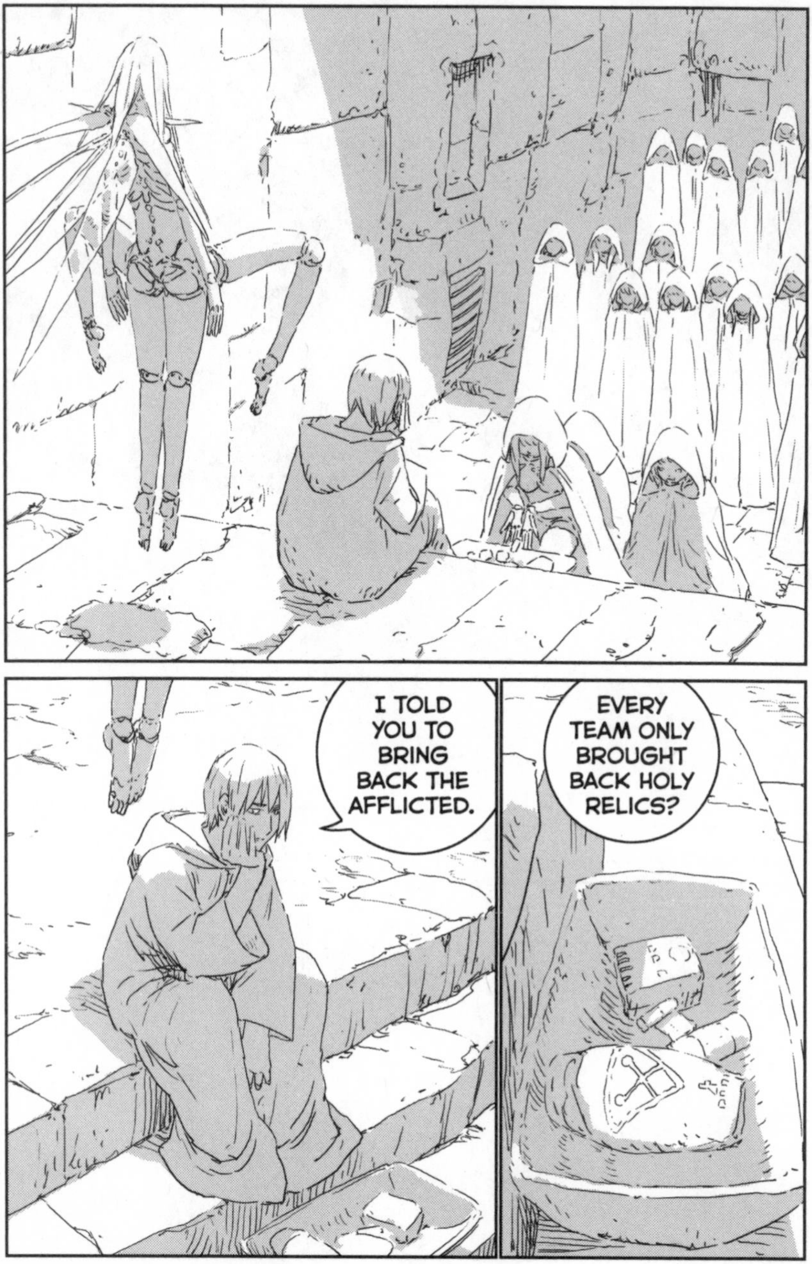
EVERY TEAM ONLY BROUGHT BACK HOLY RELICS?
I TOLD YOU TO BRING BACK THE AFFLICTED.

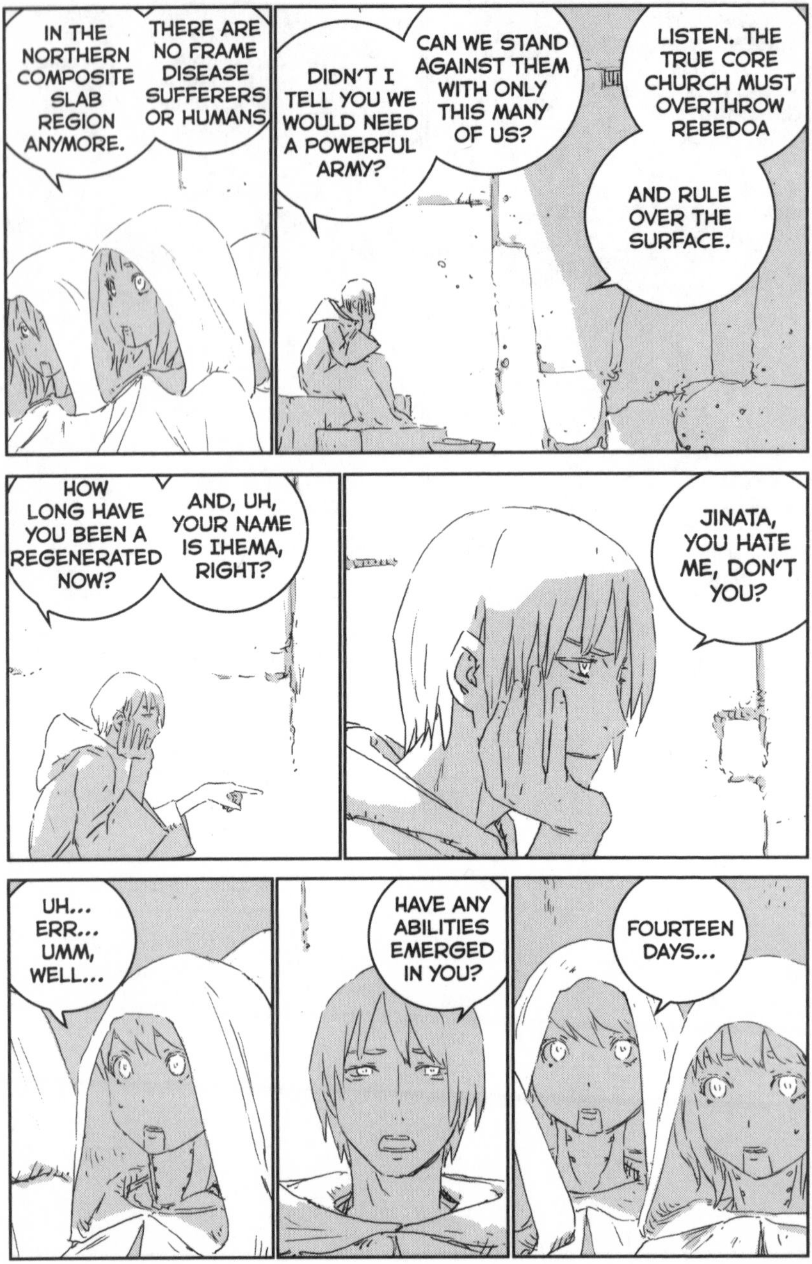
LISTEN. THE TRUE CORE CHURCH MUST OVERTHROW REBEDOA
AND RULE OVER THE SURFACE.
CAN WE STAND AGAINST THEM WITH ONLY THIS MANY OF US?
DIDN'T I TELL YOU WE WOULD NEED A POWERFUL ARMY?
THERE ARE NO FRAME DISEASE SUFFERERS OR HUMANS
IN THE NORTHERN COMPOSITE SLAB REGION ANYMORE.
JINATA, YOU HATE ME, DON'T YOU?
AND, UH, YOUR NAME IS IHEMA, RIGHT?
HOW LONG HAVE YOU BEEN A REGENERATED NOW?
FOURTEEN DAYS...
HAVE ANY ABILITIES EMERGED IN YOU?
UH... ERR... UMM, WELL...

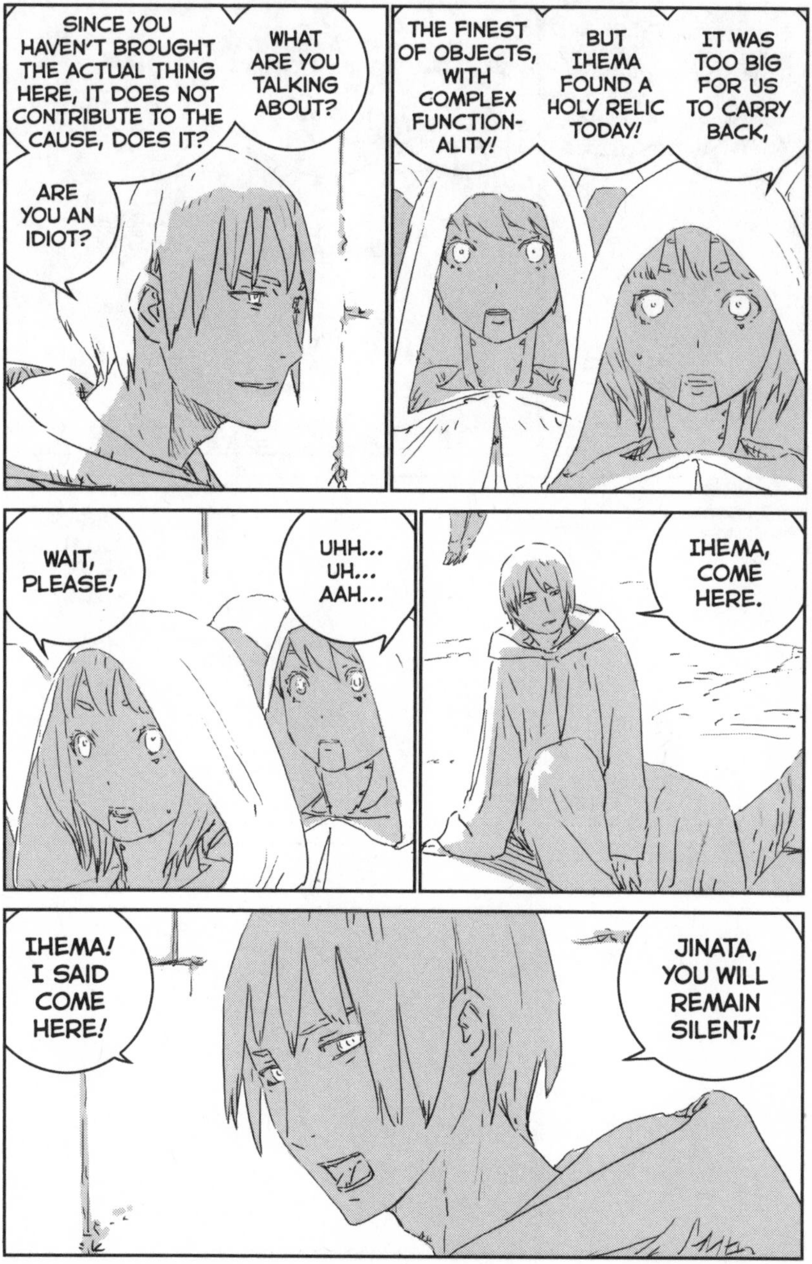
BUT IHEMA FOUND A HOLY RELIC TODAY!
THE FINEST OF OBJECTS, WITH COMPLEX FUNCTION-ALITY!
IT WAS TOO BIG FOR US TO CARRY BACK,
WHAT ARE YOU TALKING ABOUT?
SINCE YOU HAVEN'T BROUGHT THE ACTUAL THING HERE, IT DOES NOT CONTRIBUTE TO THE CAUSE, DOES IT?
ARE YOU AN IDIOT?
IHEMA, COME HERE.
UHH... UH... AAH...
WAIT, PLEASE!
JINATA, YOU WILL REMAIN SILENT!
IHEMA! I SAID COME HERE!

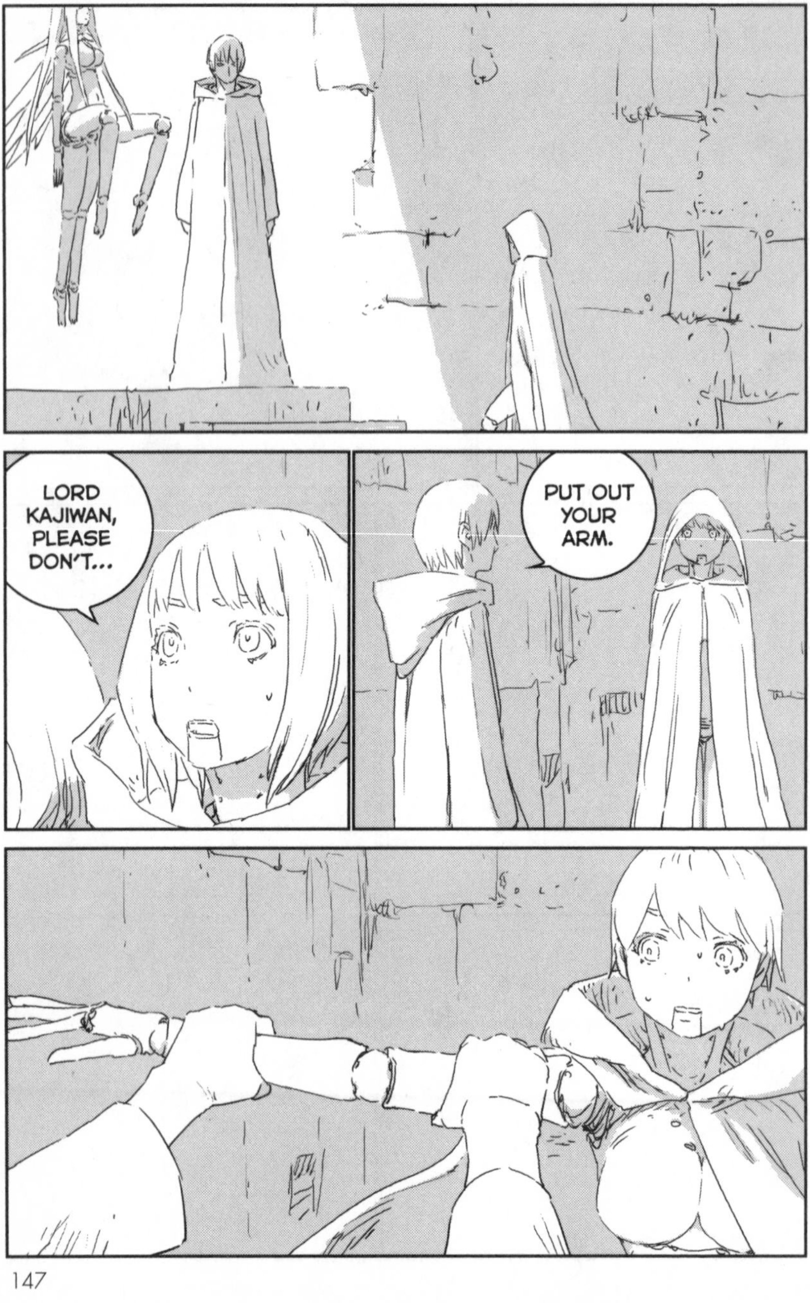
PUT OUT YOUR ARM.
LORD KAJIWAN, PLEASE DON'T...

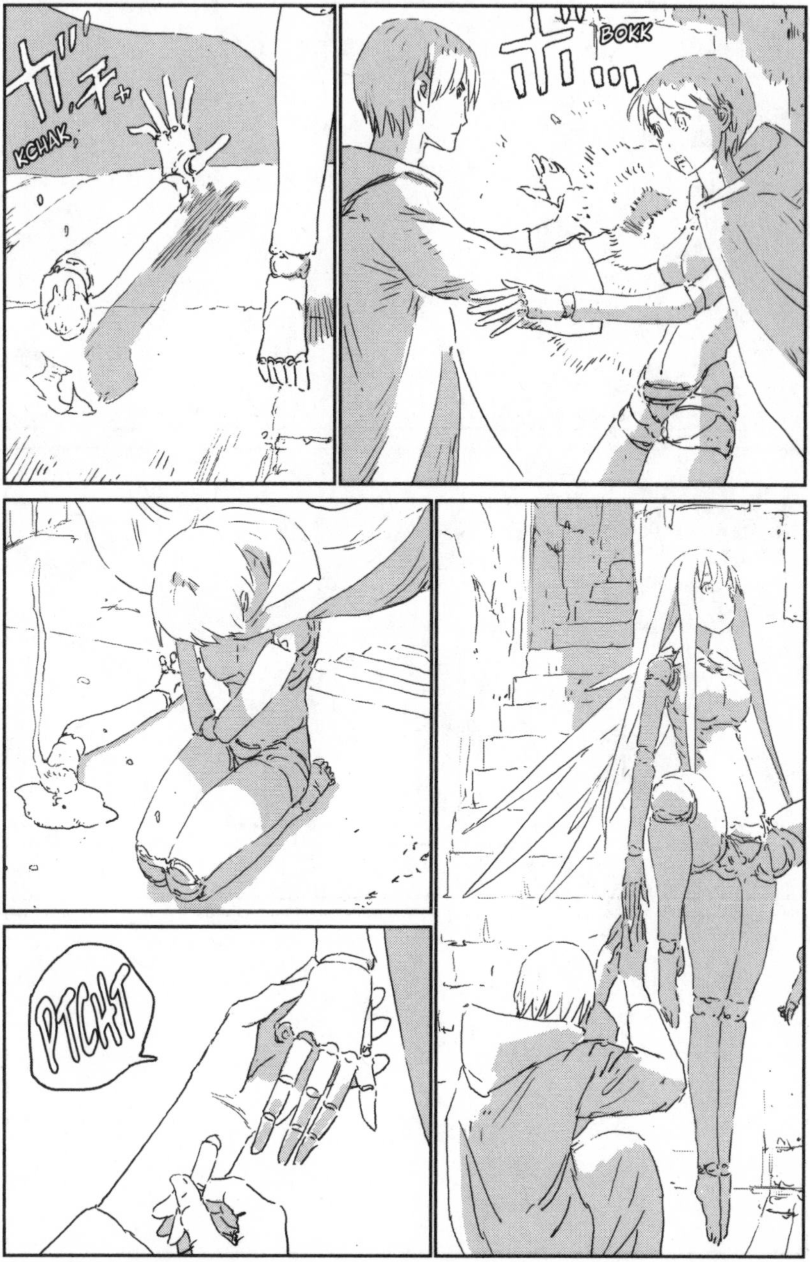
BOKK
KCHAK
PTCHT

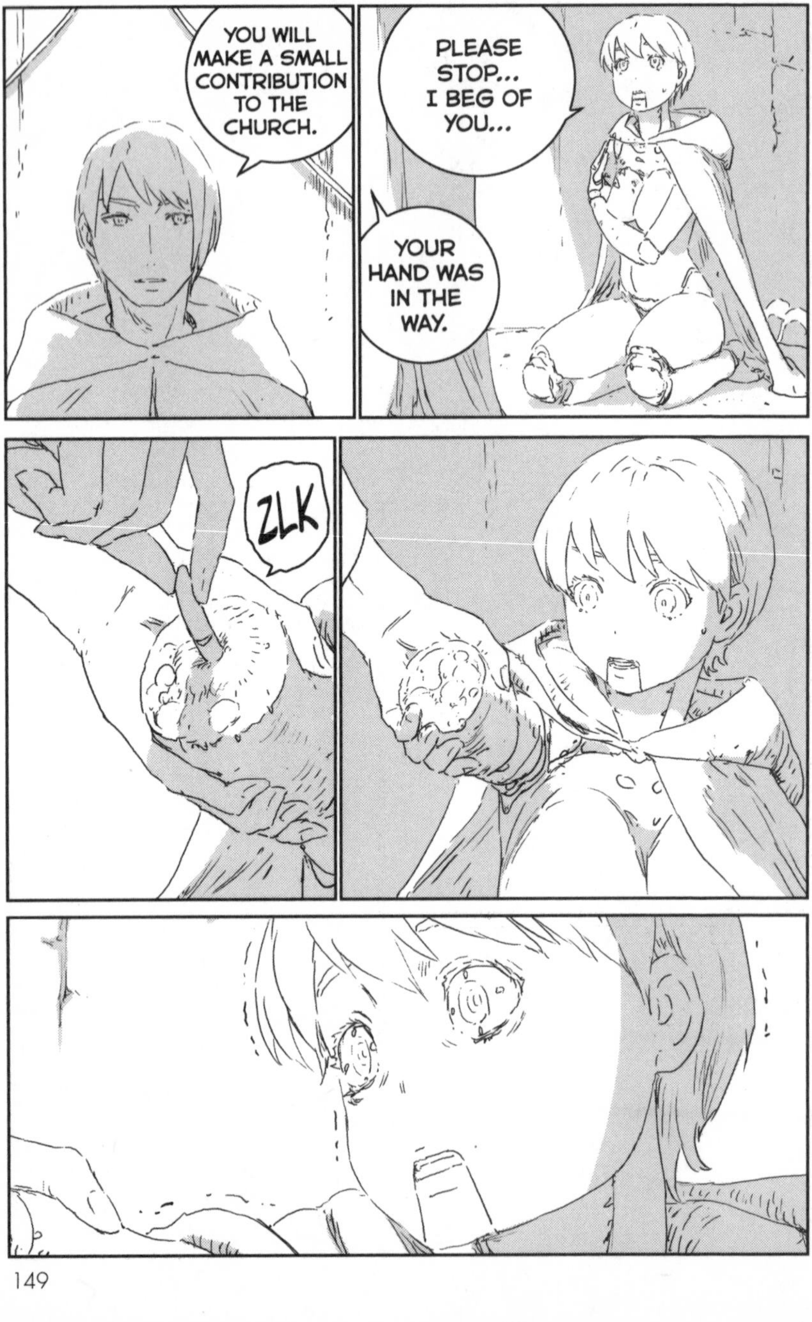
PLEASE STOP... I BEG OF YOU...
YOUR HAND WAS IN THE WAY.
YOU WILL MAKE A SMALL CONTRIBUTION TO THE CHURCH.
ZLK

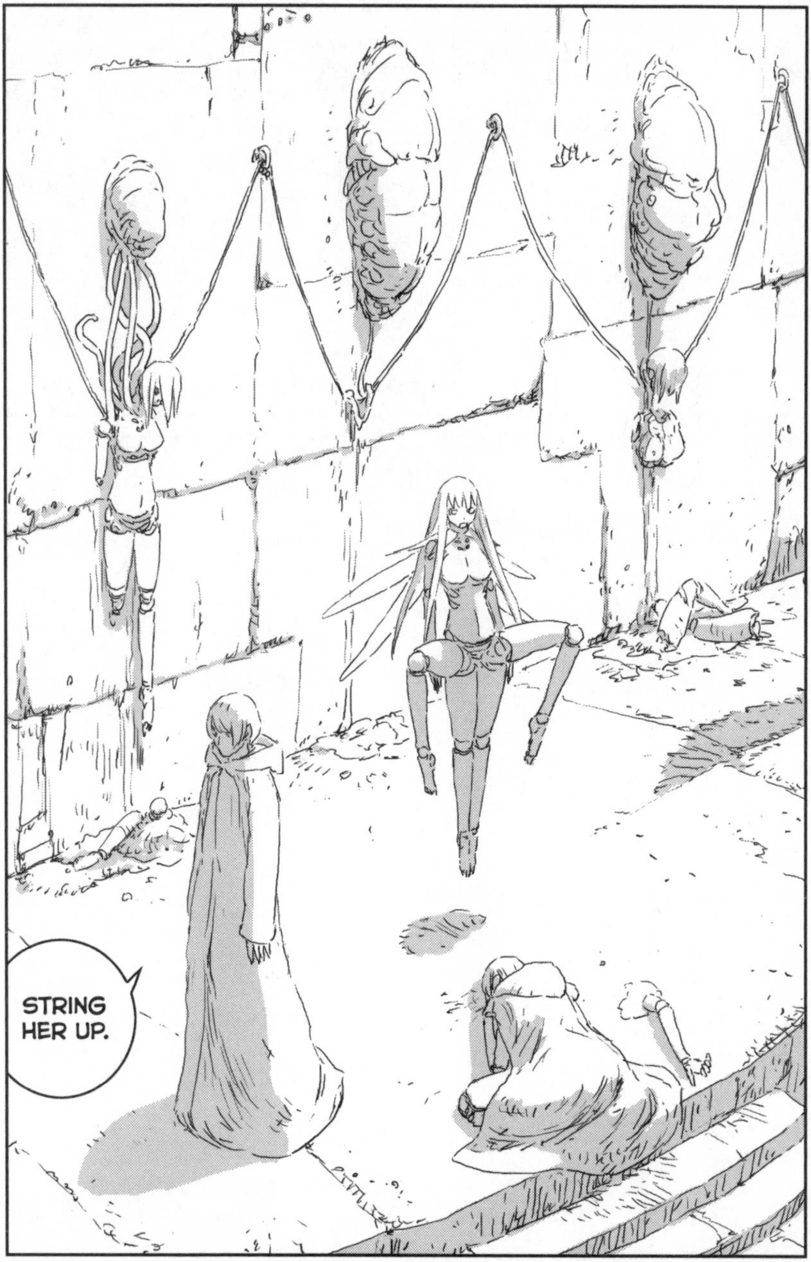
STRING HER UP.

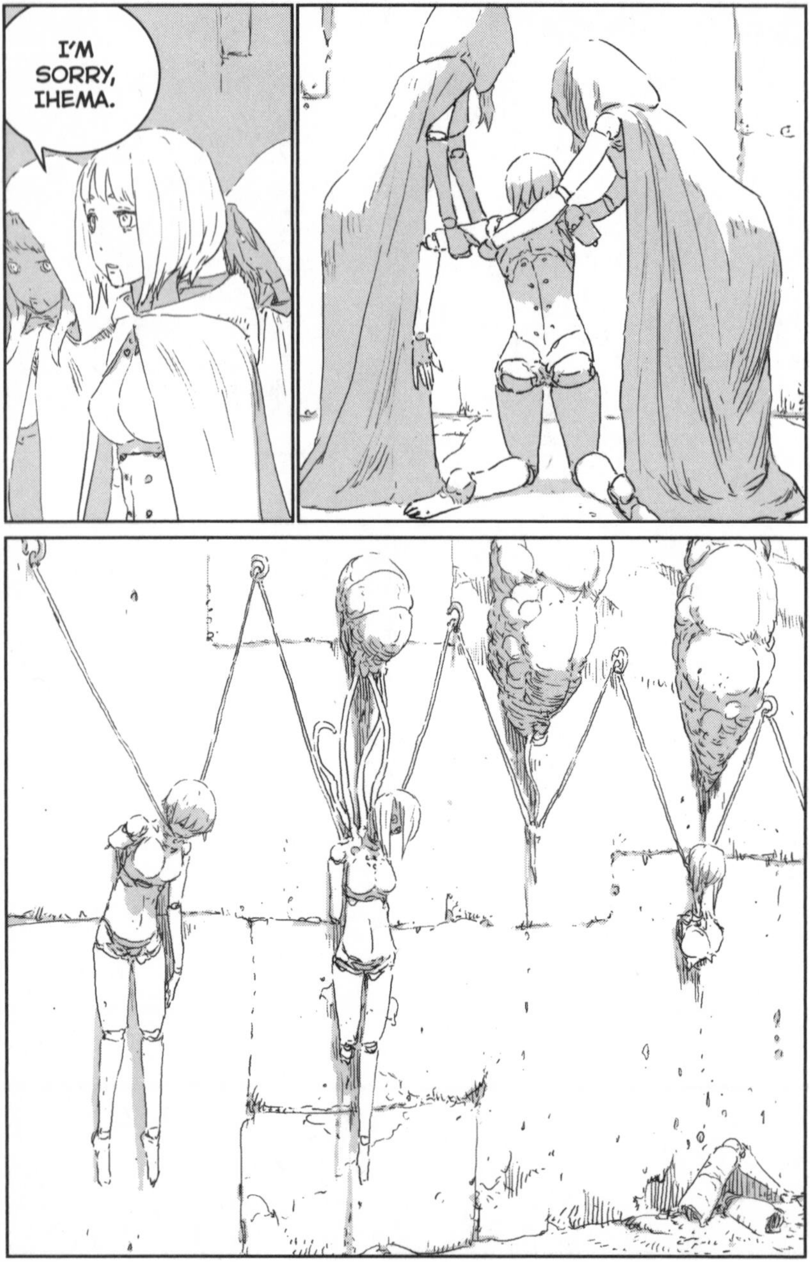
I'M SORRY, IHEMA.

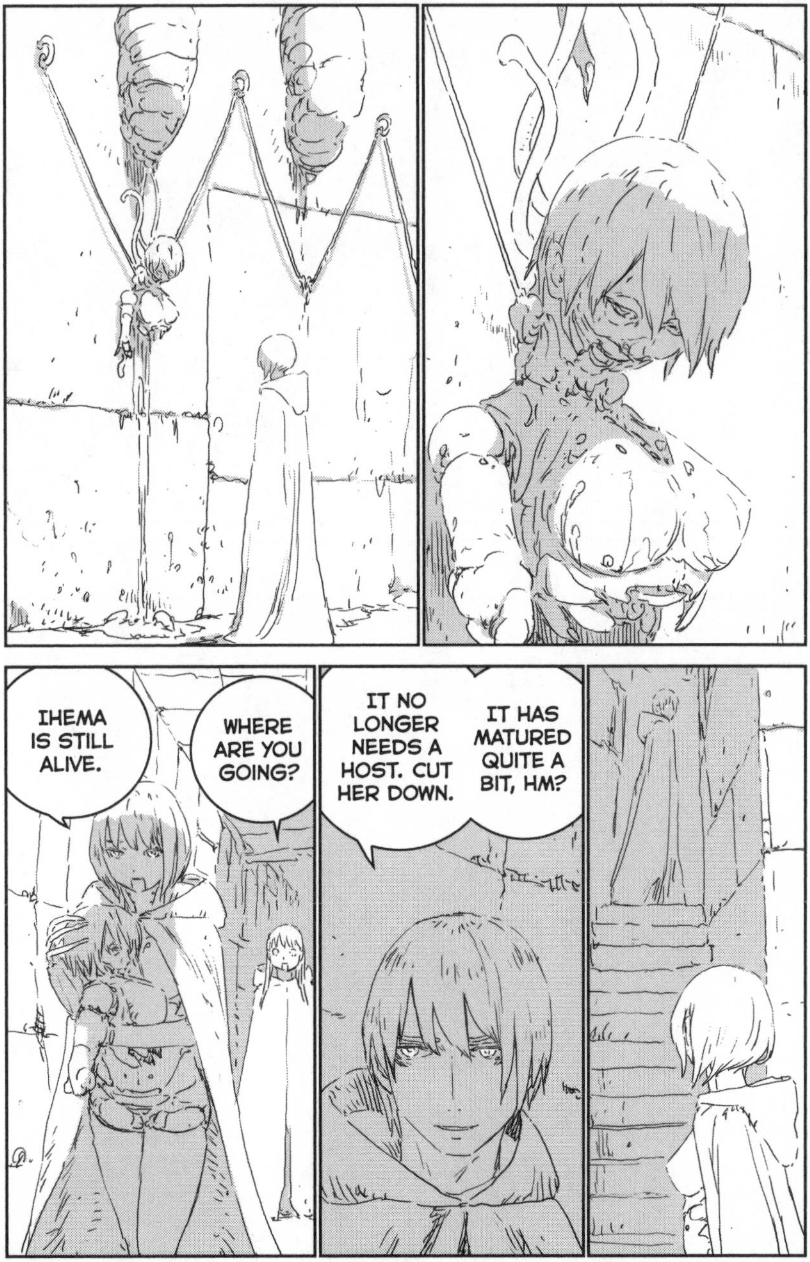
IT HAS MATURED QUITE A BIT, HM?
IT NO LONGER NEEDS A HOST. CUT HER DOWN.
WHERE ARE YOU GOING?
IHEMA IS STILL ALIVE.

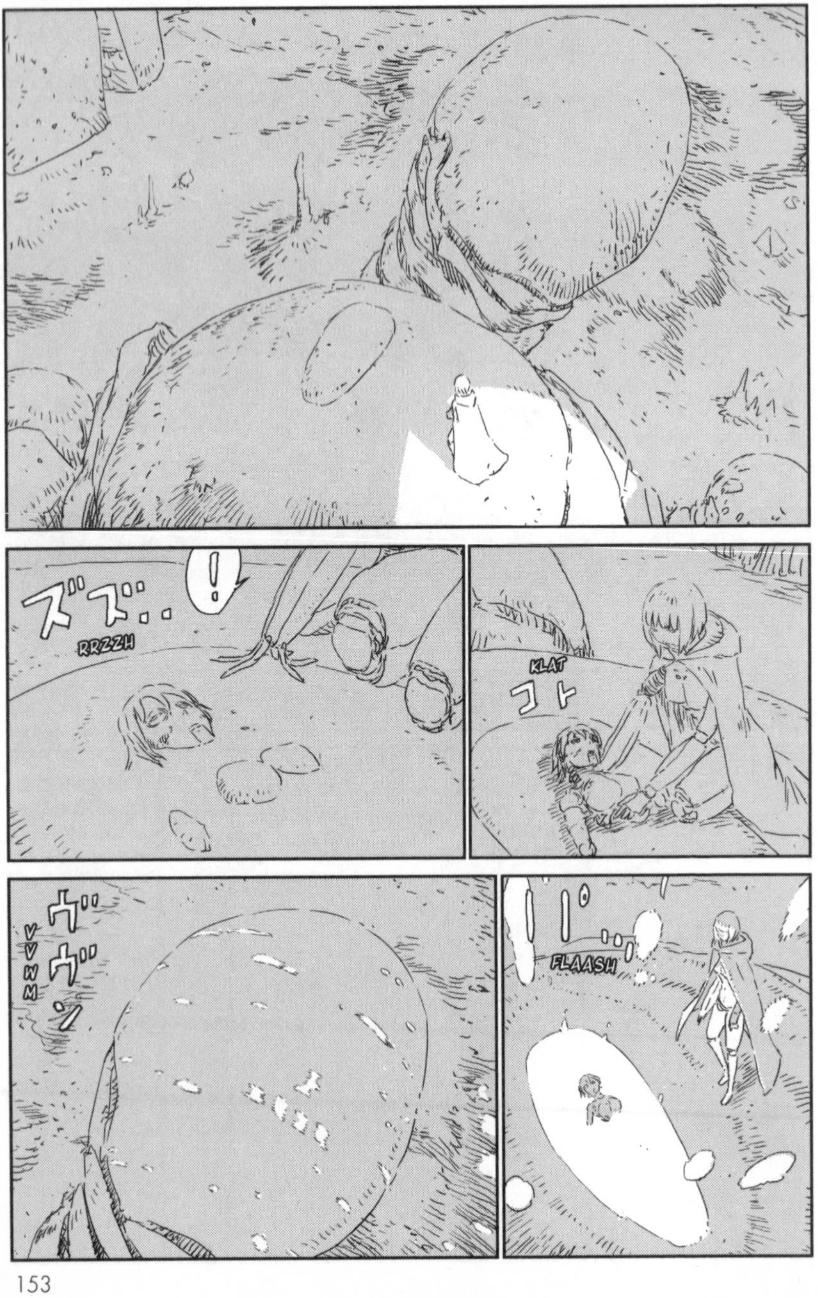

コト
KLAT
ズズ..
RRZZH
!
パ...
FLAASH
ヴヴン
VVWM

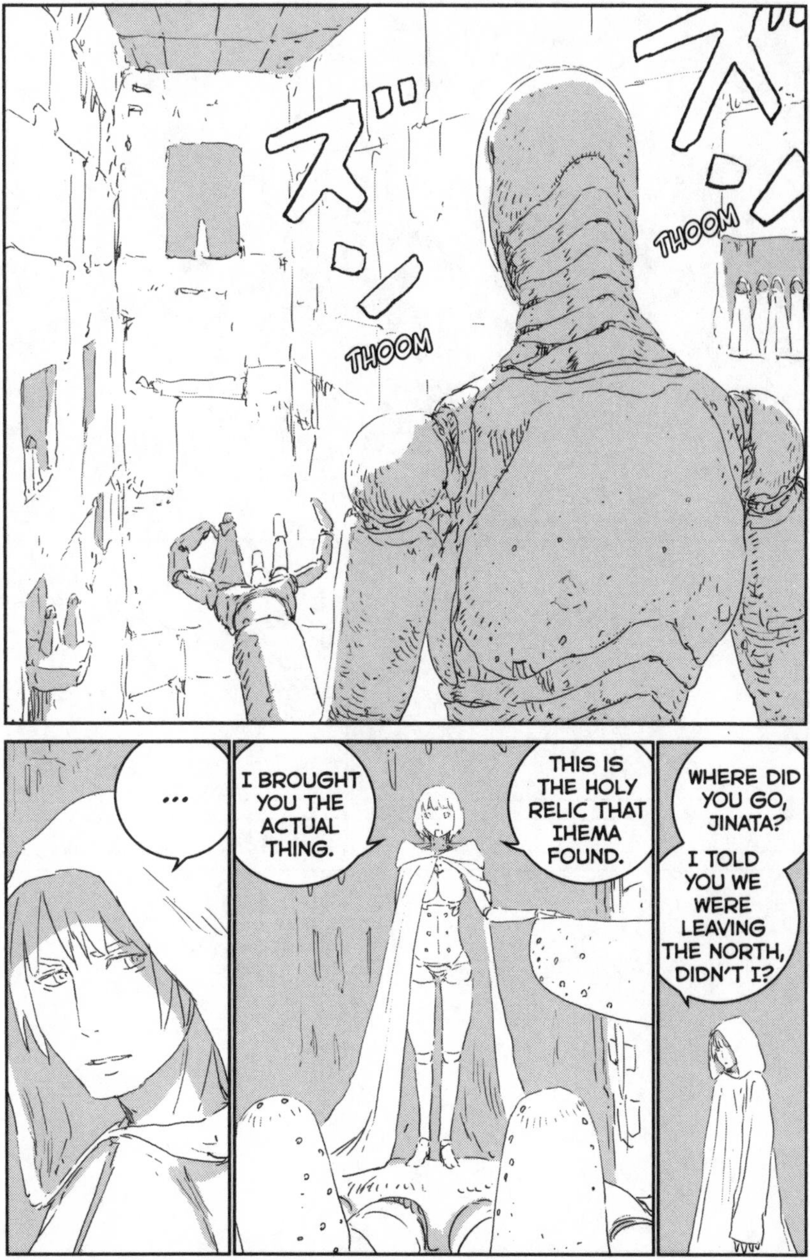
ズドン
THOOM
ズドン
THOOM
WHERE DID YOU GO, JINATA?
I TOLD YOU WE WERE LEAVING THE NORTH, DIDN'T I?
THIS IS THE HOLY RELIC THAT IHEMA FOUND.
I BROUGHT YOU THE ACTUAL THING.
...

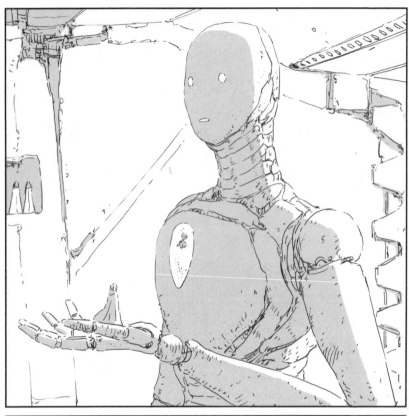

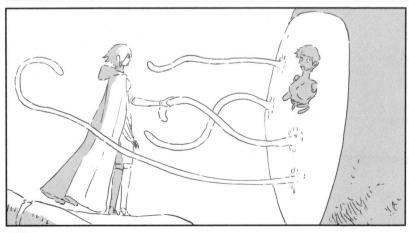

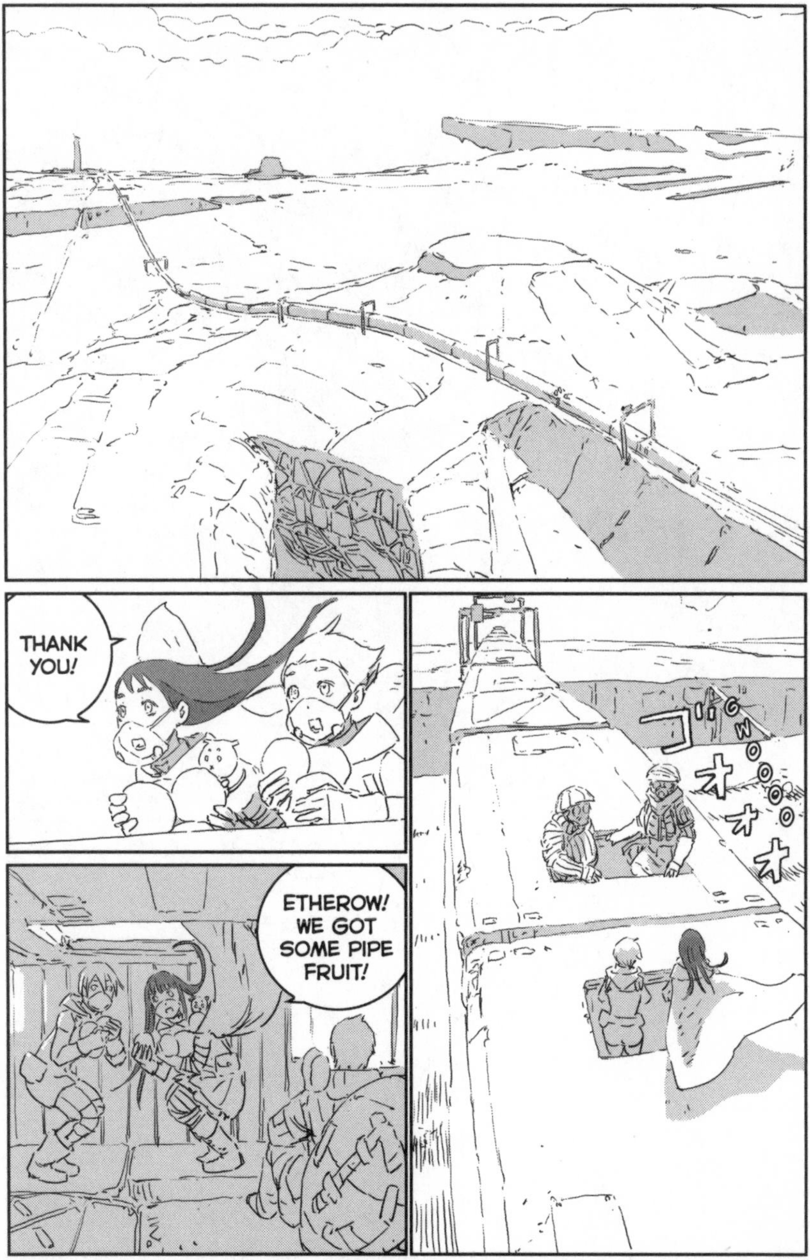
GWOOOOO
THANK YOU!
ETHEROW! WE GOT SOME PIPE FRUIT!

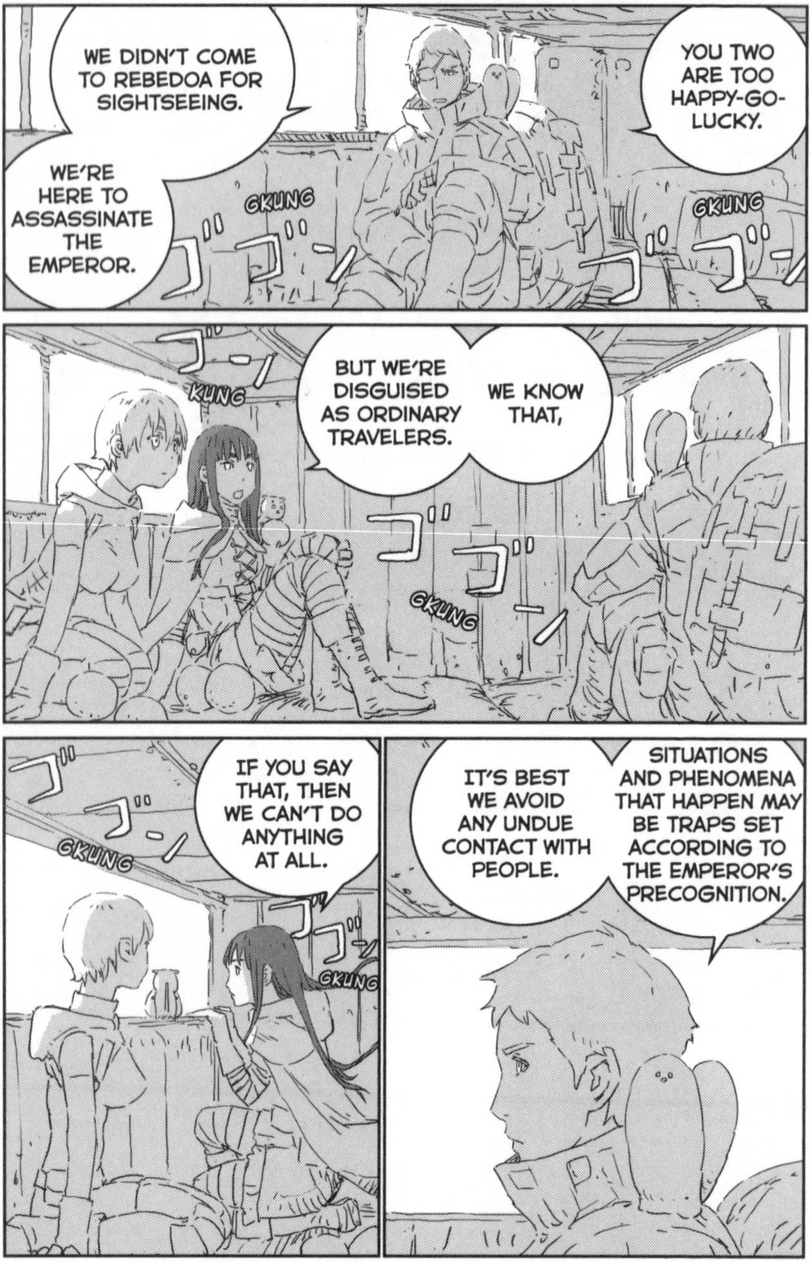
YOU TWO ARE TOO HAPPY-GO-LUCKY.
GKUNG
WE DIDN'T COME TO REBEDOA FOR SIGHTSEEING.
GKUNG
WE'RE HERE TO ASSASSINATE THE EMPEROR.
WE KNOW THAT,
BUT WE'RE DISGUISED AS ORDINARY TRAVELERS.
GKUNG
KUNG
SITUATIONS AND PHENOMENA THAT HAPPEN MAY BE TRAPS SET ACCORDING TO THE EMPEROR'S PRECOGNITION.
IT'S BEST WE AVOID ANY UNDUE CONTACT WITH PEOPLE.
IF YOU SAY THAT, THEN WE CAN'T DO ANYTHING AT ALL.
GKUNG
GKUNG

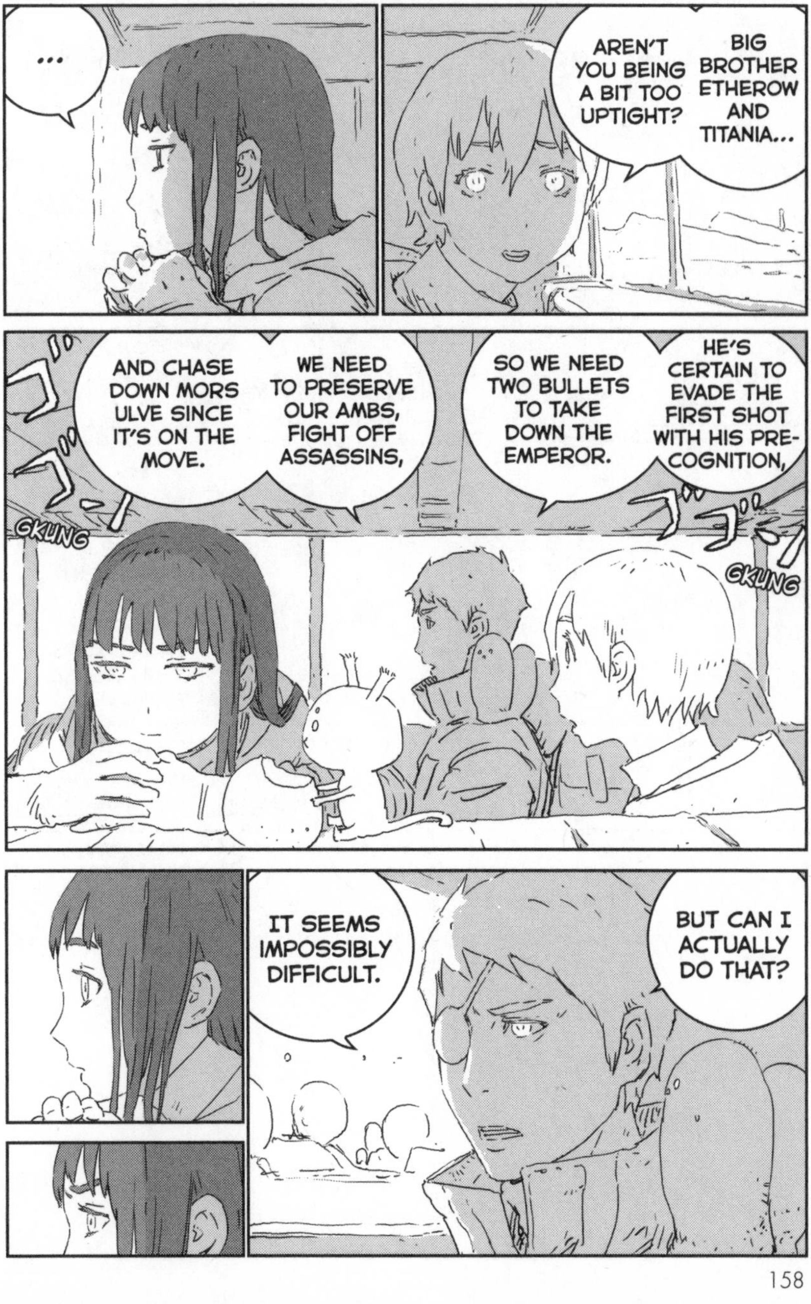
BIG BROTHER ETHEROW AND TITANIA...
AREN'T YOU BEING A BIT TOO UPTIGHT?
...
HE'S CERTAIN TO EVADE THE FIRST SHOT WITH HIS PRE-COGNITION,
SO WE NEED TWO BULLETS TO TAKE DOWN THE EMPEROR.
GKUNG
WE NEED TO PRESERVE OUR AMBS, FIGHT OFF ASSASSINS,
AND CHASE DOWN MORS ULVE SINCE IT'S ON THE MOVE.
GKUNG
BUT CAN I ACTUALLY DO THAT?
IT SEEMS IMPOSSIBLY DIFFICULT.

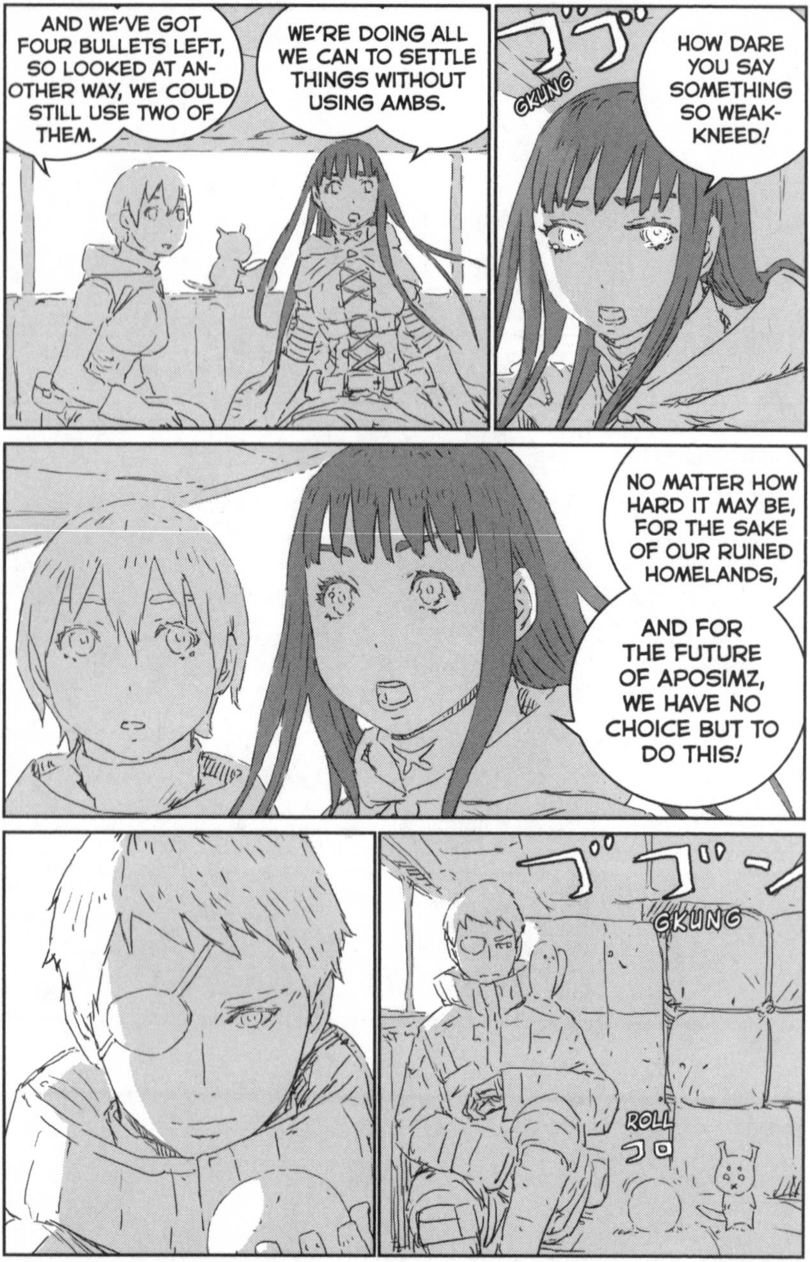
GKUNG
HOW DARE YOU SAY SOMETHING SO WEAK-KNEED!
WE'RE DOING ALL WE CAN TO SETTLE THINGS WITHOUT USING AMBS.
AND WE'VE GOT FOUR BULLETS LEFT, SO LOOKED AT AN-OTHER WAY, WE COULD STILL USE TWO OF THEM.
NO MATTER HOW HARD IT MAY BE, FOR THE SAKE OF OUR RUINED HOMELANDS,
AND FOR THE FUTURE OF APOSIMZ, WE HAVE NO CHOICE BUT TO DO THIS!
GKUNG
ROLL
コロ

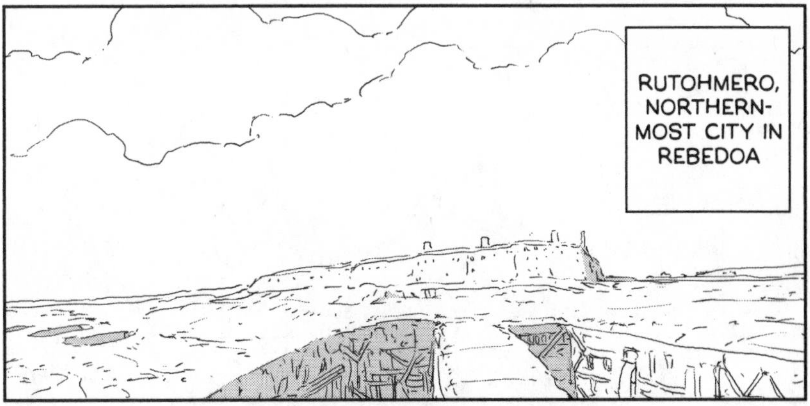
RUTOHMERO, NORTHERN-MOST CITY IN REBEDOA

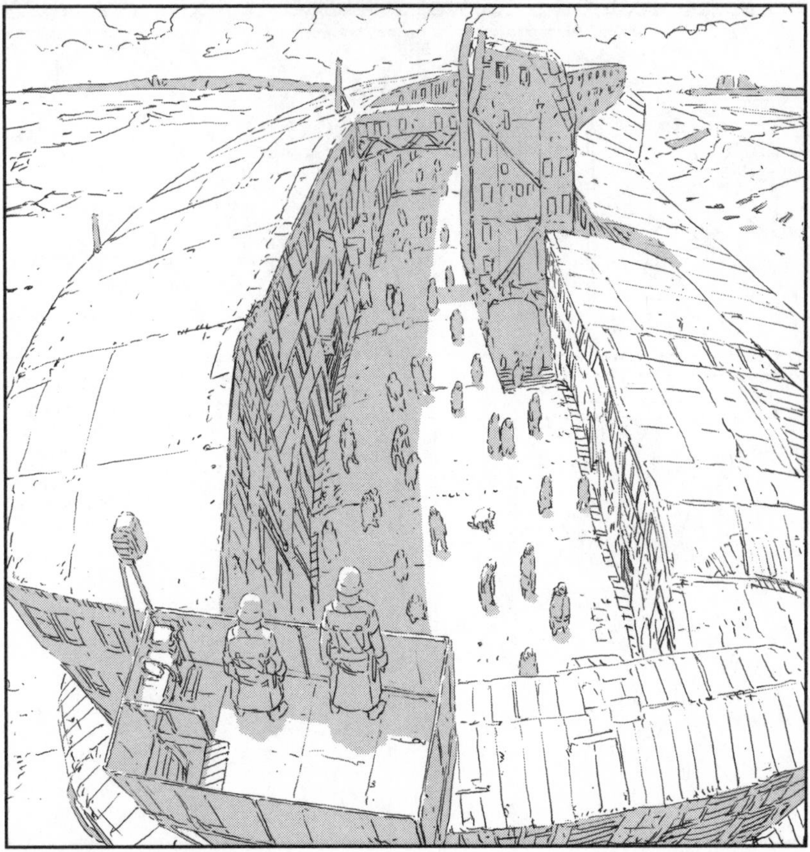

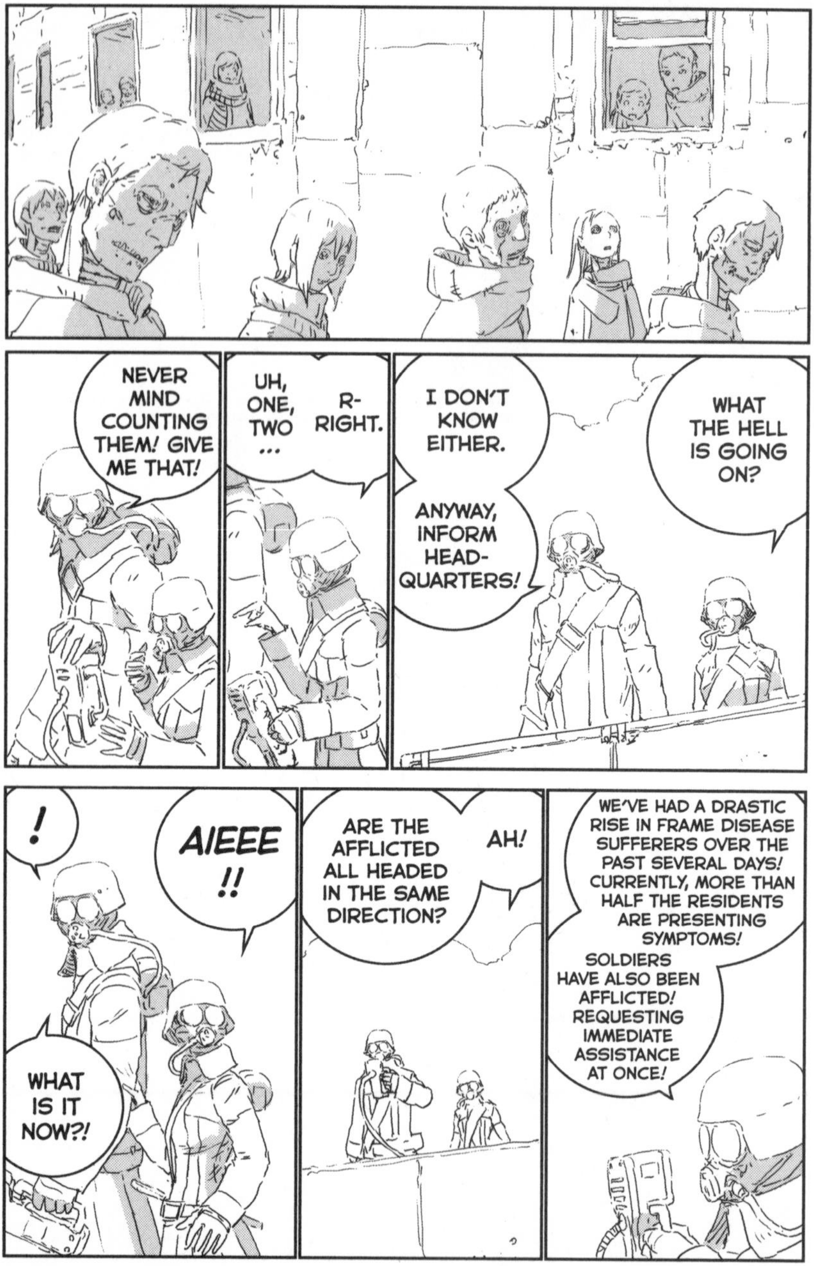
WHAT THE HELL IS GOING ON?
I DON'T KNOW EITHER.
ANYWAY, INFORM HEAD-QUARTERS!
UH, ONE, TWO ... R-RIGHT.
NEVER MIND COUNTING THEM! GIVE ME THAT!
WE'VE HAD A DRASTIC RISE IN FRAME DISEASE SUFFERERS OVER THE PAST SEVERAL DAYS! CURRENTLY, MORE THAN HALF THE RESIDENTS ARE PRESENTING SYMPTOMS!
SOLDIERS HAVE ALSO BEEN AFFLICTED! REQUESTING IMMEDIATE ASSISTANCE AT ONCE!
AH!
ARE THE AFFLICTED ALL HEADED IN THE SAME DIRECTION?
AIEEE !!
!
WHAT IS IT NOW?!

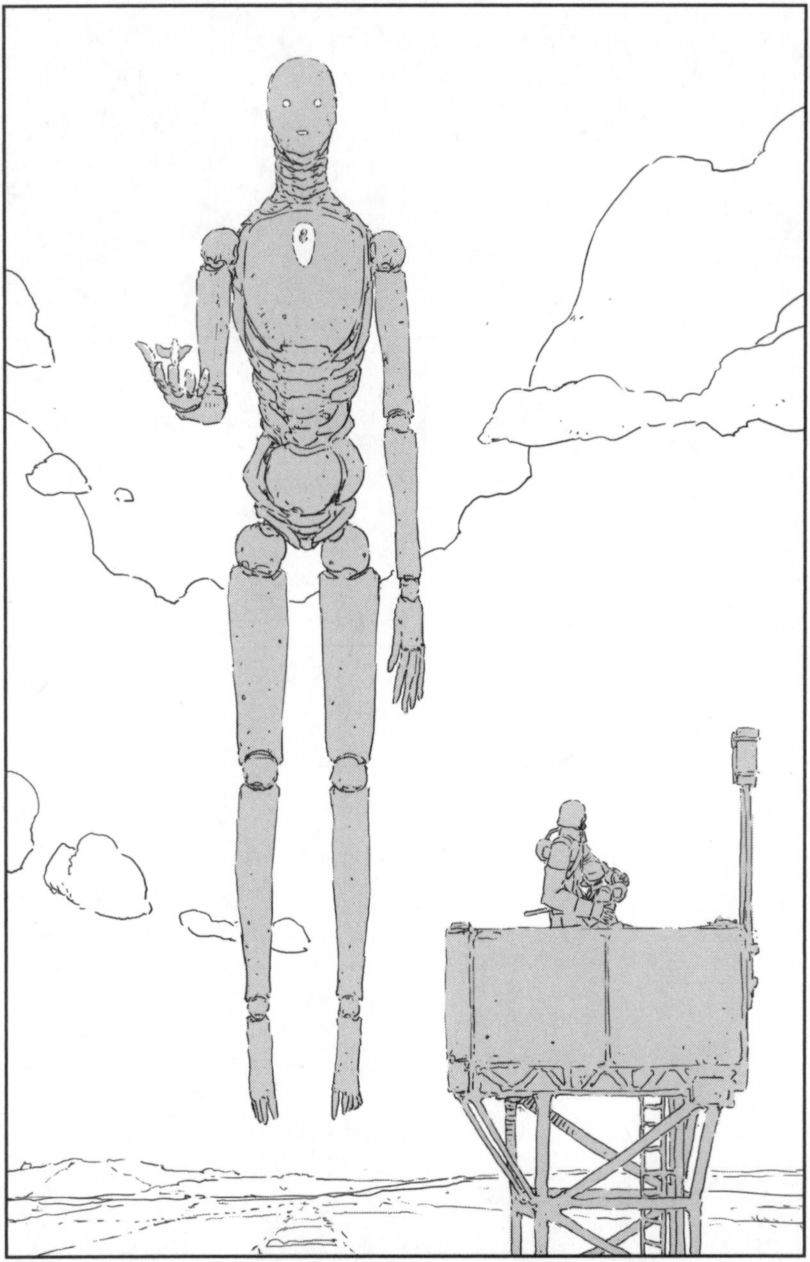

CHAPTER 42 END

WASABU'S DREAM

!!
GRIP
BIG BRO ETHEROW!
THAT'S NOT PIPE FRUIT!
AH!
NO, ETHEROW, STOP THAT!
...
WHAT A SURPRISE.
TO THINK WASABU IS THE TYPE OF REGULAR FRAME THAT CAN NAP!
ERM,
WHAT KIND OF DREAM IS HE HAVING?!

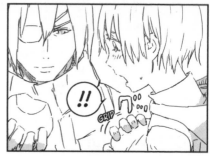

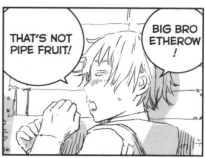

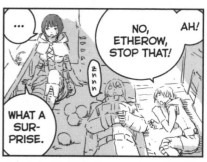

CONTINUED IN VOLUME 8

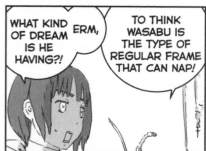

APOSIMZ volume 7

A Vertical Comics Edition

Translation: Kumar Sivasubramanian
Production: Grace Lu
Darren Smith

First published in Japan in 2020 by Kodansha, Ltd., Tokyo
Publication for this English edition arranged through Kodansha, Ltd., Tokyo
English language version produced by Vertical Comics,
an imprint of Kodansha USA Publishing, LLC

Translation provided by Vertical Comics, 2021
Published by Kodansha USA Publishing, LLC, New York

Originally published in Japanese as *APOSIMZ 7* by Kodansha, Ltd.
APOSIMZ first serialized in *Monthly Shonen Sirius*, Kodansha, Ltd., 2017-

This is a work of fiction.

ISBN: 978-1-647290-55-9

Manufactured in Canada

First Edition

Kodansha USA Publishing, LLC
451 Park Avenue South
7th Floor
New York, NY 10016
www.kodansha.us

Vertical books are distributed through Penguin-Random House Publisher Services.